13th Joint ACL-ISO Workshop on Interoperable Semantic Annotation 2017 (ISA-13)

Montpellier, France
19 September 2017

Editor:

Harry Bunt

ISBN: 978-1-5108-8133-4

Proceedings 13th Joint ISO - ACL Workshop on Interoperable Semantic Annotation (isa-13)

September 19, 2017

Montpellier, France

Harry Bunt, editor

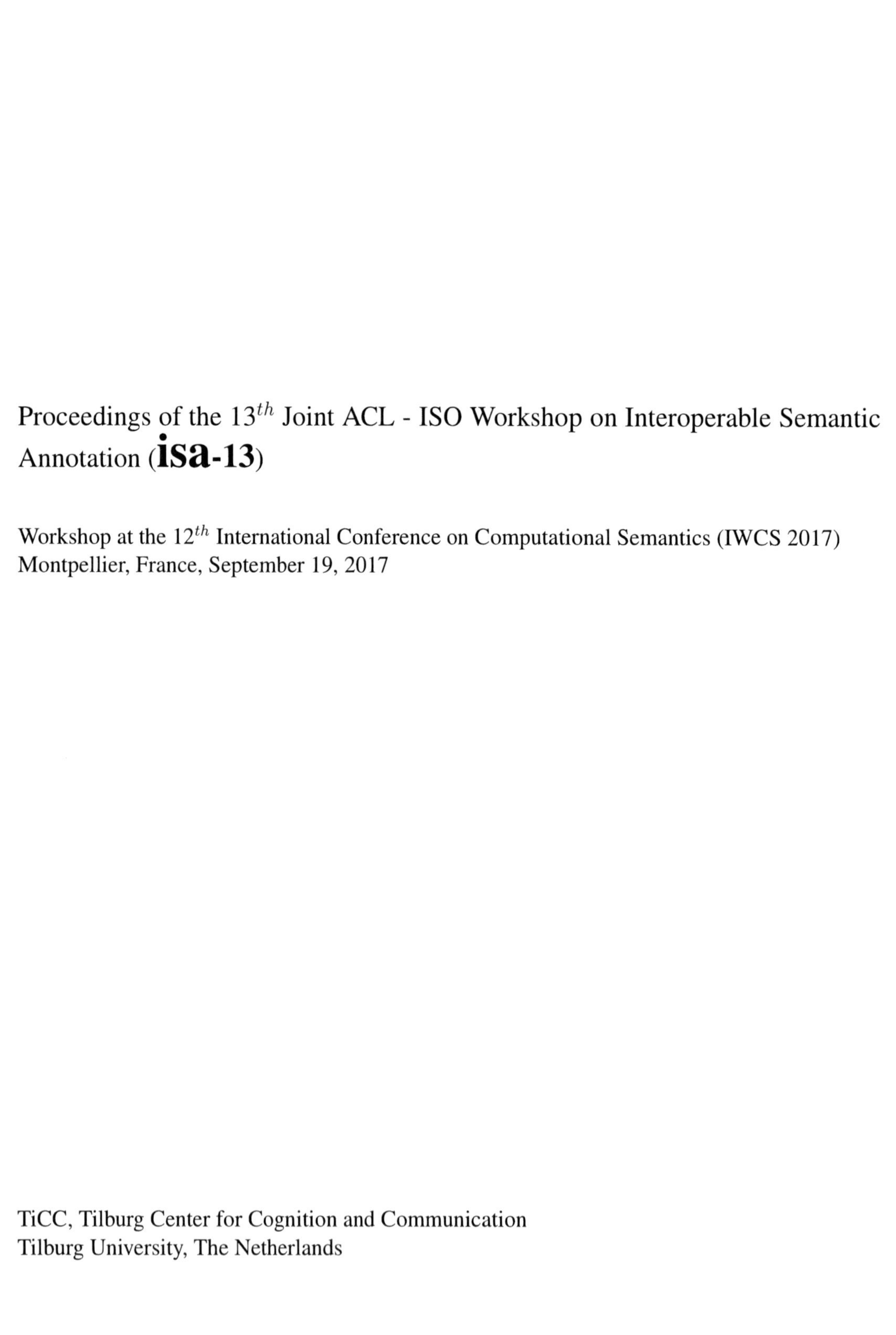

Proceedings of the 13th Joint ACL - ISO Workshop on Interoperable Semantic Annotation (**isa-13**)

Workshop at the 12th International Conference on Computational Semantics (IWCS 2017)
Montpellier, France, September 19, 2017

TiCC, Tilburg Center for Cognition and Communication
Tilburg University, The Netherlands

Workshop Programme

08.45 -- 09:00 Registration

09:00 -- 09:10 Opening by Workshop Chair

09:05 -- 09:35 Jet Hoek and Merel Scholman *Evaluating discourse annotation: Some recent insights and new approaches*
09:35 -- 10:05 Rodolfo Delmonte and Giulia Marchesini: *A semantically-based approach to the annotation of narrative style*
10:05 -- 10:35 Suzanne Mpouli: *Annotating similes in literary texts*

10:35 – 11:00 Coffee break

11:00 -- 11:30 Harry Bunt, Volha Petukhova and Alex Chengyu Fang: *Revisiting the ISO standard for dialogue act annotation*
11:30 -- 12:00 Emer Gilmartin, Brendan Spillane and Maria O'Reilly: *Annotation of greeting, introduction, and leavetaking in text dialogues*
12:00 -- 12:30 Valeria Lapina and Volha Petukhova: *Classification of modal meaning in negotiation dialogues*
12:30 -- 12:45 Andreas Liesenfeld: *Project Notes on building a conversational parser on top of a text parser: Towards a causal language tagger for spoken Chinese*

12:45 – 14:00 Lunch break

14:00 -- 14:30 Tianyong Hao, Yunyan Wei, Jiaqi Qiang, Haitao Wang and Kiyong Lee: *The representation and extraction of quantitative information*
14:30 -- 15:00 Harry Bunt: *Towards interoperable annotation of quantification*
15:00 -- 15:15 Pierre André Menard and Caroline Barrière: *PACTE: A collaborative platform for textual annotation*
15:15 -- 15:30 Loïc Grobol, Frédéric Landragin and Serge Heiden: *Interoperable annotation of (co)references in the Democrat project*

15:30 -- 16:00 Tea break

16:00 -- 16:30 Kiyong Lee: *Four types of temporal signals*
16:30 -- 16:45 Jean-Yves Antoine, Jakub Waszczuk, Anaïs Lefeuvre-Haftermeyer, Lotfi Abouda, Emmanuel Schang and Agata Savary: *Tempora@ODIL project: Adapting ISO Time-ML to syntactic treebanks for the temporal annotation of spoken speech*
16:45 -- 17:15 David Woods, Tim Fernando and Carl Vogel: *Towards efficient string processing of annotated events*
17:15 -- 17:45 James Pustejovsky and Kiyong Lee: *Enriching the Notion of Path in ISOspace*

17:45 Workshop Closing

17:45-18:30 ISO/TC 37/SC 4/WG 2 and WG 5 plenary meeting

Workshop Organizers/Organizing Committee

Harry Bunt	Tilburg University
Nancy Ide	Vassar College, Poughkeepsie, NY
Kiyong Lee	Korea University, Seoul
James Pustejovsky	Brandeis University, Waltham, MA
Laurent Romary	INRIA/Humboldt Universität Berlin

Workshop Programme Committee

Jan Alexandersson	DFKI, Saarbrücken
Harry Bunt	TiCC, Tilburg University
Nicoletta Calzolari	ILC-CNR, Pisa
Jae-Woong Choe	Korea University, Seoul
Robin Cooper	University of Gothenburg
Thierry Declerck	DFKI, Saarbrücken
Liesbeth Degand	Université Catholique de Louvain
Alex Chengyu Fang	City University of Hong Kong
Robert Gaizauskas	University of Sheffield
Koiti Hasida	Tokyo University
Nancy Ide	Vassar College, Poughkeepsie
Elisabetta Jezek	Università degli Studi di Pavia
Michael Kipp	University of Applied Sciences, Augsburg
Kiyong Lee	Korea University, Seoul
Philippe Muller	IRIT, Toulouse University
Malvina Nissim	University of Groningen
Silvia Pareti	Google Inc.
Volha Petukhova	Universität des Saarlandes, Saarbrücken
Paola Pietrandrea	Université de Tours
Andrei Popescu-Belis	Idiap, Martigny, Switzerland
Rarhmi Prasad	University of Wisconsin, Milwaukee
James Pustejovsky	Brandeis University, Waltham, MA
Laurent Romary	INRIA/Humboldt Universität Berlin
Ted Sanders	Universiteit Utrecht
Manfred Stede	University of Potsdam
Matthew Stone	Rutgers University
Thorsten Trippel	University of Bielefeld
Piek Vossen	Vrije Universiteit Amsterdam
Annie Zaenen	Stanford University
Sandrine Zufferey	Universität Bern

Proceedings Editor

Harry Bunt	Tilburg University

Table of contents

Author Index

Evaluating discourse annotation:
Some recent insights and new approaches

Jet Hoek
Utrecht Institute of Linguistics OTS
Utrecht University
j.hoek@uu.nl

Merel C. J. Scholman
Language Science and Technology
Saarland University
m.c.j.scholman
@coli.uni-saarland.de

Abstract

Annotated data is an important resource for the linguistics community, which is why researchers need to be sure that such data are reliable. However, arriving at sufficiently reliable annotations appears to be an issue within the field of discourse, possibly due to the fact that coherence is a mental phenomenon rather than a textual one. In this paper, we discuss recent insights and developments regarding annotation and reliability evaluation that are relevant to the field of discourse. We focus on characteristics of coherence that impact reliability scores and look at how different measures are affected by this. We discuss benefits and disadvantages of these measures, and propose that discourse annotation results be accompanied by a detailed report of the annotation process and data, as well as a careful consideration of the reliability measure that is applied.

1 Introduction

Linguistics researchers often make use of large amounts of data that are annotated by two or more coders. In order to draw conclusions from these data, researchers need to be sure that such data are reliable. Reliability "is the extent to which different methods, research results, or people arrive at the same interpretations or facts" (Krippendorff, 2011); data are reliable if coders agree on the labels assigned to, for instance, discourse relations (Artstein and Poesio, 2008). One way in which the reliability of annotated data can be measured is by calculating the inter-coder agreement: a numerical index of the extent of agreement between the coders.

Spooren and Degand (2010) note that sufficiently reliable annotation appears to be an issue within the field of discourse coherence. As the main reason for this, they point to the fact that coherence is a feature of the mental representation that readers form of a text, rather than of the linguistic material itself. Discourse annotation thus relies on coders' interpretation of a text, which makes it a particularly difficult task. This idea is for instance supported by studies that show that coders tend to agree more when annotating explicit coherence relations, which are signalled by a connective or cue phrase (*because, for this reason*), than when annotating implicit coherence relations, which contain no or less linguistic markers on which coders can base their decision (e.g., Miltsakaki et al., 2004; Prasad et al., 2008). Spooren and Degand (2010) argue that low agreement scores may contribute to the fact that reliability scores are often not reported in corpus-based discourse studies. They discuss several possible solutions to increase the reliability of discourse annotation tasks, including providing the annotators with more training, improving annotation protocols, and changing the definition of what a good or sufficient agreement score is.

Since Spooren and Degand (2010), there have been several new developments both in the discussion on inter-coder agreement measurement and within the field of discourse. In this paper, we address some of these insights.[1] First, we discuss a relatively new agreement measure, AC_1 (Gwet, 2002), that has

---

[1] It should be noted that although the focus of this paper will be on discourse-annotated data, some of the data characteristics we discuss are by no means unique to discourse, and all measures discussed in this paper could be used to calculate agreement for annotated data from different types of linguistic research as well.

been gaining popularity in recent years, and explore its suitability for measuring inter-coder agreement within the field of discourse annotation. AC_1 was introduced to solve some of the problems that Cohen's Kappa, the inter-coder agreement measure that is most widely used, presents.[2] Specifically, Kappa's values are sometimes relatively low, despite a high percentage of observed agreement; a problem known as the "Kappa paradox" (Feinstein and Cicchetti, 1990). As we will elaborate on in the next sections, this paradox occurs because Kappa is sensitive to certain characteristics of data that are very typical of discourse data.

After discussing AC_1 as a potential alternative for Cohen's Kappa in measuring the agreement between two (or more) expert coders, we briefly discuss some of the new methods of annotating discourse that have recently been used. These methods all involve the use of multiple naive, non-expert coders. Using non-expert coders is an attractive alternative to the conventional two-or-more expert coder scenario, since it allows researchers to obtain a lot of annotated data without extensive training sessions in a relatively fast and cheap way, especially when making use of crowdsourcing. For such annotation approaches, other methods for evaluating the reliability and quality of the annotations have been proposed.

2   Inter-coder agreement in (discourse) annotation

The discourse community makes frequent use of manually-annotated data, making inter-coder reliability a highly relevant issue for this field. However, a lot of research into reliability has been conducted by researchers from other fields, such as the medical field. These hypotheses and statistical measures have then been applied to discourse data, but differences between fields might affect the interpretation of agreement scores, as well as the appropriateness of a measure. For example, to interpret Kappa, researchers from all fields make use of Landis and Koch (1977)'s scale, which was originally designed for the medical field. Hripcsak and Heitjan (2002, p.101), however, argue that intermediate levels of Kappa cannot be interpreted consistently between fields or even within fields, because the interpretation relies heavily on the type of task and categories, the purpose of the measurement, and the definition of chance. In this section, we discuss specific characteristics of tasks and categories in the discourse coherence field, but first we address what sets apart linguistic annotation from other types of annotation, in order to highlight why different assumptions regarding reliability might be appropriate depending on the field.

Linguistic annotation differs from annotation tasks in other fields such as medicine for several reasons. In the medical field, patients are diagnosed as positive or negative, i.e., often the only two categories are 'yes' and 'no.' A data point often has an ultimate truth (the patient has the disease or does not have the disease), which can often be determined via different 'diagnostics' and for which additional evidence can emerge over time (due to the developmental course of diseases, for example). In linguistics, however, annotation tasks often consist of multiple categories. A data point never has an ultimate truth; rather, in many tasks, linguistics researchers study gradient phenomena where there are no right answers (Munro et al., 2010) and where it is not uncommon for data to be ambiguous (a coherence relation can for instance be causal and temporal at the same time). Finally, disagreements seem to be more equal in linguistics than in medicine. In the medical field, a false negative is worse than a false positive, since diagnosing a sick patient as healthy is worse than diagnosing a healthy patient as sick (e.g., Cicchetti et al., 2017). In linguistics, however, one mistake is not worse than another. These differences between domains do not at all imply that annotation tasks in discourse are easier or more difficult than those in the medical field, but they can play a role in whether a specific measure is suitable for determining agreement between coders.

In the next sections, we look at specific characteristics of typical discourse annotation tasks that influence the result of agreement measures, namely the number of categories and the distribution of categories. We illustrate our arguments using examples from discourse coherence data. However, the

---

[2]Like Kappa, AC_1 requires a simple categorical rating system. Gwet (2002) proposed a second statistic, called AC_2, for ordered categorical rating systems. This measure can be used as an alternative to weighted Kappa.

same arguments are often valid for other types of discourse annotation, including coreference coding (e.g., Van Deemter and Kibble, 2000), Translation Spotting (e.g., Cartoni et al., 2013), semantic role labeling (e.g., Palmer et al., 2005) or determining a discourse relation's segment-specific properties (e.g., Andersson and Spenader, 2014; Li, 2014; Sanders et al., 2012). Determining agreement is also relevant for experimentally obtained data, as in for instance continuation tasks or paraphrase tasks. The uneven occurrence of categories is an issue relevant to all these tasks, while the varying number of categories used in annotation is relevant mostly to the annotation of coherence relations, both in natural language and experimental data.

2.1 Number of categories

When annotating discourse relations, coders use labels to represent the way in which text segments relate to each other. Several different discourse annotation frameworks have been proposed, all of which have a different relation inventory. Frameworks differ not only in the exact labels they use, but also in the *number* of relational categories they distinguish. The DISCOR corpus (Reese et al., 2007), annotated within the framework of Segmented Discourse Representation Theory (SDRT), for example, uses 14 relation labels, while the RST Discourse Treebank (Carlson et al., 2003) uses 72 relation labels. The large variability in the number of categories between frameworks can contribute to low comparability of reliability scores between annotation efforts. A larger number of labels can for instance lead to more rare categories, which can in turn result in a lower reliability score, as we will see in the next sections.

The number of subtypes distinguished within classes in a single framework may also differ. The Penn Discourse Treebank 2.0 (PDTB 2.0, Prasad et al., 2008), for example, has 42 distinct labels, ordered in a hierarchy of four classes with three levels. The framework distinguishes 3 third-level labels within the class of TEMPORAL relations, but 11 third-level labels within CONTINGENCY relations. Such differences can make reliability scores difficult to compare between relation types even in a single framework.

2.2 Uneven distribution of categories

Regardless of the number of relation labels used, an uneven distribution of categories seems to be a common characteristic of discourse annotation. Since discourse annotation generally uses natural language as its basis, the frequency of a specific label is influenced by the frequency of the type of relation it refers to. The distribution of categories in discourse annotation can be skewed in multiple ways. For example, causal relations occur more often in natural text than non-causal relations such as LIST (e.g., Prasad et al. 2007). In addition, texts are characterized by an uneven distribution of connectives, with some connectives being very frequent (e.g., *because*), and other occurring less often (e.g., *consequently*). Finally, the distribution of relation types that specific connectives mark can also vary. Relations signaled by *so* are for instance more often RESULT than PURPOSE (e.g., Andersson and Spenader, 2014). Uneven prevalence of categories also extends beyond coherence relations. When it comes to coreference patterns, for instance, pronouns more often refer to the subject than to the object of the previous sentence.

The distribution of categories is also not stable between different types of discourse. The prevalence of relation types has been shown to differ between language modes (e.g., between spoken and written discourse, Sanders and Spooren, 2015), text genres (e.g., Demirşahin et al., 2012), and connectives (e.g., Andersson and Spenader, 2014), and between implicit and explicitly marked relations (e.g., Asr and Demberg, 2012). Similarly, coreference patterns can vary depending on the context; in the presence of an Implicit Causality verb, upcoming pronouns may more often refer back to the object than to the subject of the sentence (e.g., Garvey and Caramazza, 1974). Such variability in category distribution can reduce the comparability of reliability measures between annotation efforts, when using the same framework or the same labels.

The differences between discourse annotation efforts in the number of categories that are distinguished and the uneven distribution of categories can influence a reliability statistic such as Kappa, as will be explained in the next section. The variability in the prevalence of categories makes measuring the reliability of discourse annotations even more problematic, since it has a varying effect on the reliability scores of annotation efforts that have been done using the same relation inventory. Specifically, if the observed prevalence of items in one of the categories is low, then there is insufficient information in the data to judge coders' ability to discriminate items, and Kappa may underestimate the true agreement (Hripcsak and Heitjan, 2002). This then also complicates a comparison of reliability scores between discourse annotation frameworks, since it prevents us from determining something along the lines of a 'framework correction.' For these reasons, it is important that researchers in the field of discourse annotation understand the distribution of relations in their frameworks and the prevalence in their data, and know how the agreement measures that they apply to their annotations are affected by this data. Without such knowledge and the appropriate reporting of these qualities, agreement scores on different discourse annotation tasks cannot be compared and the reliability of the data cannot be evaluated properly.

3 Inter-coder agreement measures: Kappa and AC_1

The simplest measure of agreement between coders is the percentage of agreement, also known as the observed agreement. This measure, however, is often not suitable for calculating reliability, as it does not take into account chance agreement (Scott, 1959). Chance agreement occurs when one or both coders rate an item randomly. This type of agreement can inflate the overall agreement and should therefore not contribute to a measure of inter-coder reliability (Artstein and Poesio, 2008).

In order to get a reliable index of the extent of agreement between coders, observed agreement has to be adjusted for chance agreement. Since it cannot be known which agreements between coders occurred by chance and which agreements are real, the proportion of chance agreement must be estimated (Gwet, 2001). Kappa and AC_1 correct for chance agreement on the basis of the same idea, namely that the ratio between the observed agreement and the expected agreement reflects how much agreement beyond chance was in fact observed. This idea is expressed in the following formula, which in both cases results in a score between -1 and 1:

$$\kappa, AC_1 = \frac{P_o - P_e}{1 - P_e} \tag{1}$$

where P_o is the observed agreement, or percentage agreement, and P_e is the agreement that would be expected if the coders were acting only by chance. The crucial difference between Kappa and AC_1 lies in the way in which they estimate the expected agreement (P_e), as they have different assumptions about the coding distributions. In this section, we introduce each measure in turn, highlighting the differences between the measures as well as the respective drawbacks. We then illustrate the difference between Kappa and AC_1's scores using different annotation scenarios. The example data in this section will be used to illustrate the agreement measures, and will be reported in a two-way contingency table such as Table 1. This table represents a two-coder reliability study involving coders A and B and two categories.

It should be noted that while Kappa and AC_1 both range between 1 (complete agreement) to -1 (complete disagreement), neither score comes with a fixed value at which agreement can be considered satisfactory; guidelines and conventions on the interpretation of these measures are formed over time and can differ between fields. As mentioned above, Kappa is often interpreted using the scale proposed by Landis and Koch (1977), in which for instance $0.41-0.6 =$ moderate agreement, $0.61-0.8 =$ substantial agreement, and $0.81-1 =$ almost perfect agreement, but the cut-off point for acceptable agreement in computational linguistics is commonly set at $\kappa = 0.67$ (Di Eugenio and Glass, 2004), whereas Artstein and Poesio (2008) recommend considering $\kappa > 0.8$ as an indication of sufficient annotation quality. While these guidelines are helpful, they have no theoretical basis (Ludbrook, 2002; Xie, 2013) and are themselves subject to evaluation.

3.1 Cohen's Kappa

Cohen's Kappa assumes that "random assignment of categories to items is governed by prior distributions that are unique to each coder and that reflect individual annotator bias" (Artstein and Poesio, 2008, p.

561). In Kappa, chance agreement, or the amount of agreement that would be expected if annotators were acting only by chance ("expected agreement"), is estimated using the marginal distribution (i.e., the probability that a category is used by the coders):

$$P_e(\kappa) = (f_1 \cdot g_1 + f_2 \cdot g_2)/N^2 \tag{2}$$

where f_1, f_2, g_1 and g_2 correspond to the marginal totals in Table 1.

	Coder A		
Coder B	1	2	Total
1	a	b	g1
2	c	d	g2
Total	f1	f2	N

Table 1: Coders and response categories

3.2 Gwet's AC_1

AC_1's definition of chance agreement is based on the premises that chance agreement occurs when at least one coder guesses and that only an unknown proportion of ratings is random. AC_1 thus assumes that coders' agreements are at least in part <u>not</u> due to chance. In addition, AC_1 takes into account the prevalence of the categories for its estimation of chance agreement (Gwet, 2001).

The calculation of chance agreement in AC_1 is expressed by the following formula:

$$P_e(AC_1) = \frac{1}{(K-1)} \sum_{q=1}^{K} \left(\frac{N_q}{N} \cdot \frac{N-N_q}{N} \right) \tag{3}$$

whereby K refers to the total number of categories and q to a specific category. N_q refers to the average number of times a certain category is used by a coder and is, in case of two coders, equivalent to $(f_q + g_q)/2$. N_q/N thus represents the percentage of items labeled as category q and $(N - N_q)/N$ represents the percentage of items not labeled as category q (see also Zhao et al., 2013). Hence, whereas Kappa's formula of chance agreement is based on the chance that Coder A and B both categorize an item as '1,' the chance that both coders categorize an item as '2', etc., AC_1's chance agreement formula is based on the chance that a certain category is used.

The values from AC_1's formula for chance agreement are crucially different from those of Kappa's chance agreement formula because AC_1 does not assume a prior individual coder bias. Instead, it is based on the possibility that one or both of the coders perform a <u>random</u> classification. As such, Gwet (2002, p. 3) argues that a reasonable value for chance agreement probability should not exceed 0.5. Consequently, AC_1's chance agreement caps the probability within 0–0.5, whereas Kappa's chance agreement probability can be anywhere between 0 and 1. AC_1's limit of 0.5 aims to prevent the occurrence of a similar erratic behaviour that leads to Kappa's paradoxes. In addition, AC_1's chance agreement, unlike Kappa's chance agreement, is positively correlated with the difficulty of a task, since it includes the chance of coders annotating randomly (Feng, 2015); as a task gets more difficult, chances that coders guess increase. The next section will explore Kappa's and AC_1's behavior in different annotation scenarios.

3.3 Kappa vs. AC_1 in annotation scenarios

Because Kappa bases its chance agreement on individual coder biases, the resulting agreement score can be greatly affected by the distribution of the categories in the data. Specifically, when the marginal distributions are imbalanced, the resulting κ is lower than when the marginal distributions are balanced. In Table 2, the distribution is symmetrical and balanced; the coders agree on an equal amount of items for both categories, and category 1 is used approximately as often as category 2. The observed agreement is $100/120 = 0.83$, and the κ score for these data is 0.67 (see Table 6 for an overview of all scores).[3] In this

---

[3] All agreement scores reported in this paper were calculated using the R package agree.coeff2.r.

	Coder A		
Coder B	1	2	Total
1	50	12	62
2	8	50	58
Total	58	62	120

Table 2: Symmetrical balanced distribution

	Coder A		
Coder B	1	2	Total
1	20	12	32
2	8	80	88
Total	28	92	120

Table 3: Symmetrical imbalanced distribution

	Coder A		
Coder B	1	2	Total
1	0	12	12
2	8	100	108
Total	8	112	120

Table 4: Symmetrical imbalanced distribution
with empty target cell

	Coder A		
Coder B	1	2	Total
1	5	110	115
2	0	5	5
Total	5	115	120

Table 5: Highly imbalanced distribution in opposite
direction

scenario, AC_1's chance agreement is the same. Consequently, the agreement scores are also the same. Hence, when the data is distributed evenly, Kappa and AC_1 give comparable scores.

In Table 3, the distribution of categories is also approximately the same for each coder (i.e., 30/90), but category 2 is used more often than category 1, and the distribution is therefore symmetrical but imbalanced. For these types of distributions, AC_1 and Kappa yield different scores. Kappa assumes that both coders have a bias toward category 2 and that, as such, they would agree often if they guessed according to their biases. The observed agreement is the same as for the data in Table 2 (0.83), but Kappa's chance agreement is higher (0.62), resulting in a lower κ score (0.56).[4] AC_1, by contrast, assumes that uneven categories are a property of the data. Consequently, AC_1 assumes a lower value for chance agreement than Kappa (0.38), which results in a higher agreement score (0.73).

Table 4 illustrates a scenario in which two coders have reached a high observed agreement (0.83), but have not managed to agree on a single case for category 1 (resulting in an empty target cell). The κ score for this annotation task is -0.09, which indicates that agreement was around chance level. Kappa estimates chance agreement at 0.85. This is an extreme case of a low Kappa score for a task with a high observed agreement. The fact that the Kappa score is much lower than the observed agreement is in this case not completely unreasonable, since even though both coders used category 1 several times, they did not agree on a single case for this category. On the other hand, having a reliability score around chance implies that coders did no better than if they were guessing, even though it seems plausible to assume that at least part of the items that were classified as category 2 were assigned this label because the coders were certain that the item belonged to this category.

Because AC_1, unlike Kappa, takes into account both the number of categories and the prevalence of those categories, the chance agreement is much lower than Kappa's (0.22) and the resulting reliability score is higher (0.80). Note that AC_1's estimation of chance agreement for Table 4 is lower than for Tables 2 and 3, and that its reliability score for 4 is therefore higher than for the other two scenarios. This can be considered counter-intuitive; after all, there is only one category in Table 4 on which the coders have managed to agree. The coders have not been able to reliably assign any items to the other category, which constitutes 50% of the categories in a 2×2 table. One would expect that the corresponding agreement score is affected by this. Zhao et al. (2013) note that this is an abnormality in AC_1: in case of a very skewed distribution with an empty target cell, AC_1 turns out higher than what seems justified.

A similar abnormality in AC_1 is that unused categories influence the reliability score. For instance,

---

[4]Sometimes, KappaMAX is used to correct Kappa in case of uneven categories. KappaMAX is calculated using the same formula as Kappa, but the '1' in formula 1 is replaced by the maximum value for observed agreement possible (if f_1 is the smallest marginal total, $maxp_o = (f_1 + g_2)/N$; if f_2 is the smallest marginal total, $maxp_o = (f_2 + g_1)/N$ (see also Feinstein and Cicchetti, 1990)). Although KappaMAX can correct Kappa's prevalence problem, it has been reported to overcorrect in case of coder bias (Feinstein and Cicchetti, 1990).

Table	P_o	Kappa		AC_1	
		P_e	κ	P_e	AC_1
2	0.83	0.50	0.67	0.50	0.67
3	0.83	0.62	0.56	0.38	0.73
4	0.83	0.85	-0.09	0.22	0.80
5	0.08	0.08	0.004	0.50	-0.83

Table 6: Values for observed agreement, chance agreement and reliability scores for Tables 2-5.

if we were to add an empty category ('3') to Table 2, the AC_1 score would rise from 0.67 to 0.78. Kappa, by contrast, is not affected by the unused category, and gives a score of 0.67 in both cases. This may be perceived as a positive feature of AC_1, since the measure can reflect that coders have successfully not attributed any of the items to a certain category. On the other hand, it makes AC_1 vulnerable to inflation through the inclusion of useless categories in an annotation task. It should, however, be noted that the inflation effect of unused categories decreases as the number of used categories increases.

Instead of being low relative to the observed agreement, Kappa can also be high. Table 5 presents an extreme case of coder disagreement. The observed agreement is very low (0.08), but κ is 0.0004, which suggests that agreement was around chance. Looking at the table, however, it appears that there is almost perfect disagreement. It could be argued that this too is a type of agreement; even though the coders did not use the same label, they did make the same categorization of the data. The agreement should therefore close to -1. AC_1's agreement score for the data in Table 5 (0.80) therefore much better reflects the almost perfect disagreement that the coders showed. Although such extreme cases of disagreement are rare in annotation, this example demonstrates Kappa's potential to be relatively high when coders disagree on many items. Ideally, a measure would be able to deal properly with all possible scenarios, including one of almost perfect disagreement.

3.4 Using AC_1 to evaluate discourse annotations

As discussed in Section 2, skewed data are fairly common in discourse annotation tasks and distributions can vary depending on the context or the task. This variation complicates a comparison of reliability scores between annotation efforts. In addition, discourse frameworks often have many categories and the prevalence of these categories in a text or dataset is unknown. Empty categories are therefore very likely to occur in discourse annotation tasks. Disagreements on a rare category can have a big impact on the Kappa score, especially when the target cell for that category remains empty. AC_1 is more robust to skewedness and variability in the distribution of categories, and therefore seems promising as a measure for evaluating agreement in discourse annotation. Results from several studies and simulations have suggested that AC_1 is a reliable alternative measure for calculating inter-coder agreement (e.g., Gwet, 2001; Wongpakaran et al., 2013; Xie, 2013). Moreover, AC_1 has been applied often in the medical field (e.g., Bryant et al., 2013; Crowle et al., 2017; Fuller et al., 2017; Marks et al., 2016) and has also been used in the computational linguistics field (Besser and Alexandersson, 2007; Haley, 2009; Hillard et al., 2007; Kranstedt et al., 2006; Purpura and Hillard, 2006; Yang et al., 2006), but no research in the field of discourse annotation has used AC_1 as of yet.

It is important that researchers are aware that both Kappa and AC_1 behave abnormally under some conditions. Zhao et al. (2013) point out that we cannot be entirely sure exactly when a measure like AC_1 – which assumes that coding happens randomly only part of the time – overestimates reliability or by how much and, vice versa, when a measure like Kappa – which assumes maximum-randomness – underestimates reliability. The choice for any agreement statistic should be well-motivated and researchers should be transparent about the distributions in their data. It might also be warranted that the guidelines for what constitutes satisfactory agreement are slightly stricter for AC_1 compared to those for Kappa, whether they be 'formalized' guidelines such as Landis and Koch (1977), framework-specific guidelines, or practices developed over annotation efforts.

Since AC_1 is still a relatively new agreement measure, it is possible that more frequent use and more examination will uncover more issues. We encourage discourse researchers to consider using both AC_1 and Kappa, and to be explicit about the characteristics of their data that might influence the suitability of their inter-coder agreement measure. Regardless of which measure researchers choose for their data, we advise them to include contingency tables to make annotation results more transparent and to allow readers to evaluate the results as well.

4   Multiple coders and crowdsourcing

Traditional annotation tasks consist of two expert coders. However, as Krippendorff (2004) notes, using more, non-expert coders can help ensure the reliability of the annotated data. In recent years, studies have begun to explore whether non-expert, non-trained (also referred to as naive) coders can also be employed for discourse annotation tasks (compared to expert coders). There are several advantages in employing such coders: non-experts are easier to come by, making it easier to employ a large number. Multiple annotators reduce the risk of coder bias in the data (Artstein and Poesio, 2005). Moreover, employing non-expert coders allows for a cost-effective and fast approach to collecting large amounts of data.

For non-expert annotations to be valuable, researchers have to be sure that they are sufficiently reliable (compared to expert annotations). There are several ways to evaluate annotations generated by non-expert, non-trained coders. For example, coders can be compared to each other based on their performance (Peldszus and Stede, 2013). Alternatively, they can be compared to a gold standard developed by an expert (Scholman et al., 2016). Typically, an adapted version of Kappa (i.e., Fleiss' Kappa, Davies and Fleiss, 1982) is used to calculate agreement for tasks with multiple coders, but AC1 could in fact also be used. Recall, precision, and F-scores can also provide valuable insights into problematic categories in the framework that is used.

To facilitate crowdsourced annotation projects without a gold standard set by experts, new methods of coding evaluation have been proposed, such as models that can extract a gold standard from crowdsourced data. Aroyo and Welty (2013), for instance, propose creating binary annotation vectors for all annotated items. These vectors then function as a gold standard to which individual annotations can be compared: comparing individual coder vectors to the total item vectors (minus the data supplied by that coder) gives an indication of coder disagreement, or the quality of each individual coder, whereas comparing all coder vectors for a single item to the averaged item vector functions as a measure of sentence clarity, or sentence ambiguity (for details, see Aroyo and Welty, 2013).

Another, more commonly used method is an approach using probabilistic item-response models that draw inferences about annotated data (Hovy et al., 2013; Passonneau and Carpenter, 2014). Such models use unsupervised learning to estimate the probability of labels for every item and coder. The utility of such a model lies in its ability to support meaningful inferences from the data, such as an estimate of the true prevalence of each category. Specifically, two features of probabilistic models make them an attractive alternative to more traditional reliability measurement methods. First, the models allow researchers to differentiate between coders; specifically, they can adjust for annotations from noisy coders, since some coders perform better than others. This is for instance done by giving different weights to annotators that answer correctly less often than others (Hovy et al., 2013). Second, probabilistic models cannot only identify the correct label for an item based on the crowdsourced annotations, they can also provide a confidence measure that indicates how likely it is that this label is indeed the correct label (cf. Hovy et al., 2013; Passonneau and Carpenter, 2014). This allows researchers to balance between coverage, i.e., the amount of data that is annotated, with accuracy, i.e., the trustworthiness of each annotation; as Hovy et al. 2013 explain, researchers can favor a different trade-off between coverage and accuracy depending on their research purposes. With the exception of Kawahara et al. (2014), no work has evaluated crowdsourced discourse relation annotations using probabilistic models. This seems a promising topic for future research.

The use of multiple (naive) coders also opens up other possibilities for representing the data. It allows researchers to study the distribution of responses over many coders, rather than specific data points

(Munro et al., 2010). This can be beneficial in unsupervised approaches where it is assumed that there is no one ground truth. Rohde et al. (2016) and Scholman and Demberg (2017), for example, present confusion matrices, percentage agreement and distribution plots to show that, often, multiple interpretations are possible for a single discourse relation. Rohde et al. (2016) argue that without gathering judgements from a crowd of coders, differences in annotation might be written off as coder error or bias, or a low level of inter-coder agreement. Based on their crowdsourced data, they conclude that disagreements on the interpretation of certain relations might be due to the fact that not every item can be assigned one right answer. Using the distribution of responses from multiple coders to determine whether disagreements are due to biases or errors, or caused by genuine ambiguity or double meanings could in the future lead to valuable insights for the evaluation of discourse annotation efforts by a limited number of expert annotators as well, especially if we can determine a subset of relations (or relation characteristics) that tend to allow multiple interpretations.

While there are many benefits to crowdsourcing annotations, using a large number of naive coders to annotate discourse relations may not be without its difficulties. As discussed in Sections 1 and 2, annotating discourse relations is a highly complicated task. Expert annotators usually spend a long time developing or acquainting themselves with an annotation framework and its relation inventory, annotation manuals tend to be very extensive, and annotation tasks often involve practice phases and discussion. Replicating this process in a crowdsourcing setting may be difficult, if not inconceivable. Instead of trying to use existing annotation manuals and procedures, however, researchers should consider developing methods that allow them to reap the benefits of crowdsourcing, while at the same time approximating the results yielded by a traditional annotation scenario. They may, for instance, opt for connective/cue phrase insertion tasks (cf. Rohde et al., 2016; Scholman and Demberg, 2017), in which case the connectives coders can choose from should be reliably associated with a specific type of relation. In addition, the annotation process could be simplified by cutting it up into several different steps, as in Scholman et al. (2016), or by including only a limited set of relations, as in Kawahara et al. (2014). Alternative solutions could be training coders to annotate only a small subset of relations, such as temporal relations, or teaching them to annotate only a single distinction, for instance the difference between RESULT and PURPOSE relations, between contrastive and temporal *while*, or between inclusive and exclusive DISJUNCTION relations.

5 Conclusion

This paper reviewed some recent developments concerning reliability evaluation within linguistic annotation in general and discourse annotation in specific. We explored the suitability of a relatively new agreement measure, AC_1, to evaluate the reliability of discourse annotation. This measure could be considered as a possible alternative for, or be used in addition to Cohen's Kappa. In general, the comparison demonstrated how agreement statistics can be influenced by properties of the data. We also discussed some annotation methods that have been used as alternatives to the two-or-more expert coders procedure, how the reliability can be determined for these methods, and how findings from these studies could help further our understanding of the practice of discourse annotation.

When reporting the results of a study that involves annotation, it is advisable to be transparent about the annotation process and to carefully consider which agreement measure is reported. Reporting (multiple) agreement scores and making raw annotation data available would facilitate other researchers to judge the reliability of the annotated data and, consequently, the findings of a study. In addition, it would enable a comparison between different annotation efforts and frameworks.

Acknowledgements

This research was funded by the SNSF Sinergia project MODERN (CRSII2_147653) and the German Research Foundation (DFG) as part of SFB 1102 "Information Density and Linguistic Encoding". We are grateful to the anonymous reviewers for their helpful suggestions.

References

Andersson, M. and J. Spenader (2014). Result and purpose relations with and without 'so'. *Lingua 148*, 1–27.

Aroyo, L. and C. Welty (2013). Crowd truth: Harnessing disagreement in crowdsourcing a relation extraction gold standard. *WebSci2013. ACM 2013*.

Artstein, R. and M. Poesio (2005). Bias decreases in proportion to the number of annotators. *Proceedings of the Conference on Formal Grammar and Mathematics of Language (FG-MoL)*, 141–150.

Artstein, R. and M. Poesio (2008). Inter-coder agreement for computational linguistics. *Computational Linguistics 34*(4), 555–596.

Asr, F. T. and V. Demberg (2012). Implicitness of discourse relations. In *Proceedings of the International Conference on Computational Linguistics (COLING)*, pp. 2669–2684. Citeseer.

Besser, J. and J. Alexandersson (2007). A comprehensive disfluency model for multi-party interaction. In *Proceedings of SigDial*, Volume 8, pp. 182–189.

Bryant, J., L. E. Skolarus, B. Smith, E. E. Adelman, and W. J. Meurer (2013). The accuracy of surrogate decision makers: Informed consent in hypothetical acute stroke scenarios. *BMC Emergency Medicine 13*(1), 18.

Carlson, L., D. Marcu, and M. E. Okurowski (2003). Building a discourse-tagged corpus in the framework of Rhetorical Structure Theory. In *Current and new directions in discourse and dialogue*, pp. 85–112. Springer.

Cartoni, B., S. Zufferey, and T. Meyer (2013). Annotating the meaning of discourse connectives by looking at their translation: The translation-spotting technique. *Dialogue and Discourse 4*(2), 65–86.

Cicchetti, D. V., A. Klin, and F. R. Volkmar (2017). Assessing binary diagnoses of bio-behavioral disorders: The clinical relevance of Cohen's Kappa. *The Journal of Nervous and Mental disease 205*(1), 58–65.

Crowle, C., C. Galea, C. Morgan, I. Novak, K. Walker, and N. Badawi (2017). Inter-observer agreement of the general movements assessment with infants following surgery. *Early Human Development 104*, 17–21.

Davies, M. and J. L. Fleiss (1982). Measuring agreement for multinomial data. *Biometrics 38*(4), 1047–1051.

Demirşahin, I., A. Sevdik-Çallı, H. Ö. Balaban, R. Çakıcı, and D. Zeyrek (2012). Turkish discourse bank: Ongoing developments. In *Proceedings of the First Workshop on Language Resources and Technologies for Turkish Languages*, pp. 15–19. Citeseer.

Di Eugenio, B. and M. Glass (2004). The kappa statistic: A second look. *Computational linguistics 30*(1), 95–101.

Feinstein, A. R. and D. V. Cicchetti (1990). High agreement but low kappa: I. The problems of two paradoxes. *Journal of clinical epidemiology 43*(6), 543–549.

Feng, G. C. (2015). Mistakes and how to avoid mistakes in using intercoder reliability indices. *Methodology 11*(1), 14–22.

Fuller, G., S. Kemp, and M. Raftery (2017). The accuracy and reproducibility of video assessment in the pitch-side management of concussion in elite rugby. *Journal of science and medicine in sport 20*(3), 246–249.

Garvey, C. and A. Caramazza (1974). Implicit causality in verbs. *Linguistic Inquiry 5*(3), 459–464.

Gwet, K. (2001). *Handbook of inter-rater reliability: How to estimate the level of agreement between two or multiple raters.* Gaithersburg, MD: STATAXIS Publishing Company.

Gwet, K. (2002). Kappa statistic is not satisfactory for assessing the extent of agreement between raters. *Statistical methods for inter-rater reliability assessment 1*(6), 1–6.

Haley, D. (2009). *Applying latent semantic analysis to computer assisted assessment in the computer science domain: A framework, a tool, and an evaluation.* Ph. D. thesis, The Open University.

Hillard, D., S. Purpura, and J. Wilkerson (2007). An active learning framework for classifying political text. In *Annual Meeting of the Midwest Political Science Association, Chicago.*

Hovy, D., T. Berg-Kirkpatrick, A. Vaswani, and E. H. Hovy (2013). Learning whom to trust with mace. In *HLT-NAACL*, pp. 1120–1130.

Hripcsak, G. and D. F. Heitjan (2002). Measuring agreement in medical informatics reliability studies. *Journal of Biomedical Informatics 35*(2), 99–110.

Kawahara, D., Y. Machida, T. Shibata, S. Kurohashi, H. Kobayashi, and M. Sassano (2014). Rapid development of a corpus with discourse annotations using two-stage crowdsourcing. In *Proceedings of the International Conference on Computational Linguistics (COLING)*, pp. 269–278.

Kranstedt, A., A. Lücking, T. Pfeiffer, H. Rieser, and M. Staudacher (2006). Measuring and reconstructing pointing in visual contexts. In *Proceedings of the Brandial*, pp. 82–89.

Krippendorff, K. (2004). Reliability in content analysis. *Human communication research 30*(3), 411–433.

Krippendorff, K. (2011). Agreement and information in the reliability of coding. *Communication Methods and Measures 5*(2), 93–112.

Landis, J. R. and G. G. Koch (1977). The measurement of observer agreement for categorical data. *Biometrics 33*(1), 159–174.

Li, F. (2014). *Subjectivity in Mandarin Chinese: The meaning and use of causal connectives in written discourse.* Netherlands Graduate School of Linguistics. Ph.D. Dissertation.

Ludbrook, J. (2002). Statistical techniques for comparing measurers and methods of measurement: A critical review. *Clinical and Experimental Pharmacology and Physiology 29*(7), 527–536.

Marks, D., T. Comans, M. Thomas, S. K. Ng, S. O'Leary, P. G. Conaghan, P. A. Scuffham, and L. Bisset (2016). Agreement between a physiotherapist and an orthopaedic surgeon regarding management and prescription of corticosteroid injection for patients with shoulder pain. *Manual Therapy 26*, 216–222.

Miltsakaki, E., R. Prasad, A. K. Joshi, and B. Webber (2004). The Penn Discourse TreeBank. In *Proceedings of the International Conference on Language Resources and Evaluation (LREC)*. Citeseer.

Munro, R., S. Bethard, V. Kuperman, V. T. Lai, R. Melnick, C. Potts, T. Schnoebelen, and H. Tily (2010). Crowdsourcing and language studies: The new generation of linguistic data. In *Proceedings of the NAACL HLT 2010 Workshop on Creating Speech and Language Data with Amazon's Mechanical Turk*, pp. 122–130. Association for Computational Linguistics.

Palmer, M., D. Gildea, and P. Kingsbury (2005). The proposition bank: An annotated corpus of semantic roles. *Computational linguistics 31*(1), 71–106.

Passonneau, R. J. and B. Carpenter (2014). The benefits of a model of annotation. *Transactions of the Association for Computational Linguistics 2*, 311–326.

Peldszus, A. and M. Stede (2013). From argument diagrams to argumentation mining in texts: A survey. *International Journal of Cognitive Informatics and Natural Intelligence (IJCINI) 7*(1), 1–31.

Prasad, R., N. Dinesh, A. Lee, E. Miltsakaki, L. Robaldo, A. K. Joshi, and B. Webber (2008). The Penn Discourse TreeBank 2.0. In *Proceedings of the International Conference on Language Resources and Evaluation (LREC)*. Citeseer.

Prasad, R., E. Miltsakaki, N. Dinesh, A. Lee, A. K. Joshi, L. Robaldo, and B. Webber (2007). *The Penn Discourse Treebank 2.0 annotation manual*. University of Pennsylvania.

Purpura, S. and D. Hillard (2006). Automated classification of congressional legislation. In *Proceedings of the 2006 International Conference on Digital government Research*, pp. 219–225. Digital Government Society of North America.

Reese, B., J. Hunter, N. Asher, P. Denis, and J. Baldridge (2007). *Reference manual for the analysis and annotation of rhetorical structure (version 1.0)*. Technical report. Austin: University of Texas, Departments of Linguistics and Philosophy. Available online: http://timeml. org/jamesp/annotation_manual. pdf.

Rohde, H., A. Dickinson, N. Schneider, C. N. Clark, A. Louis, and B. Webber (2016). Filling in the blanks in understanding discourse adverbials: Consistency, conflict, and context-dependence in a crowdsourced elicitation task. In *Proceedings of the 10th Linguistic Annotation Workshop (LAW X)*, pp. 49–58.

Sanders, T. J. and W. P. Spooren (2015). Causality and subjectivity in discourse: The meaning and use of causal connectives in spontaneous conversation, chat interactions and written text. *Linguistics 53*(1), 53–92.

Sanders, T. J., K. Vis, and D. Broeder (2012). Project notes of CLARIN project DiscAn: Towards a discourse annotation system for Dutch language corpora. In *Workshop on Interoperable Semantic Annotation (ISA)*, pp. 61–65.

Scholman, M. C. and V. Demberg (2017). Examples and specifications that prove a point: Identifying elaborative and argumentative discourse relations. *Dialogue & Discourse 8*(2), 56–84.

Scholman, M. C., J. Evers-Vermeul, and T. J. Sanders (2016). Categories of coherence relations in discourse annotation: Towards a reliable categorization of coherence relations. *Dialogue & Discourse 7*(2), 1–28.

Scott, W. A. (1959). Reliability of content analysis: The case of nominal scale coding. *Public Opinion Quarterly 19*(3), 321–325.

Spooren, W. P. and L. Degand (2010). Coding coherence relations: Reliability and validity. *Corpus Linguistics and Linguistic Theory 6*(2), 241–266.

Van Deemter, K. and R. Kibble (2000). On coreferring: Coreference in MUC and related annotation schemes. *Computational Linguistics 26*(4), 629–637.

Wongpakaran, N., T. Wongpakaran, D. Wedding, and K. Gwet (2013). A comparison of Cohen's Kappa and Gwet's AC1 when calculating inter-rater reliability coefficients: A study conducted with personality disorder samples. *BMC Medical Research Methodology 13*(61), 1–7.

Xie, Q. (2013). Agree or disagree? A demonstration of an alternative statistic to Cohen's kappa for measuring the extent and reliability of agreement between observers. Unpublished manuscript.

Yang, H., J. Callan, and S. Shulman (2006). Next steps in near-duplicate detection for eRulemaking. In *Proceedings of the 2006 International Conference on Digital Government Research*, pp. 239–248. Digital Government Society of North America.

Zhao, X., J. S. Liu, and K. Deng (2013). Assumptions behind intercoder reliability indices. *Annals of the International Communication Association 36*(1), 419–480.

A Semantically-Based Computational Approach to the Annotation of Narrative Style

Rodolfo Delmonte
Ca' Foscari University of Venice
(delmont@unive.it)

Giulia Marchesini
Ca' Foscari University of Venice
(giuliamarches@gmail.com)

Abstract

This work describes the annotation of the novel "The Solid Mandala" (Patrick White, 1966), carried out combining sentiment and opinion mining on character level with the Appraisal Theory framework, here used to identify evaluative statements and their contribution to the social dimension of the text. Our approach was inspired by research on the correlation between White's style and the personality of his main characters. The annotation was manually executed by second author using an XML standard markup system and double-checked by first author. In this paper we comment on the selected features, focusing on the ones acquiring specialized meaning in the context of the novel, and provide results in terms of quantitative data. Comparing them, we are able to extract story units in which *special or significant events* take place, and to predict the presence or similar units in the narrative by detecting concentrations of features. Eventually collecting all annotations has made available a lexicon where all ambiguities are clearly identifiable and verifiable. The lexicon will be used in the future for the automatic annotation of other novels.

1 Introduction

In this paper we will demonstrate the use of deep semantic features in the annotation of a complex narrative text, the novel "The Solid Mandala", by White (1966), in an effort to prove the main tenet of White's style as purported by G. Collier in his "The Rocks and Sticks of Words" (Collier (1992) hence, GC1992). The theory states that White makes use of linguistic features to define his characters more accurately and at a deeper level, deliberately using specific words, phrases, syntactic structures and semantic features to profile each main character in the narrative and to highlight personality traits. Collier defines many interesting recurring features which seem to be prominent in the novel, features which we therefore incorporated in our annotation scheme.

"The Solid Mandala" is a particularly interesting sample for analysis because of the peculiarity of its structure and of its style. It is in fact divided into four distinct sections, each written as if through the eyes of one of the main characters. Using such a narrative as a starting point, we aim in the future to expand the limitations of the current annotation system, which is now partly tailored to the novel, to include many other kinds of narrative texts. This will be made possible by the collected annotations in a lexicon where head words are associated to their lemmata (see Delmonte and Marchesini (2017)).

In our case, White's style always maintains internal consistency, but it does so adapting its qualifying linguistic elements according to the lens of the narrating point of view – there are three main characters, and each of them is tasked with narrating a portion of the same story. Other elements impacting linguistic features are the nature of the relationships between the characters and the specificity of the events in their lives, and all of them are considered in the evaluation of the annotation.

As for the elements chosen for analysis, we started from semantic features connected to psychology and affection and included particularly meaningful syntactic structures, as we will see in more detail below. Predicates and verbs in general, for example, are often crucial to interpret many layers of textual analysis. Different aspects, tenses and modes all influence reader interpretation: an imperfective psychological verb might be related to a conscious, lasting mental process, while a perfective one might indicate unconscious realization and can come back later in the form of recognition.

For a general overview, we want to give a first quantitative outline of the novel. Its text has been divided into 131 **narremes**, defined as minimal independent story units as in GC1992 (p, 35-36) (see also Bonheim (2000)), each of independent size and connected to a specific event.[1] Table 1 indicates the total number of tokens considered and the number of annotations, both of single tokens (as in "thinks") and of compounds (as in "is thinking").

The manual annotation made on a text editor took around three months of work to complete, including revision and evaluation of the preliminary results. The contents of this paper refer to these evaluations. We are currently looking for trained annotators in order to provide data on inter-annotator agreement on at least a subset of the novel.

Items	Total	Standard Deviation
Tokens	120,249	1149.3
Annotations	8616	84.26

Table 1: Number of tokens (including punctuation), annotations, and their standard deviation

2 Semantic Features as Inherent Items of White's Style

As mentioned, we considered semantic features (see Bos and Delmonte (2008), Delmonte and Pallotta (2011)) as the main elements used to link the style and the personality of the three main characters. They are the twins Waldo and Arthur Brown, each narrating one of the two main sections of the book, and their neighbour Mrs Poulter, who instead narrates the shorter first and last sections corresponding to prologue and epilogue.

Both the fabula – the chronological order of events – and the sujet – their stylistic rearrangement, or plot, here a complex back and forth of memories alternated with actional present – were taken in consideration, mostly thanks to the fragmentation of the text in single events (narremes). After the annotation it is simpler to look at the narrative stream and to immediately spot evident concentrations of features, signaling highly relevant and symbolic events.

As for the annotation task itself, it was organized in three main meta-tags and a number of hierarchically related more specific ones, as shown in the table below. The annotation scheme is original and based on characteristics of the XML markup standard (elements, attributes and values). In this section we will discuss the reasoning behind the chosen categories.

2.1 Commenting Features and Their Relevance to the Storyline

Our three high level features, the meta-tags, are *uncertainty*, *subjectivity* and *judgement*. Additionally, we annotated with the element *negative* all negative forms in the novel.

With "uncertainty" we mark all the parts of the text which carry in their syntactic, semantic or pragmatic value a sense of interpretation of the storyworld by the characters (e.g. "it seems"). This interpretation may express the more or less conscious doubts in the minds of the protagonists. At the opposite end, it can also signal a judgement of certainty, which – ironically – generates in turn insecurity in the reader and raises the question: 'Is the narrator reliable?'. In this analysis the element of uncertainty, abbreviated

---

[1] By *narreme* we (and he) mean here a basic story unit and a microstructure covering one independent event, as conveyed via a single or multiple points of view. As Collier notes (Collier (1992) pp. 37-43), it is important to remember that these narremes are merely heuristic abstractions, albeit very useful ones when it comes to psychological narrative. Not so is the opinion of other narratologists, who claim a structural causal relation intervening between each narreme (Wittmann (1975) pp. 19-28). In his analysis, Collier only takes action-oriented narremes, or "process statements", as opposed to "stasis statements". The latter passages of the novel are mostly a-temporal, descriptive, and purely psychological; in any case, they are never tied to a specific event or series of events, unlike the former. Since we needed to cover the whole text of the novel, and not only the process statements, an expansion of the original list was needed. So eventually we passed from 124 narremes of Collier to 131

Uncertainty	Subjectivity	Judgement
Non-factual	*Psychology*	*Social-esteem*
Seeming	Perception	Positive/Negative
Gnomic	Precognition	*Social-sanction*
Concessive	Cognition	Positive/Negative
Conditional	PerformWill	
DefDesire	*Affect-emot*	
Will	Positive/Negative	
Possibility	*Affect-inclin*	
Ability	Positive/Negative	
Obligation	*Affect-secur*	
Assumption	Positive/Negative	
	Affect-satisf	
	Positive/Negative	

Table 2: Hierarchy of deep semantic features used in the annotation

as *uncertnty* in the annotation, has only one obligatory attribute: non-factual (see Sauri and Pustejovsky (2012)). It is in fact crucial in this case to establish the annotated expression as non-real, non-factual, as something that is only going on in the character's mind and which does not have an equivalent in the 'real world' of the story.

"Subjectivity" (see Taboada et al. (2011), Pang and Lee (2004)) focuses instead on various facets of character psychology. The main difference between *uncertainty* and *subjectivity* lies in the fact that the first category is about how the protagonists rationalize their reality, while the second marks the modalities in which they actively and subjectively contribute to the narrative. The former is non-factual in nature, but the latter always has consequences. *Subjectivity* includes active psychological processes both conscious and unconscious as studied by the cognitive sciences, as well as expressions of emotion and different kinds of feelings. These sub-categories are grouped into five attributes: *psychology, affect-emotivity, affect-inclination, affect-security* and *affect-satisfaction*. While psychology can have different values, the other four can only have two: positive or negative.

The last element is "judgement", abbreviated as *judgmnt* in the annotation, which marks all evaluative expressions and aims at highlighting social and personal reactions to the storyworld. The theoretical basis of this category can be found in the so-called "Appraisal Theory" (see Martin and White (2005) (hence M&W2005), Read and Carrol (2012), Taboada and Grieve (2004)). This theory emphasizes the relevance of impressions and judgements in the formation of feelings, emotions, and complex thoughts. Environment and psychology are here understood as being in a relation of mutual dependency, with the reactions of each individual to stimuli evoking different responses. Since we are talking about a novel, this system is of course artificial and created by the author. From a general standpoint we can say that *judgement* and the above-mentioned *affect* have a lot in common, both dealing with indices of emotion and sentiment (see Kim and Hovy (2004), Kao and Jurafsky (2012). In this specific study, however, it was decided to annotate *judgement* as an independent element for two main reasons: firstly in order to stress our interest in evaluative language, and secondly in order to allow a more detailed internal differentiation between the attributes of *social-esteem* (personal dimension, e.g. appreciated/unappreciated) and *social-sanction* (social dimension, e.g. allowed/forbidden).

A more detailed description of attributes and values follows.

2.2   Features in Detail: Uncertainty

<uncertnty non-factual= "seeming">

Seeming is the probably the most representative of all the values of *non-factual*, and *uncertainty* in general. It is in fact the class that most refers to irrealia – indices referring to non-real elements of the storyworld. These figural and stylistic indices, meant to mark the internalization of experience by the characters of the novel, are defined as indices of *figural apperception* (see GC1992, pp. 140-141)[2]. This value covers indicative verbs (e.g. "seemed"), modal statements (e.g. "must have"), adverbial clauses (e.g. "as though") and discourse markers (e.g. "perhaps"). In the case of modal verbs cases of ambiguity can arise, particularly with "must have" and the *assumption* class. To keep the distinction clear, modal verbs were only marked as *seeming* when their meaning was obviously indexical to character judgement.

<uncertnty non-factual= "gnomic">

Gnomic sentences are characterized by frequent use of the present tense, sententious tone, and generalization. Their use in White's style has been largely controversial in academic discussions and often interpreted as authorial intrusiveness, but in this analysis we choose to consider it as another element of apperception: through the formulation of generalizations and conclusions the characters rationalize their reality. In this interpretation gnomic expressions, either complete sentences or significant parts of larger ones, are read as the manifestation in the style of a psychological process.

<uncertnty non-factual= "concessive">

Fragments of text annotated as *concessive* always have a clear semantic value and structure. We made a distinction between 'true' concessives (e.g. "even if/though") and *if-concessives* or *pseudo-concessives* (e.g. "good, if bitter") (see GC1992; p. 187), not to be confused with the similar *if-conditional* type. Their occurrence in the novel is so high that we can talk about it as a pervasive characteristic of White's writing, at least in this particular novel.

<uncertnty non-factual= "conditional">

Conditional markers are another example of how a common syntactic structure can carry significant stylistic and narratological weight. In our case hypotheticals are particularly tied to character psychology and provide differentiations between the narrating characters. They see different applications in varying degrees of rationalization and justification, both real and putative, depending on the case.

<uncertnty non-factual= "defdesire">

Defdesire is here short for "desire defeated by grammar". It is a peculiar way of using conditionals, when a character's desire is negated by the structure of the sentence itself. Because of this high level of specialization and its importance for character psychology – it carries in fact negative semantic traits connected to pessimism and failure – we considered it as a separate value in the current annotation.

<uncertnty non-factual= "will">

Expressions of *will* represent the first of five groups of non-factual modal – or in this case, modal-like – values. We selected for this category all verbs of will and wish (including "like", "would like to" and "would have liked to" when synonyms of "want") and the noun "will". More difficult to solve were expressions of "be willing to", potentially overlapping with *inclination* or even *psychology* (see below). In order to disambiguate, we selected only the expressions stressing the verb and the result – action or inaction, highlighted by the presence of "to".

<uncertnty non-factual= "possibility">

Possibility is connected to prospects, odds, and opportunities. It consists of a variety of different elements, from modal verbs to nouns, from adjectives to adverbs, all of them playing a similar role in conveying the concepts of 'option' or 'likelihood' as seen from the point of view of the protagonists (e.g. "may", "might", "can", "could", "possibility", "possible", "possibly"...).

<uncertnty non-factual= "ability">

Ability (e.g. "can", "be able to") is a class of modality which can sometimes be confused with the previous one, *possibility*. Its range of meaning is generally described as varying between general abilities (e.g. "I can swim" – always) and specific abilities (e.g. "You can do this" – now), and this distinction is maintained in the present research. Additionally, in "The Solid Mandala" we annotated as *ability* a specific "would", which seems to be a linguistic irregularity associated with Australian slang.

---

[2] *Seeming* and *uncertainty* in general can sometimes be judged as ironic statements, as well, but Collier chooses not to cover this possibility in his analysis and we in turn follow his suggestion. (Collier (1992) pp. 44-45, Reyes et al. (2012))

<uncertnty non-factual= "obligation">

It is dedicated to expressions of obligation and need, including commitments, duties, necessities, coercions, and sometimes even a sense of inevitability (e.g. "must", "ought to", "be forced to", "necessity", "necessary"...). Ambiguous occurrences were the expressions of "need": when followed by "to" they usually express obligation, and when on their own (e.g. "need something") they are not synonyms of "have to" and were marked as *inclination*. Another ambiguous case was the resolution of "should", which can also indicate *assumption*.

<uncertnty non-factual= "assumption">

Assumption (e.g. "should/should have", "must/must have") can have a twofold scope of meaning: the first is related to hypotheses, speculations, deductions, beliefs and abstract ideas; the second refers to suggestions or offers. The psychological value of assumption relates to two kinds of processes: rationalization for the first range of denotations, and preparations of future events for the second.

2.3   Features in Detail: Subjectivity

Four of the values of *subjectivity*, the ones connected to *affect* (inspired by Martin and White (2005), see also Wiebe et al. (2005), Turney and Littman (2003), Kao and Jurafsky (2012)) can be defined with a positive/negative polarity of values, while only one of them, *psychology* can take four different values. *Psychology* contains all cognitive indices, including terms indicating perception, memory, thought, imagination, metacognition, and so on.

<subjectivity psychology= "perception">   *Perception* can mark two groups of terms: those directly connected to the physical five senses (e.g. "hear", "see", "the sound"), and those related to the primary mental processes tasked with interpreting them (such as basic attention, e.g. "noticeably").

<subjectivity psychology= "precognition">

Unconscious or semi-conscious mental processes, represented by psychological verbs, belong to this value (e.g. "listen", "wonder"), and often tend to overlap with other classes, as is the case for instance with expressions of fear or doubt. In order to maintain the distinction as clear as possible, we have marked under *precognition* all generic expressions of feeling, wondering, wide-ranging ideas and immediate impressions, as well as interpretations of stimuli (e.g. forms of listen) and thoughts (when they take the form of feelings, intuitions, or impressions; e.g. thinking something of someone's attitude). Moreover, the concept of knowledge is here considered as a cognitive function instead of precognitive.

<subjectivity psychology= "cognition">

This value mostly describes psychological verbs connected to consciousness and awareness (e.g. "remember", "realize", "understand"). As occurs in precognition, cognition is a category of psychological verbs only, despite their great variety. For this reason the concept of "knowledge" is considered to involve consciousness and to be more similar to the idea of awareness, and therefore as a part of the cognitive group, while perfective and "one-time" uses of verbs like "think" (when it indicates feelings etc.; see above) are classified as precognitive. The goal is to distinguish more clearly between the domain of the "spirit" – feelings, impressions and abstract thought, all precognitive – and the domain of the "mind" – with awareness, memory, decisional processes, hopes and knowledge (both theoretical and with a semantic substrate of "acquaintance") among its most important functions. Another reason for the distinction is, then, the implementation of the "emotional" categories that we shall witness in the following sections, which may cause overlapping and confusion between the groups.

<subjectivity psychology= "performwill">

Short for "performative cognition and will", *performwill* marks expressions of extreme self-control and imposition of personal will on reality (e.g. special use of "decide"). The storyworld isn't rationalized as it is, but as the character wills it. Expressions of performwill are not simply cognitive indices but represent an extreme form of self-control as for instance for Waldo and his perpetual attempt to control reality and the ways in which this influences how he perceives external stimuli and other people. This strong manifestation of will can be either positive or negative: it is positive when a character – usually Waldo – more or less consciously forces himself to say something or to act in a certain way, and it is negative when the same willpower is directed at restraining oneself from doing something or at avoiding and negating some realization or other.

<subjectivity affect-emot= "positive/negative">

The attribute *affect-emot* (emotion) marks all the expressions indicating happiness or unhappiness in the novel, the former distinguishing between cheer and affection (e.g. "jovially", "love") and the latter between misery and antipathy (e.g. "sorry", "despise").

<subjectivity affect-inclin= "positive/negative">

The positive aspect of *affect-inclin* (inclination) expresses varying degrees of desire and longing, all with comparable active traits of optimism and eagerness (e.g. "desire", "waiting"). Its negative end is instead annotated when someone is shown as far from eager to do, experience, or say something. It involves feelings of suspicion, mistrust and concern, if not outright anxiety or even terror (e.g. "afraid", "had feared"). As with the other affect categories, affect-inclin (inclination) covers an emotional spectrum. Its positive end usually expresses varying degrees of desire and longing, all with comparable active traits of optimism and eagerness. In this respect, this category was mentioned earlier in the context of the annotation of uncertnty non-factual="will"; the two aspects are alike in their general acceptation of "desire" and "will", but while the category under uncertnty non-factual deals with the modal side of the semantic field, affect-inclin marks projections of eagerness and feelings of longing or craving.

<subjectivity affect-secur= "positive/negative">

Short for security, it refers in its positive value to expressions of self-assurance, calm, hope and reliance (e.g. "trust", "confidence", "relief") and in it negative one to the reverse: disquiet, insecurity, anxiety, lack of confidence, and sometimes indices of fear (e.g. "surprise", "sweat"). A surprise is not always negative per se, but in this case always shows some degree of lack of security for a character, and is therefore part of the negative value. Affect-secur (security) marks yet another aspect of the varied overview of sensations. Its positive value is referred to in expressions of self-assurance, calm, hope and/or reliance, while the negative indicates the reverse: insecurity, anxiety, lack of confidence, and sometimes indices of fear. It is at this point necessary, focusing on fear, to establish a difference between this "security fear" and the "inclination fear" presented in the previous section, which are part of the same semantic field and can sometimes overlap – in a similar way to "non-factual will" and "inclination will". The main divergence between the two classes is in the semantic traits associated with each category: while "inclination fear", as we saw, expresses "not wanting to do something", often a concern for the future or inward rebellion against an idea, "security fear" indicates a sense of alarm and fright. It is not apprehension, but a nervousness caused by a lack of security, be it self-confidence or danger coming from the outside world.

<subjectivity affect-satisf= "positive/negative">

Affect-satisf (satisfaction) deals with the last aspect of the emotive sphere as it is considered in the current analysis. The positive value of this attribute marks all indices of approval, pleasure, agreement and curiosity, (e.g. "appeal") all deeply connected with the idea of "happiness" explored above and sometimes slightly overlapping with positive inclinations. At the opposite pole we find the negative connotations of dissatisfaction, including bother, sense of monotony, disapproval, impatience and anger (e.g. "yawned", "furious"). Expressions based on the notion of "satisfaction", in fact, are deeply connected with self-fulfillment and the possible lack thereof, which are among the most relevant themes of the whole novel. We can distinguish among four self-explanatory subcategories, Interest (satisfaction); Pleasure (satisfaction); Ennui (dissatisfaction); Displeasure (dissatisfaction).

2.4   Features in detail: judgement

The last content-related element introduced in the annotation is, as was the case with the affect attributes, an addition to the original theory formulated by Collier. In this annotation, judgmnt (judgement) marks all evaluative expressions relating to the characters of the novel, aimed at highlighting both social and personal reactions to the storyworld and particularly to the other characters and their behavior. The theoretical basis of this category can be found in the so-called "appraisal theory",(see Martin and White

(2005) p.111) which underscores the relevance of impressions and judgments in the formation of feelings, emotions, and complex thoughts. Environment and psychology are here understood as standing in a relation of mutual dependency, with the reactions of each individual to events and stimuli evoking different responses. Speaking of the characters of a novel, in this case, we can say that the "artificially created" psychology of every character reacts in substantially different ways to what happens in the storyworld. From a general point of view we can say that judgmnt and affect as categories have a lot in common, both dealing as they do with indices of emotion and sentiment. In this specific study, however, it was decided to annotate judgmnt as an independent element, for two main reasons: the first was to emphasize our interest in the evaluative language used by the author, and the second was to allow a more detailed internal differentiation between the categories of social-esteem and social-sanction and their respective polarities. For this very reason the element has two attributes with two values each. Both social-esteem and social-sanction are characterized by a social and a personal component. The social one is predominant, since in both attributes something is evaluated as positive when it is socially acceptable, and is considered negative when it does not respect social norms. The personal approach to the evaluation is as important, however, particularly in a novel like The Solid Mandala in which the protagonists are rarely socially accepted themselves, and were raised in a rather closed and secluded environment.

<judgmnt social-esteem= "positive/negative">

This category is used to mark adjectives and a few adverbs indicating respect and admiration (e.g. "healthy-looking", "reliable") or, at the negative pole, criticism and denigration (e.g. "peculiar", "capricious"). We identified three subcategories of this attribute, each with the internal polarity positive/negative: Normality ("how special?"), including lucky, predictable, fashionable / unlucky, eccentric, obscure, etc.; Capacity ("how capable?"), including robust, experienced, competent / weak, stupid, ignorant, etc.; Tenacity ("how dependable?"), including brave, thorough, faithful / timid, reckless, inconstant, etc.

<judgmnt social-sanction= "positive/negative">

In the case of *social-sanction*, the annotation focuses on particularly strong expressions of admiration or social denounce (see Martin and White (2005)). Similar in nature to social-esteem instances, these indices tend to be more general and often deal with moral and ethical issues, labeling adjectives and adverbs which refer to universal appraisal (e.g. "kindly", "honest") or universal condemnation (e.g. "indecent", "dishonest"). Two subclasses distinguished by semantic traits can be found under this attribute: Veracity ("how honest?"), deals with issues of truth and general trust, including truthful, candid, tactful / deceitful, manipulative, blunt, etc.; Propriety ("how far beyond reproach?"), deals with ethical issues. It includes moral, law-abiding, humble / evil, mean, irreverent, etc.

<negative= "/negative">

Negative is the last element in this annotation, and its characteristics lead it to be considered as separate from the others. It does not represent, in fact, a textual tag (like narreme, p and s) but a content-related one, and at the same time it is much "simpler" than the other elements explained above (uncertnty, subjectivity and judgmnt). It marks all the negations in the novel, in all their possible forms - taking care of double negations which are not regarded as such. The annotation often includes the complete form of the verb being negated (e.g. <negative>did not say</negative>), but not necessarily whole expressions, especially when dealing with modals (e.g. <negative>did not want</negative> to go). While in this particular study the frequency of negative versus positive verbs is particularly relevant because of the numerous verbal tags, these are not the only elements to be annotated. The negative tag was applied to many adjectives, pronouns and adverbs when appropriate, as well as to colloquial forms of "no" – both in direct and in indirect speech. A last comment must be made on the annotation of negative as applied to verbs. In the case of never (see the second example) and in some cases of not (fourth example), it was decided not to include the verbs they depended on, in order to highlight the negation in itself. This decision relied on the fact that "never" and "not", the latter when followed by an adjective, mostly occur independently. Tagging them by themselves is the easiest way to make quantitative evaluations about their distribution in the text.

3 Discussion of Experimental Data

The first thing to notice is the still-high level of ambiguity in our extracted lexicon. All our extracted information was collected in a lexicon with each occurrence (e.g. "here") followed by a compound feature label, or series of labels, (e.g. "subjct-psychology-cognition") and the narreme index. From this general lexicon we derived another one, this time only composed of unique forms. High ambiguity was then apparent. As seen in Table 1, the total number of extracted features amounts to 8646, but the non-repeated count only amounts to 1584. This means that there are forms which are present in the lexicon more than once and within different categories. An example is the form "hear", which can belong to *cognition*, *perception* or *precognition* depending on the case. We calculated a total of 121 entries having double or triple meaning.[3] This final lexicon, made of word-forms associated with lemmata, potentially makes ambiguity a resource: it allows in fact to check for possible associated meaning in other meaning repositories. One of our goals is to use this principle to try and automatically tag other texts by the same author, checking the level of coverage and eventually moving on to other kinds of texts.

Back to the current analysis, extracting information from the annotated text allowed us to confirm our starting hypothesis: the style exhibits different characteristics depending both on the profile of the narrating character and on the nature and context of the specific event in the narrative. In the extraction of data and subsequent discussion the categories employed in the annotation system are referred to as *traits*. Their names (seeming, cognition, affect-secur...) stay the same, but each and every one of them is hereby envisioned as a psychological trait to be investigated.

We applied quantitative information about trait distribution to every main character – Waldo Brown, Arthur Brown and Mrs Poulter – using the above-mentioned narremes (story units), which provide us with the narrator for each event. With three distinct portions of text, each related to a protagonist, we were able to study which traits prevailed and therefore to draw conclusions about character profiling.

For each trait we calculated a ratio using the formula:

[annotations of trait X for given character / total of annotations of trait X]

We then considered the length of the three sections, with Waldo's being the longest by far and Mrs Poulter's the shortest, and established as *significant* for our analysis every trait with a ratio of more than 0.65 for Waldo, 0.3 for Arthur, and 0.11 for Mrs Poulter. You can see a list of these *significant traits* for each character in Table 3.

The distribution of traits gives us valuable data on character profiling. We can see, for example, that Waldo Brown almost has exclusive access to *performative will* (with a ratio of more than 0.9) and that many of his significant traits are connected to appraisal with a negative polarity – manifesting a tendency to judge himself and/or others, and a feeling of being judged. It is not by chance if we find the negative declinations of *affect-inclination* and *affect-security*, as well, since they both deal with indices of apathy, anxiety, insecurity and fear. Moreover, the high frequence of *precognition* and *seeming* suggests that the character uses indices of interpreting phenomena before interiorizing them, raising the chance that we are dealing with a particularly unreliable narrator. Even for someone who has not read the novel, the general profile of the character is at this point established.

The same principle is valid for the other main characters, even with less significant traits. Arthur Brown's highest value is assigned to *defeated desire* which, along with the positive value of *inclination*, *ability*, *assumption* and both values of *satisfaction*, suggests a character striving to do something, pondering his abilities and those of others, and mostly exhibiting a pessimistic note about final impossibility

---

[3] A few more examples, as they appear in our Prolog-compiled lexicon:
lx(confused,confuse,[subjct-affect-secur-negative,subjct-psychology-cognition]).
lx(contemplate,,contemplate,[subjct-psychology-perception,subjct-psychology-precognition]).
lx(could-not-have-been,be,[uncrtn-non-factual-ability,uncrtn-non-factual-possibility]).
lx(embarrassing,embarass,[subjct-affect-emot-negative,subjct-affect-secur-negative]).
lx(frustration,frustrate,[subjct-affect-emot-negative,subjct-affect-satisf-negative]).
lx(intended,intend,[subjct-affect-inclin-positive,subjct-psychology-cognition,-psychology-performwill]).

Waldo	Arthur	Mrs Poulter
1. PerformWill	1. DefDesire	1. S-sanction (p)
2. Possibility	2. Inclin (p)	2. Gnomic
3. S-sanction (p)	3. Ability	3. S-esteem (p)
4. Precognition	4. Gnomic	4. Possibility
5. S-esteem (n)	5. Satisf (n)	5. Inclin (p)
6. Seeming	6. Satisf (p)	
7. S-sanction (n)	7. Assumption	
8. Inclin (n)		
9. Secur (n)		
10. S-esteem (p)		

Table 3: Significant traits for each character

to reach the goal. Interestingly, the sad and more realistic meaning of *defeated desire* is almost diametrically opposite to the wishful thinking of Waldo's *performative will*. Experience in Arthur's section is mostly expressed by positive *inclination* – opposed to Waldo's negative – towards life and others, and by a more generalized *gnomic* approach. These traits are present in Mrs Poulter, as well, indicating an important similarity between the two characters, but the differences are even more interesting. Mrs Poulter's section lacks all the dynamism and the interpretation of the world seen in Arthur's, using more basic *gnomic* rationalization and the positive appraisal values of *social sanction* and *social esteem*.

Additionally, distribution of traits was extremely useful to identify *significant events* (i.e. narremes with a high concentration of traits) and to investigate the nature of different relationships between main and secondary characters of the story. All these pieces of information contributed to an even more detailed psychological profile of the protagonists.

You can see the distribution of the occurrences in Table 4.

4 Conclusion

We presented the annotation of the whole text of "The Solid Mandala", by Patrick White, which was carried out by second author and double-checked by first author. The research was inspired by Gordon Collier's book about the same novel, "The Rocks and Sticks of Words", and it is based on many features suggested in it, with many changes and additions due to the specificity of our task. Suggestions from Martin & White's Appraisal Theory were included as well, introducing new features related to judgement and affect. The final results are here summarised with the help of tables and diagrams, clearly showing the effectiveness of this approach in highlighting psychological profiles of characters. The connection between profiles, authorial style and narratological level of analysis was also proved to be very strong. We intend to use the lexicon derived from the XML annotation to try and automatically annotate another novel by the same author, in order to evaluate the results in terms of coverage and precision. A second related goal is to use this analysis as a starting point to expand the annotation scheme to a larger target of narrative texts.

Tags/Chars	Waldo	Arthur	Mrs Poulter
Perception	674	303	109
Precognition	379	141	39
Cognition	953	460	140
PerformW	39	3	0
Seeming	512	198	56
Will	74	33	8
Possibility	224	54	42
Gnomic	32	20	9
Ability	347	195	51
Obligation	178	79	28
Concessive	150	75	26
Conditional	264	117	32
DefDesire	49	35	2
Assumption	73	36	9
Emot-Pos	400	183	43
Emot-Neg	247	107	30
Inclin-Pos	83	50	17
Inclin-Neg	75	26	12
Secur-Pos	133	65	19
Secur-Neg	297	116	40
Satis-Pos	136	66	10
Satis-Neg	215	112	25
Esteem-Pos	223	71	47
Esteem-Neg	346	129	39
Sanct-Pos	80	19	18
Sanct-Neg	127	47	16

Table 4: Distribution of semantic linguistic features for the three main characters

References

Bonheim, H. (2000). Shakespeare's narremes. *Shakespeare Survey: Shakespeare and narrative 53*.

Bos, J. and R. Delmonte (2008). *STEP '08 - Proceedings of the 2008 Conference on Semantics in Text Processing*. Semantics. London: College Publications.

Collier, G. (1992). *The Rocks and Sticks of Words Style, Discourse and Narrative Structure in the Fiction of Patrick White*. Amsterdam Atlanta: Editions Rodopi B. V.

Delmonte, R. and G. Marchesini (2017). A semantically based computational approach to narrative structure. In *Proceedings of IWCS, International Workshop on Computational Semantics*, Stroudsburg, PA, USA, pp. 8–17. ACL.

Delmonte, R. and V. Pallotta (2011). *Opinion Mining and Sentiment Analysis Need Text Understanding*, pp. 81–95. Berlin, Heidelberg: Springer Berlin Heidelberg.

Kao, J. and D. Jurafsky (2012). A computational analysis of style, affect, and imagery in contemporary poetry. In *Proceedings of NAACL Workshop on Computational Linguistics for Literature*, Stroudsburg, PA, USA, pp. 8–17. ACL.

Kim, S.-M. and E. Hovy (2004). Determining the sentiment of opinions. In *Proceedings of the 20th international conference on computational linguistics - COLING*, Stroudsburg, PA, USA, pp. 1367–1373. ACL.

Martin, J. and P. White (2005). *Language of Evaluation, Appraisal in English*. London and New York: Palgrave Macmillan.

Pang, B. and L. Lee (2004). A sentimental education: sentiment analysis using subjectivity summarization based on minimum cuts. In *Proceedings of the 42nd annual meeting of the Association for Computational Linguistics*, Stroudsburg, PA, USA, pp. 271–278. ACL.

Read, J. and J. Carrol (2012). Annotating expressions of appraisal in english. *Language Resources and Evaluation 46*, 421–447.

Reyes, A., P. Rosso, and D. Buscaldi (2012). From humor recognition to irony detection: The figurative language of social media. *Data & Knowledge Engineering*.

Sauri, R. and J. Pustejovsky (2012). Are you sure that this happened? assessing the factuality degree of events in text. *Computational Linguistics 38*(2), 261–299.

Taboada, M., J. Brooke, M. Tofiloski, K. Voll, and M. Stede (2011). Lexicon-based methods for sentiment analysis. *Computational Linguistics 37*(2), 267–307.

Taboada, M. and J. Grieve (2004). Analyzing appraisal automatically. In *Proceedings of the AAAI Spring Symposium on Exploring Attitude and Affect in Text: Theories and Applications*, pp. 158–161. AAAI Press.

Turney, P. D. and M. L. Littman (2003). Measuring praise and criticism: Inference of semantic orientation from association. *ACM Trans. Inf. Syst. 21*(4), 315–346.

White, P. (1966). *The Solid Mandala*. London: Eyre & Spottiswood.

Wiebe, J., T. Wilson, and C. Cardie (2005). Annotating expressions of opinions and emotions in language. *Language Resources and Evaluation 39*(2), 165–210.

Wittmann, H. (1975). Thorie des narrèmes et algorithmes narratifs. *Poetics 4*(1), 19–28.

APPENDIX
Figures of Deep Semantic Features and their Distribution in Narremes

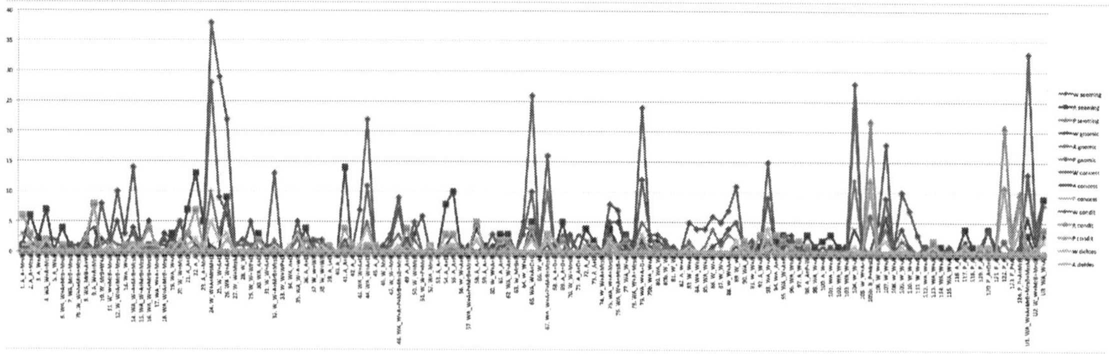

Figure 1: Distribution of uncertainty in 131 narremes

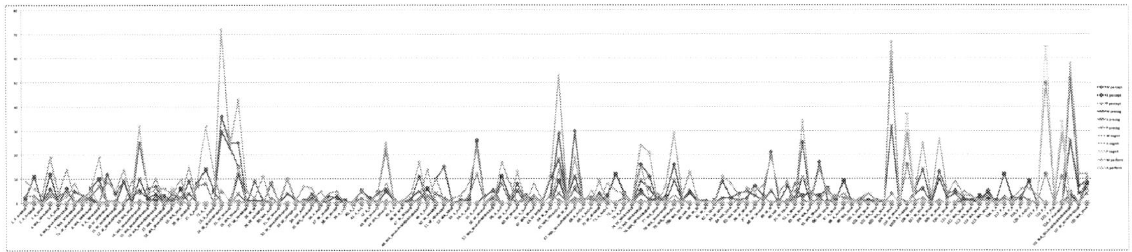

Figure 2: Distribution of psychology in 131 narremes

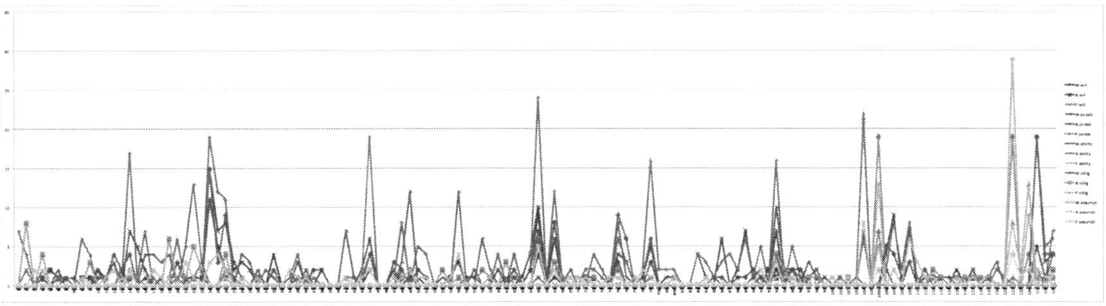

Figure 3: Distribution of modality in 131 narremes

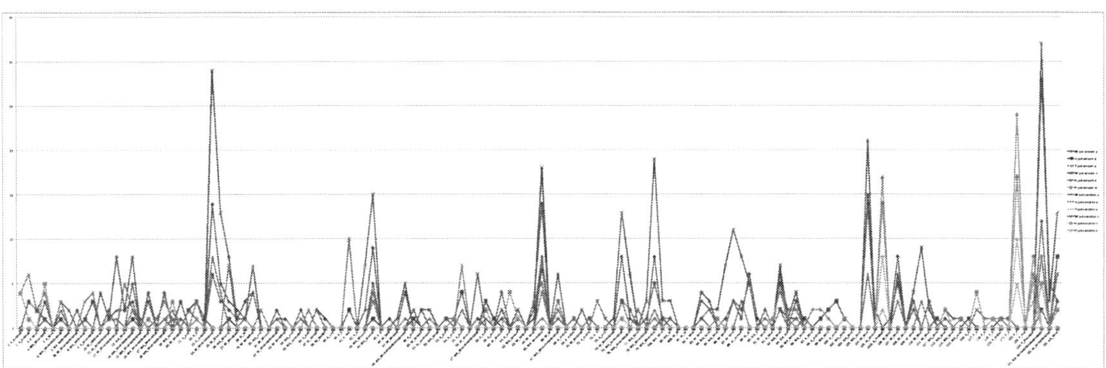

Figure 4: Distribution of judgement in 131 narremes

Annotating Similes in Literary Texts

Suzanne Mpouli
Université de Lyon, Lyon 2, ERIC EA 3083
`suzanne.mpouli@eric.univ-lyon2.fr`

Abstract

Annotated corpora are invaluable resources for researchers in the humanities: on the one hand, for natural processing tasks, they can serve as standards against which results from new automatic methods can be measured; on the other hand, in corpus-based studies, they enable either to answer existing research questions or to explore original ones. In this respect, some annotation frameworks such as the Text Encoding Initiative (TEI) attempt to standardise annotation practices in order to facilitate data reuse and exchange. However, despite the crucial role played by figurative language in general and similes in particular in language, no consensus has been reached so far on how to comprehensively annotate them in literary texts. The present paper proposes a framework for annotating similes in literary texts which takes into consideration their semantic and syntactic characteristics as well as the challenges inherent to the automatic detection of similes.

1 Introduction

Be them written or spoken, human-produced sentences are fraught with figures of speech, which possibly explain why, in recent years, various annotated corpora and annotation schemes have been elaborated to describe several of these figures from a linguistic perspective:

- metonymy in Markert and Nissim (2002);

- metaphor in Steen et al. (2010), Shutova and Teufel (2010), and Gordon et al. (2015);

- irony in Gianti et al. (2012), Trevisan et al. (2014), Van Hee et al. (2016), and Karoui et al. (2017);

- figures of repetition in Gawryjolek (2009), and Ruan et al. (2016).

However, despite the important place that figures of speech occupy in literary analysis and the linguistic creativity that particularly characterise fictional writings, literary texts have rarely been at the centre of these research endeavours. Similarly, generally speaking, the automatic detection of figures of speech has mostly been focused on general texts, consumer reviews and social media. Although, especially as far as figurative language is concerned, the quality of the results obtained and the coverage of these detection methods still need to be further improved, it is undeniable that digital versions of literary texts could tremendously benefit from the presence of stylistic annotations of figures of speech both for research and teaching purposes .

Rather than attempting to propose a framework that takes into consideration all existing figures of speech, this paper focuses on the simile, defined as a figure of speech which relies on a linguistic marker to draw a parallel between two or more distinct entities or processes based on stated or implied (dis)similarities, so as to build up a specific image in another person's mind. If like the metaphor, the simile is based on resemblance and exemplifies figurative language, it is also structurally identical to literal comparisons, which are very effective to sustain an argumentation. In addition, the simile is flexible enough to be combined with other figures of speech, as illustrated by the following examples:

- Simile + personification/animation: *Diseases* **like** **snakes** *crawling over the earth, leaving trails of slime.* [Lowell (1916)]

- Simile + alliteration: [...] The spring *will come back* like **a blooming bride** [...] [Mason (1914)].

- Simile + humour: For statesmen are as *thick* as **fleas**, and poets, they are between [...] [Mason (1916)].

Therefore, with respect to their pervasiveness in language and the wide spectrum of figures of speech they can be associated with, similes provide a large framework to study in detail the issues related to the annotation of figures of speech in literary texts.

The present paper is divided into four main parts. So as to better understand how similes are described stylistically in scholarly texts, Section 2 presents the main simile types and structures. Section 3 reviews two existing annotated corpora while Section 4 describes the simile annotation scheme that has been developed to produce a standard corpus based on the data collected from the (Dis)Similitudes platform.[1] Finally, Section 5 concludes the paper and discusses future work.

2 Simile Types and Structures in Stylistics

Using the terminology introduced by Richards (1936) to designate the elements of a metaphor, excluding the marker of comparison, a simile comprises at most three elements:

- the tenor, which is the entity or process that is compared;

- the ground or "the basis on which the comparison is made" (Strachan and Terry (2000));

- and the vehicle or standard that is used to establish the comparison.

In practice, at the sentence level, apart from the marker and the vehicle, the remaining components could be omitted; for example, as opposed to a close simile that contains a ground, a simile without any ground is called an open simile as it leaves more room for imagination. Thus, a close simile such as "She is soft, crinkled like a fading rose" [Lowell (1916)] would be analysed as follows:

She   is *soft, crinkled*   like   **a fading rose**
```
tenor       ground       marker     vehicle
```
As a comparative sentence, such a simile, of course, has the canonical structure of the comparative construction in most Indo-European languages: **object of comparison + shared quantity/quality + marker of comparison + standard of comparison**. When putting side by side the simile "She is soft, crinkled like a fading rose" and the literal comparison "Her hands are soft, crinkled like her sister's", it becomes obvious that a simile and a literal comparison differ only in terms of semantics: a simile uses world knowledge to help deduce and picture specific features of an entity in relation to another entity which generally belongs to a different semantic domain while a comparison merely states whether two entities are equal or not. In addition, on the surface, a third type of grammatical constructions, referred to as pseudo-comparisons, has exactly the same syntactic structure as literal comparisons and consequently, similes. As a matter of fact, in some cases, markers of comparison convey an estimation ("approximation"), highlight a function ("identification"), introduce a hyponym ("exemplification") or coordinate terms ("coordination").
Example of an identification: And so he yielded to his fate, and came forth as a candidate. [Mason (1916)].

Unlike similes and literal comparisons, although metaphors can be introduced by some signalling words (Goatly (2011)), they do not altogether require any comparative marker as the comparison they establish is implied and mostly takes place in the mind. Furthermore, metaphors correspond to a number of rather different syntactic patterns among which:

- the stand-alone vehicle: The surgeon toiled the livelong night above the gory **wreck**; he got the ribs adjusted right, the wishbone and the neck [Mason (1916)];

---

[1] English version: dissimilitudes.lip6.fr:8180; French version: dissimilitudes.lip6.fr:8181

Similes comparing entities	Similes involving processes
. . . sad and **corpse**-like is his face, as he carves his ancient veal. [Mason (1916)]	Miniature rockets peppering the black bricks with golden stars, as though **a gala flamed a night of victorious wars.**[Lowell (1916)]
The great gift the gods bestowed on mortal was his dome of thought [. . .]; it sometimes seems a trifling thing, less *useful* than **one's lungs or slats**. [Mason (1916)]	The empty form drops from a cloud, like **a gourd from a vine** [. . .] [Williams (1920)]
No more of his triumphs he *lilted*, like **Spartacus spieling in Rome**; the steel hearted warrior wilted, and followed his conquerer. [Mason (1914)]	I gazed upon that mighty flood, that *writhed* as though **in pain or woe**. [Mason (1916)]

Table 1: Examples of similes based on the nature of the compared elements

- a nominal vehicle and a verb : Every hour that's **gone**'s a dead one, and another **comes** and **goes** / **Lasso**, then, the hour that's with you, **ride** it till its back is sore. [Mason (1916)];

- a genitive link: [. . .] in **the graveyard** of the ages hours will find their last repose [Mason (1916)];

- an adjective and a noun: Every hour that's gone's a **dead** one, and another comes and goes [Mason (1916)];

- a copula: [. . .] her eyes were **stars, from heaven torn**, and she was guiltless of a corn upon her sweet angelic toes. [Mason (1916)]

Similarly, within the confines imposed by the comparative sentence, similes can be expressed through various markers and syntactic constructions. In this respect, despite the lack of consensus between scholars, the stylistic analysis of similes in literary texts has mainly been developed around two non-mutually exclusive paradigms: their syntactic structure and their semantic components. While the former encompasses word order as well as the length and number of simile components, the latter describes the semantic leap at work in similes in terms of semantic categories, animacy or abstractedness.

2.1   Syntactic Description of Similes

Based solely on the simile structure and the grammatical category of the vehicle, it is possible to distinguish between similes that compare entities and those that involve processes. While the first type is mostly restricted to nominal vehicles, vehicles in the latter one can be prepositional phrases, whole or elliptical clauses (see Table 1).

Authors can also create very simple stylistic effects by changing the canonical sentence word order, for instance by inverting the vehicle or even the tenor.

Examples: And behind her *came, slowly* as **a hunter**, a young man who wore a cloak of two colours. [Wilde (2000)]

His brawn stands out in hummocks, he like **a lion** *treads*; he sits on foemen's stomachs and stands them on their heads. [Mason (1914)]

Furthermore, so as to emphasise a particular point or to make an image more vivid, a simile can have more than one tenor, ground or vehicle. In this respect, Pistorius (1971) calls a simile with two grounds such as "The big black dog *went stalking on*, as *calm and tranquil* as **the dawn** [. . .] [Mason (1916)]" a "doubled simile", whereas Kirvalidze (2014) refers to it as a "polymotivated simile". If the simile rather has a ground related to more than one vehicle, or two grounds with different vehicles, a different effect is created as a second image is created to reinforce or to enhance the first one.

Examples: Like **a blow, a kiss, a caress**, my songs *shall came*. [Anderson (1918)]

It's freighted with a gentle woe as *old* as **all the seas that flow**, as *young* as **yesterday**; as *changeless* as **the stars above**, as *yearning* as **a woman's love for true knight far away**. [Mason (1916)]

Degree of abstraction	Degree of animacy
abstract tenor-concrete vehicle Lord has no use for the twenty-cent skate, whose <u>courage</u> is *weak* <u>as</u> **the foam** [...] [Mason (1916)]	inanimate tenor-animate vehicle So <u>the hours</u> <u>like</u> **spotted ponies** *trot along in single file* [...] [Mason (1916)]
abstract tenor-abstract vehicle ...when <u>failure</u> is as *certain* <u>as</u> **the coming of the dusk**, then it's wise to take your fiddle. [...] [Mason (1916)]	inanimate tenor-inanimate vehicle So does <u>his fame</u>, <u>like</u> **that lone mountain**, *rise, cleaving the mists and reaching the skies*[...] [Mason (1916)
concrete tenor-abstract vehicle Time to make a showing that your trade is growing, time to show your grit and *rustle round* <u>like</u> **the sin.** [Mason (1914)]	animate tenor-inanimate vehicle There's the man with hands so horny that <u>they</u> feel <u>like</u> **chunks of slate** [...] [Mason (1916)]
concrete tenor-concrete vehicle There's the man <u>whose hand</u> is *clammy* <u>as</u> **a fish that lately died** [...] [Mason (1916)]	animate tenor-animate vehicle And <u>the neighbors</u> come and chaff me, *laugh* <u>like</u> **horses at the door** [...] [Mason (1916)]

Table 2: Possible semantic combinations in similes

Besides increasing the number of similes components, creating a lack of balance between the length of the tenor and that of the vehicle often enables to shape a full-fledged image, typically by extending the vehicle with a relative clause.

Example: [...] I looked <u>as</u> *slick* <u>as</u> **a cabbage rose that's kissed by the nice wet dew.** [Mason (1916)]

Still on the structure of similes, Quintilian (Watson (1856)) observes that "sometimes the simile stands by itself and is unconnected; sometimes, as is preferable, it is joined with the object of which it is the representation, resemblances in the one answering to resemblances in the other". In the latter case, one would easily recognise the prototypical simile of the type "The spring will come back like a blooming bride" while the former case corresponds to elliptical similes devoid of tenor such as in: "*Firm* <u>as</u> **that mountain in the day of dread, when Freedom wept**, and pointed to her dead; *grim* <u>as</u> **that mountain to the ruthless foe, wasting the land that wearied of its woe** ; *strong* <u>as</u> **that mountain, 'neath his load of care, when brave men faltered in a sick despair.**"[Mason (1916)]

In some cases, anticipation can be induced by running the simile on more than one sentence.

Example: He lay still, for the ash stick held him in place. Six months! Then <u>her face</u> came out of a mist of green. *Pink and white and frail* <u>like</u> **Dresden china**, lilies-of-the-valley at her breast, puce-coloured silk sheening about her. [Lowell (1916)]

2.2   The Semantic Dimension of Similes

Traditionally, the semantics of the similes is concerned with measuring the semantic distance between the tenor and the vehicle using semantic categories which can me more or less well-defined. Brooke-Roose (2002) summarises the various predominant theories that classify similes based on its content by distinguishing: first, Aristotle with the species/genus classification, then Aristotle's successors among whom Quintilian, who introduced the animate/inanimate classification. Afterwards, came the classification by domain of thought or activity used in the 19th and the 20th century for linguistic and literary analysis, and finally, the analysis by dominant trait which focused on the resemblances between the vehicle and the tenor. Therefore, it can be said that describing similes based on the semantic traits of the tenor and the vehicle or specific only to the vehicle has been a fixed feature of literary studies. Table 2 illustrates the various types of simile that are often used in scholarly literary texts about literature, depending on the degree of abstraction or animacy of the tenor and the vehicle.

3   Review of Existing Simile Annotation Schemes

Obviously, when talking about digital publishing and the annotation of literary texts, the first resource that comes to mind is the Text Encoding Initiative (TEI), which, in recent years, has imposed itself as the standard in the humanities for encoding additional information in texts. However, despite their exhaustive coverage of the encoding of various textual elements such as places or characters, the TEI P5 Guidelines[2] only address figurative language briefly and leave entirely the choice to the encoder:

> For other features it must for the time being be left to encoders to devise their own terminology. Elements such as `<metaphor tenor="..." vehicle="...">...</metaphor>` might well suggest themselves; but given the problems of definition involved, and the great richness of modern metaphor theory, it is clear that any such format, if predefined by these Guidelines, would have seemed objectionable to some and excessively restrictive to many. (6.7)

In the case of the simile, apart from the fact that the ground needs to be added, determining a posteriori how the different components are related in a sentence with more than one simile could be an issue.

Unlike what is suggested by the TEI, existing annotated corpora of similes have operated mainly at the word level. Niculae and Danescu-Niculescu-Mizil (2014) propose a corpus of annotated similes identified in Amazon product reviews which consists of 2,400 sentences in which a comparison between two common nouns has been automatically detected.[3] Each sentence is presented in the CoNLL format, the output format of the dependency parser used (TurboParser),[4] to which the mentions "TOPIC" for the tenor, "EVENT" for the verbal ground, "PROPERTY" for the adjectival ground, "COMPARATOR" for the marker and "VEHICLE" have been added when suitable. Before each sentence, metadata are given about the domain of the review, the annotators score about its figurativeness, the title of the review, the price of the article, the author of the comment...

Example: {"category": "Music", "figurativeness": [4, 4, 4], "title": "Siempre", "price": "unknown", "userId": "A20AEO9CWVD7JY", "score": "5.0", "helpfulness": "0/0", "time": "1182902400", "profileName": "Hilda Gonzalez Gonzalez", "productId": "B000NI3G8W"}

Their	their	PRP\$	1	2	NMOD	_
voices	voice	NNS	2	3	SUB	TOPIC
blend	blend	VBP	3	0	ROOT	EVENT
like	like	IN	4	3	VMOD	COMPARATOR
magic	magic	NN	5	4	PMOD	VEHICLE
....	....	:	6	3	P	_

Clearly, because of the chosen output and of the information it contains, this corpus is mostly aimed at NLP researchers interested in the automatic detection of similes. Besides, in addition to its restrictive scope and the fact that all sentences are presented as stand-alone entities devoid of any context, this annotation scheme suffers from various other shortcomings: a principle of unicity (one simile per sentence and only one simile component annotated) and incorrect annotations resulting from parsing errors which were not rectified because the crowdsourcing task only dealt with figuativeness. Moreover, still in compliance with the parser's output, auxiliaries and modal verbs preceding another verb are wrongly tagged as main verbs.

The second corpus, the VUAMC (Vrije Universiteit Amsterdam Metaphor Corpus) Online[5] (Steen et al. (2010)) is a manually annotated corpus of fragments of academic texts, conversations, fiction and news taken from the BNC Baby, a subset of the British National Corpus (BNC). It contains 16,202 sentences in which each word has been scanned to find out if it is used metaphorically or not. In addition, it

---

[2] http://www.tei-c.org/Guidelines/P5/

[3] http://vene.ro/figurative-comparisons/

[4] http://www.cs.cmu.edu/~ark/TurboParser/

[5] This corpus is searchable online (http://www.vismet.org/metcor/search/showPage.php?page=start) or can be freely downloaded as an XML file (http://ota.ahds.ac.uk/headers/2541.xml).

distinguishes between direct metaphors, implicit metaphors and words signalling metaphors also called "metaphor flags" into which fall simile markers. However, some of these metaphor flags such as "appearance", "call", "symbolically" and "types", only precede an analogy or a metaphor. As a matter of fact, although as its name implies this corpus deals with the metaphor in its broadest sense, it devotes a rather small space to similes as exemplified by the discrepancy between the number of identified metaphorical words (more than 25,000) and the number of true similes (113 in total, 40 in the fiction fragments).

The downloadable version of this corpus is TEI-compliant and makes use of XML tags to delimit each sentence. Those tags also indicate for each word or punctuation mark, its part-of-speech tag, its lemma and whether it is a metaphorical word (`function="mrw"`) or a metaphorical signal (`function="mFlag"`). Furthermore, cases in which doubts subsist are also clearly indicated with the attribute `WIDLII` (when in doubt, leave it in). If this corpus constitutes a good basis to study metaphoricity in general, it does not say much about the reason why a particular word is metaphorical in a specific context or give information on the semantic structure of the identified similes.

```
<s n="88">
    <w lemma="the" type="AT0">The </w>
    <w lemma="result" type="NN2">results </w>
    <w lemma="be" type="VBB">are </w>
    <w lemma="terse" type="AJ0">
        <seg function="mrw" type="met" vici:morph="n">terse</seg>
    </w>
    <w lemma="and" type="CJC">and </w>
    <w lemma="sharply" type="AV0">sharply </w>
    <w lemma="etch" type="VVN">
        <seg function="mrw" type="met" vici:morph="n">etched</seg>
    </w>
    <c type="PUN">, </c>
    <w lemma="like" type="PRP">
        <seg function="mFlag" type="lex">like</seg>
    </w>
    <w lemma="the" type="AT0">the </w>
    <w lemma="good" type="AJS">best </w>
    <w lemma="line" type="NN1">
        <seg function="mrw" xml:id="alh-fragment05-cn2" type="lit" vici:morph="n">line</seg>
    </w>
    <w lemma="drawing" type="NN2">
        <seg function="mrw" corresp="#alh-fragment05-cn2" type="lit" vici:morph="n">drawings
        </seg>
    </w>
    <c type="PUN">.</c>
</s>
```

4 The Proposed Annotation Scheme

This annotation framework has been designed with two main purposes in mind: to constitute the final output of a simile detection algorithm for prose literary texts written in English or in French (Mpouli (2016)) and to describe the similes and (pseudo-)comparisons that volunteers have annotated online. Built with scribeAPI [6], the (Dis)Similitudes crowdsourcing platform proposes 1,456 fragments of French, British and American prose poems published between the 18th and the 21st century. A fragment, here, refers to a sentence which contains one or more comparison markers and its surrounding sentences. Each fragment is presented as an image accompanied by a series of questions concerning the structure to analyse. To facilitate the annotation process, the corresponding marker has been coloured in blue beforehand.

Each volunteer can choose between two main tasks:

- answer questions on the structure to analyse (decide whether it is a comparison or a pseudo-comparison, give its function or pragmatic value, identify and describe its components);

- transcribe already annotated elements and indicate their semantic categories.

---

[6]`http://scribeproject.github.io/`

As the annotation process is still in progress, few conclusions can presently be drawn with certitude on the difficulty of the task as the whole or on the relevant information that it will reveal about the origin of figuration in similes. However, the data collected has enabled to confirm that indeed the whole phrase plays a role in creating and understanding the image conveyed by the simile since most annotators tend to mark phrases and not simple words.

To accurately render the different levels of analysis traditionally found in stylistics, similes in the developed annotation framework are annotated at a more general level and at the level of each of their components. The sentence constitutes the upper level of analysis and as such, each sentence is numbered and enclosed within a tag `<sentence>`. Then, the nature of the simile is specified: clausal similes (`<simile nature="clausal" >...</simile>`) or nominal similes (`<simile nature="nominal">... </simile>`). Five types of similes are distinguished:

- idiomatic similes (`<type= "idiomatic">...</type>`);

- perceptual similes which occur with a verb of perception like "look", "sound", "taste", "smell" (`<type="perceptual">...</type>`);

- proverbial similes which occur with the verb "to be", a nominal tenor and a nominal vehicle (`<type="proverbial">...</type>`);

- reinvented idiomatic similes (`<type="reinvented">...</type>`) in which the adapted form is of course mentioned with the attribute `source` followed by the typical form of the idiomatic simile.

- original similes (`<type="original">...</type>`) which are the creative ones.

Unlike what has been done so far, the tenor, the ground and the vehicle are annotated both at the word and at the phrase level. Concretely for each of these components, the mark up delimits the boundaries of the phrase to which it belongs, links it to the corresponding marker in the sentence and gives the grammatical category and the lemma of its head(s) as well as its position. Each marker in a sentence is identified by its position in the sentence which is encoded by the attribute `marker_id`. For multiword markers, only the position of the head lexeme is considered. Furthermore, additional stylistic information is given about the marker, whether it occurs at the beginning of the sentence, after a comma or a coordinating conjunction. Such information is introduced by an attribute `syntax`. Similarly, a tag `<rel>` signals vehicles that are followed by a relative clause while the tag `<neg>` indicates a negated ground.

The semantic category of the tenor and the vehicle is also specified via an attribute `category`. Even though some categories such as "humans" and "animals" seem to be quite agreed upon, it remains rather difficult to define semantic categories. After consulting lexical resources such as Fellbaum (1998) and the SIMPLE-CLIPS,[7] we opted for a set of categories neither too broad nor too refined which consists in the following semantic categories:

	Man-made objects
	Natural objects
	Body parts
Concrete	Human beings
	Animals
	Plants, fruits and vegetables
	Temporal elements
	Concepts
Abstract	Feelings and emotions
	Acts and processes
	Attributes and qualities

Collective nouns

---

[7] `http://webilc.ilc.cnr.it/clips/Ontology.htm`

At the moment, for automatically generated annotations, when the tenor or the vehicle is not a common noun, the value of its semantic category is marked as "undetermined". Based on the annotations that have been collected so far, we checked the relevance of the selected semantic categories. In the French counterpart of the (Dis)Similitudes platform, the broader semantic categories fit almost perfectly with human annotations (98%) whereas the score drops significantly (67%) when it comes to further semantic distinctions especially as far as abstract entities are concerned. Such differences, of course, could be attributed to the polysemy of some words but also to personal sensibility. For instance, although all annotators agree that the term "cri" ("shout") is an abstract entity, for some it denotes an act or process and for others an emotion. It is worth noting that annotators can also choose "Others" if they disagree with all the listed subcategories.

Example of an annotated simile:

** It's freighted with a gentle woe as *old* as **all the seas that flow**, as *young* as **yesterday**; as *changeless* as **the stars above**, as *yearning* as **a woman's love for true knight far away** [Mason (1916)].

```
<sentence id="2">
It's freighted with
<simile nature="nominal" type="original">
<tenor marker_id="8,17,22,29">a gentle <head id="7" lemma="woe" postag="NN" category="abstract
    , emotions and feelings">woe</head>
</tenor>
<marker marker_id="8" lemma="as" syntax="null">as</marker>
<ground marker_id="8"><head id="9" lemma="old" postag="JJ">old</head>
</ground>
<marker marker_id="8" lemma="as">as</marker>
<vehicle marker_id="8">all the<head id="13" lemma="sea" tag="NNS" category="concrete,natural
    objects">seas</head><rel>that</rel></vehicle> flow,
</simile>
<simile nature="nominal" type="original">
<marker marker_id="17" lemma="as" syntax="juxt">as</marker>
<ground marker_id="17"><head id="18" lemma="young" postag="JJ">young</head></ground>
<marker lemma="as" marker_id="17">as</marker>
<vehicle marker_id="17"><head id="19" lemma="yesterday" tag="NN" category="abstract, temporal
    elements">yesterday</head>;</vehicle>
</simile>
<simile nature="nominal" type="original">
<marker marker_id="22" lemma="as" syntax="juxt">as</marker>
<ground marker_id="22"><head id="23" lemma="changeless" postag="JJ">changeless</head></ground>
<marker marker_id="22" lemma="as"  syntax="null">as</marker>
<vehicle marker_id="22">the<head id="26" lemma="star" tag="NN" category="concrete, natural
    objects">stars</head>above,</vehicle>
</simile>
<simile nature="nominal" type="original">
<marker marker_id="29" lemma="as"  syntax="null">as</marker>
<ground marker_id="29"><head id="30" lemma="yearning" postag="JJ">yearning</head></ground>
<marker marker_id="29" lemma="as" syntax="null">as</marker>
<vehicle marker_id="29">a woman's<head id="36" lemma="love" postag="NN" category="abstract,
    emotions and feelings">love</head> for true knight far away.</vehicle>
</simile>
</sentence>
```

In addition, specifically for simile detection gold standards, two main types of structures can be distinguished:

- literal comparisons (`<comparison>`) and their three components `<comparee_NP>`, `<quantity_quality>` and `<standard_NP>`;

- and pseudo-comparisons with their respective values (exemplification, identification, coordination and approximation) and components.

Like simile components, all these components are described with the attributes `id` and `marker_id` as well as a child element `head`.

Examples:

1/ It was ten cents cheap<u>er than</u> suits I'd bought, from local dealers... [Mason (1916)]

```
<sentence id="2">
<comparison>
<comparee_NP marker_id="6">
<head id="1" lemma="it" postag="PRP" category= concrete, man-made objects">It</head>
</comparee_NP>
was
<quantity_quality  marker_id="6">ten cents <head id="5" lemma="cheap" postag="JJR">cheaper</
    head>
</quantity_quality>
<marker marker_id="6" lemma="than" syntax="null">than</marker>
<standard_NP marker_id="6"><head id="7" lemma="suit" tag="NNS" category="concrete, man-made
    objects">suits</head></standard_NP>
</comparison>
I'd bought, from local dealers...
</sentence>
```

2/ You yet may have a chance to serve <u>as</u> juryman, in court [Mason (1916)].

```
<sentence id="7">
<pseudo_comparison type= identification >
<identified_element marker_id="9">
<head id="1" lemma="you" postag="PRP" category= concrete, human beings">You</head>
</identified_element>
yet may have a chance to
<verb marker_id="9"><head id="8" lemma="serve" postag="VB">serve</head>
</verb>
<marker marker_id="9" lemma="as" syntax="null">as</marker>
<complement_marker marker_id="9"><head id="10" lemma="juryman" tag="NN" category="concrete,
    human beings">juryman</head></complement_marker>
</pseudo-comparison>
, in court.
</sentence>
```

5 Conclusion

This paper proposed a simile annotation framework that has been developed to produce a gold standard from the (Dis)Similitudes crowdsourcing platform and which takes into account stylistic practices as well the challenges specific to the automatic detection of similes. In this respect, it presents a multi-layered annotation scheme that describes each simile in the sentence and its respective components. As other figures of speech are not currently taken into consideration, the next step is to consider how to combine the current framework with the annotation scheme for irony, metaphor, metonymy and figures of repetition mentioned in the Introduction so as to accurately represent how these rhetorical figures are interconnected. Furthermore, it could be interesting to go beyond the sentence level as some similes can cover more than one sentence. Finally, to adequately single out creative similes, by mining literary corpora, it will be possible to separate original similes from cliché or frozen ones, i.e. those similes that are widely used among authors without being idiomatic such as the combination heart + beat + marker of comparison + hammer.

Acknowledgements

This work was supported by French state funds managed by the ANR within the Investissements d'Avenir programme under reference ANR-11-IDEX-0004-02.

References

Anderson, S. (1918). *Mid-American Chants*. New York: B. W. Huebsch, Inc.

Brooke-Roose, C. (2002). *Invisible Authors: Last Essays*. Ohio State University Press.

Fellbaum, C. (1998). *WordNet: An Electronic Lexical Database*. Cambridge: The MIT Press.

Gawryjolek, J. J. (2009). Automated annotation and visualization of rhetorical figures. Master's thesis, University of Waterloo.

Gianti, A., C. Bosco, V. Patti, A. Bolioli, and L. Di Caro (2012). Annotating irony in a novel Italian corpus for sentiment analysis. In *Proceedings of the 4th Workshop on Corpora for Research on Emotion Sentiment and Social Signals*, pp. 1–7.

Goatly, A. (2011). *The Language of Metaphors*. London & New York: Routledge.

Gordon, J., J. R. Hobbs, J. May, M. Mohler, F. Morbini, B. Rink, M. Tomlinson, and S. Wertheim (2015). A corpus of rich metaphor annotation. In *Proceedings of the Third Workshop on Metaphor in NLP*, pp. 56–66.

Karoui, J., B. Farah, V. Moriceau, V. Patti, C. Bosco, and N. Aussenac-Gilles (2017). Exploring the impact of pragmatic phenomena on irony detection in tweets: A multilingual corpus study. In *Proceedings of the 15th Conference of the European Chapter of the Association for Computational Linguistics: Volume 1, Long Papers*, Volume 1, pp. 262–272.

Kirvalidze, N. (2014). Three-dimensional world of similes in English fictional writing. *Sino-US English Teaching 11*(1), 25–39.

Lowell, A. (1916). *Men, Women and Ghosts*. New York: Macmillan.

Markert, K. and M. Nissim (2002). Towards a corpus annotated for metonymies: The case of location names. In *LREC*, pp. 1385–1392.

Mason, W. (1914). *Rippling Rhymes*. Chicago: A. C. McClurg & Co.

Mason, W. (1916). *His Book*. New York: Barse & Hopkins Publishers.

Mpouli, S. (2016). *Automatic annotation of similes in literary texts*. Ph. D. thesis, Université Pierre et Marie Curie-Paris VI.

Niculae, V. and C. Danescu-Niculescu-Mizil (2014). Brighter than gold: Figurative language in user generated comparisons. In *EMNLP*, pp. 2008–2018.

Pistorius, G. (1971). La structure des comparaisons dans Madame Bovary. *Cahiers de l'Association internationale des études francaises 23*(1), 223–242.

Richards, I. A. (1936). *The Philosophy of Rhetoric*. London, Oxford & New York: The Oxford University Press.

Ruan, S., C. Di Marco, and R. A. Harris (2016). Rhetorical figure annotation with XML. In *Proceedings of the 16th Workshop on Computational Models of Natural Argument*, pp. 23–33.

Shutova, E. and S. Teufel (2010). Metaphor corpus annotated for source-target domain mappings. In *LREC*, Volume 2, pp. 3255–3261.

Steen, G. J., A. G. Dorst, J. B. Herrmann, A. Kaal, T. Krennmayr, and T. Pasma (2010). *A method for linguistic metaphor identification: From MIP to MIPVU*, Volume 14. Amsterdam & Philadelphia: John Benjamins Publishing.

Strachan, J. R. and R. Terry (2000). *Poetry*. Edinburgh University Press.

Trevisan, B., M. Neunerdt, T. Hemig, E.-M. Jakobs, and R. Mathar (2014). Detecting ironic speech acts in multilevel annotated German web comments. In *Proc. Workshop NLP 4 CMC*, pp. 34–41.

Van Hee, C., E. Lefever, and V. Hoste (2016). Exploring the realization of irony in Twitter data. In *LREC*, pp. 1795–1799.

Watson, J. S. (1856). *Quintilian's Institutes of Oratory*. London: George Bell and Sons.

Wilde, O. (2000). *The Complete Works: Poems and Poems in Prose*. Oxford University Press.

Williams, W. C. (1920). *Kora in Hell: Improvisations*. Boston: The Four Seas Company.

Revisiting the ISO standard for dialogue act annotation

Harry Bunt
Tilburg Center for Cognition and Communication (TiCC)
Tilburg University, Tilburg, The Netherlands
`harry.bunt@uvt.nl`

Volha Petukhova
Spoken Language Systems
University of Saarland, Germany
`v.petukhova@lsv.uni-saarland.de`

Alex Fang
Dialogue Systems Group
City University of Hong Kong
`alex.fang@cityu.edu.hk`

Abstract

Based on experiences using the ISO standard for dialogue act annotation (ISO 24617-2:2012), this paper proposes to correct certain deficiencies in the standard, and discusses some extensions that would increase the standard usefulness and usability. More specifically, it is suggested to add the annotation of non-functional segments that are relevant for the accurate annotation of some feedback acts and speech editing acts, and to import devices from the newly established ISO standard for the annotation of discourse relations (ISO DR-Core) in order to improve the annotation of rhetorical relations between dialogue acts. The latter kind of extension is argued to be interesting for also joint annotation of different kinds of semantic information by combining different annotation schemes.

1   Introduction

ISO standards are examined every five years for the need of corrections, extensions, or other updates. This means that the ISO standard for dialogue act annotation, ISO 24617-2,[1] which was published in September 2012, is up for possible revision in September 2017. Application of ISO 24617-2 in annotation efforts in recent years, for example in the construction of the DialogBank,[2] has brought some deficiencies to light, as well as some unwelcome limitations. So far, the following issues have been identified as deserving discussion and possibly revising (and discussions with users and analysts of the annotation scheme may be expected to give rise to further issues):

- the treatment of segments that are relevant for dialogue act annotation but that do not carry a communicative function;
- the addition of certain dimensions and communicative functions that are felt to be missing;
- the accurate annotation of rhetorical relations between dialogue acts or their semantic contents;
- the status of functional and feedback dependence relations;
- the combination of dialogue act annotation with that of other semantic information, such as semantic roles, time and space;
- the use of representation formats other than the reference format of the standard.

Section 2 of this paper gives a very brief summary of the ISO 24617-2 standard. Section 3 discusses some limitations and deficiencies, and outlines possible corresponding changes. Section 4 discusses the combination of dialogue act annotations with the annotation of other semantic information, e.g. using other standard ISO annotation schemes. Section 5 discusses the use of representation formats other than the XML format defined in ISO 24617-2.

---

[1] ISO 24617-2, Language Resources Management, Semantic Annotation Framework, part 2: Dialogue acts.
[2] See `https://dialogbank.uvt.nl` and Bunt (2016)

2 The ISO 24617-2 Standard

ISO 24617-2 provides a comprehensive, application-independent annotation scheme, building on previously designed annotation schemes such as DAMSL, DIT^{++}, MRDA, HCRC Map Task, Verbmobil, SWBD-DAMSL, and DIT.[3] For most of these annotation schemes, dialogue act annotation consists of segmenting a dialogue into certain grammatical units and marking up each unit with one or more communicative function labels. The ISO 24617-2 scheme is intended for semantically more complete annotation, including the following aspects:

1. 'Dimension', or category of semantic content: the annotation scheme supports multidimensional annotation, i.e. multiple communicative functions may be assigned to dialogue segments; different from DAMSL and other multidimensional schemes, an explicitly defined notion of 'dimension' is used that corresponds to a certain category of semantic content. The nine ISO scheme distinguishes nine dimensions: (1) *Task:* dialogue acts that move the task or activity forward which motivates the dialogue; (2-3) *Feedback*, divided into *Auto-* and *Allo-Feedback*: acts providing or eliciting information about the processing of previous utterances by the current speaker or by the current addressee, respectively; (4) *Turn Management:* activities for obtaining, keeping, releasing, or assigning the right to speak; (5) *Time Management:* acts for managing the use of time in the interaction; (6) *Discourse Structuring:* dialogue acts dealing with topic management, opening and closing (sub-)dialogues, or otherwise structuring the dialogue; (7-8) *Own-* and *Partner Communication Management:* actions by the speaker to edit his current contribution or a contribution of another current speaker, respectively; (9) *Social Obligations Management:* dialogue acts for dealing with social conventions such as greeting, introducing oneself, apologizing, and thanking.

2. 'Qualifiers' may be added for expressing that a dialogue act is performed conditionally, with uncertainty, or with a particular sentiment.

3. Dependence relations are defined for expressing semantic relations between dialogue acts, e.g. for indicating which question is answered by a certain answer act (functional dependence relation), or which utterance a feedback act responds to (feedback dependence relation).

4. Rhetorical relations may be annotated to indicate for example that one dialogue act explains the performance of another dialogue act.

The ISO 224617-2 schema defines 56 communicative functions, which are listed in Appendix A. Some of these are specific for a particular dimension; for instance *Turn Take* is specific for Turn Management; *Stalling* is specific for Time Management, and *Self-Correction* is specific for Own Communication Management. Other functions can be applied in any dimension; for example, *You misunderstood me* is an *Inform* in the Allo-Feedback dimension. All types of question, statement, and answer can be used in any dimension, and the same is true for commissive and directive functions, such as *Offer, Suggest,* and *Request*. The later functions are called *general-purpose* functions, as opposed to the former ones which are *dimension-specific* functions.

ISO 24617-2 annotations assume that a dialogue act has one sender, one or more addressees, zero or more other participants, one semantic content category (or 'dimension'), one communicative function, zero or more functional and feedback dependence relations, possibly one or more qualifiers, and possibly one or more rhetorical relations to other dialogue acts.

ISO 24617-2 includes the markup language DiAML (Dialogue Act Markup Language), designed in accordance with the ISO Linguistic Annotation Framework (LAF)[4] and the ISO Principles of Semantic Annotation ('SemAF Principles').[5] LAF makes a fundamental distinction between *annotation* and *representation*: 'annotation' refers to the linguistic information that is added to segments of language

---

[3]See Allen & Core (1997); Bunt (2007); Shriberg et al. (2004); Anderson et al. (1991); Alexandersson et al. (1998); Jurafsky et al. (1997); and Bunt (1994; 2000), respectively.

[4]ISO 24612:2012; see also Ide & Romary (2004).

[5]ISO 24617-6; see also Bunt (2015).

data, independent of format; 'representation' refers to the rendering of annotations in a particular format. Following SemAF Principles, this distinction is implemented in the DiAML definition in the form of an *abstract syntax* that specifies a class of abstract *annotation structures*, which are set-theoretical constructs like pairs and triples, and a *concrete syntax* that specifies a rendering of these annotation structures using XML. This format is called DiAML-XML. It uses abbreviated XML-expressions, and is complete and unambiguous relative to the abstract syntax, i.e. (1) the concrete syntax defines a representation for every structure defined by the abstract syntax; and (2) every expression defined by the concrete syntax represents one and only one structure defined by the abstract syntax. A format with these properties is called *ideal*. Any ideal representation format can be converted through a meaning-preserving mapping to any other ideal format (see Bunt, 2010 for formal definitions and proofs).

According to ISO 24617-2, dialogue acts correspond to 'functional segments', defined as *minimal stretches of communicative behaviour that have a communicative function and a semantic content*, 'minimal' in the sense of not including material that does not contribute to the expression of the function or the semantic content of the dialogue act. Functional segments are mostly shorter than turns, may be discontinuous, may overlap, and may contain parts contributed by different speakers. A segment carrying a feedback function for instance frequently overlaps with a segment that carries a task-related function.

The requirement of being 'minimal' has been added in order for communicative functions to be assigned as accurately as possible to those stretches of behaviour which express these functions. The following example illustrates this:

(1) Can you tell me what time the train to *ehm,...* Viareggio leaves?

The small interrupting segment *ehm,...* is not really part of the question, so according to the minimality condition it does not belong to the corresponding functional segment. The utterance in (1) is thus analysed as consisting of two functional segments: the discontinuous segment *"Can you tell me what time the train to Viareggio leaves?"*, and the segment *"ehm,..."* corresponding to a Stalling act. This can be annotated in DiAML as follows:

(2)
```
<dialogueAct xml:id="da1"target="#fs1" speaker="#s" addressee="#a"
    dimension="task" communicativeFunction="request" conditionality="conditional"/>
<dialogueAct xml:id="da2" target="#fs2" speaker="#s" addressee="#a"
    communicativeFunction="stalling" dimension="timeManagement"/>
```

Example (3b) illustrates the annotation of relations among dialogue acts for the dialogue fragment in (3a), which contains a rhetorical relation (Elaboration) between the dialogue acts in utterances 1 and 3, and a feedback dependence between the dialogue acts in utterances 3 and 4.

(3)
1. G: go south and you'll pass some cliffs on your right
2. F: uhm...
3. G: and some adobe huts on your left
4. F: oh okay

```
<diaml xmlns="http://www.iso.org/diaml">
<dialogueAct xml:id="da1" target="#fs1" sender="#g" addressee="#f"
    dimension="task" communicativeFunction="instruct"/>
<dialogueAct xml:id="da2" target="#fs2" sender="#f" addressee="#f"
    dimension="turnManagement" communicativeFunction="turnTake"/>
<dialogueAct xml:id="da3" target="#fs2" sender="#f" addressee="#g"
    dimension="timeManagement" communicativeFunction="stalling"/>
<dialogueAct xml:id="da4" target="#fs3" sender="#g" addressee="#f"
    dimension="task" communicativeFunction="inform"/>
<rhetoricalLink dact="#da4" rhetoAnteceden="#da1" rhetoRel="elaboration"
<dialogueAct xml:id="da5" target="#fs4" sender="#f" addressee="#g"
    dimension="autoFeedback" communicativeFunction="autoPositive"
    feedbackDependence="#da1 #da4"/>
</diaml>
```

It should be noted that the DiAML format is just a compact way of using XML. The compactness of the representation is an obvious advantage, still, its equivalence with a full XML form is important for the possible combination of dialogue act annotation with other semantic or pragmatic information. This is discussed in Section 4.

3   ISO 24617-2 Limitations and Extensions

3.1   Annotating Feedback Dependence Relations

Feedback acts are about the processing of something that was said earlier in the dialogue; this 'something' is indicated by the value of the 'feedbackDependence' attribute. The nature of this 'something' depends on the kind or 'level' of the feedback. The DIT^{++} taxonomy of communicative functions, which has been a major source of inspiration for ISO 24617-2, distinguishes between feedback at five different levels of processing: (1) attention; (2) perception; (3) understanding; (4) evaluation; and (5) execution.

Feedback about paying attention to another speaker is mostly given in nonverbal form, such as by eye contact. Positive feedback at the level of perception can be expressed by echoing what the previous speaker said; negative feedback by repeating part of what was said with a questioning intonation, like *Tuesday?*, or *"John WHO?"*. Feedback at the level of understanding can be expressed for example by *"I see"* or by paraphrasing something that was expressed. Positive feedback at the level of evaluation can be expressed by *"Excellent!"*, *"True"*, or *"Good question"*. Negative feedback, e.g. by *"Really?"* Positive feedback at the level of execution can be expressed by *"Sure"*; negative feedback by *"I don't know"* in response to a question.

Feedback by means of expressions such as *"OK"*, *"Uh-huh"*, or *"Really?"* says something about a previous dialogue act, while feedback by means of *"Tuesday?"* or *"John WHO?"* is about a particular word or dialogue segment. The ISO 24617-2 annotation scheme therefore allows both dialogue acts and functional segments as antecedents for feedback dependence relations.

The ISO scheme is not quite correct at this point, since segment-related feedback is not necessarily about a *functional* segment; it may be about *any* previous segment, functional or not, such as a single word. The DBOX annotations (see Petukhova et al., 2014) in the DialogBank deviate in this respect from the ISO standard, since for feedback dependences special non-functional segments have been introduced. The ISO standard should be corrected in this respect, and should include segments ('reference segments') in their segmentation, to allow more accurate markup of feedback dependences.

3.2   Functional and Feedback Dependence Relations

Besides the feedback dependence relation, ISO 24617-2 defines the functional dependence relation as the *"relation between a given dialogue act and a preceding dialogue act on which the semantic content of the given dialogue act depends due to its communicative function.* An example is the relation between an answer and the question that was answered. The importance of this relation is semantic: the meaning of an answer cannot be determined fully if one doesn't know the question that was asked. This is because an answer is inherently responsive in character (as opposed to a question). The ISO scheme includes the following responsive types of dialogue acts: Answer, Confirm, Disconfirm, Agreement, Disagreement, Correction, Accept Request, Address Request, Reject Request, Accept Suggest, Address Suggest, Reject Suggest, Accept Offer, Address Offer and Reject Offer.

ISO 24617-2 is not entirely clear about the assignment of functional and feedback dependence relations, partly due to a certain vagueness in the definition of the feedback dependence relation, which reads as follows: *"relation between a feedback act and the stretch of communicative behaviour whose processing the act provides or elicits information about"*. The vagueness is in the term 'feedback act', which is sometimes understood as "dialogue act in one of the two feedback dimensions" and sometimes as "dialogue acts with a feedback-specific communicative function". In the former interpretation, feedback acts include feedback questions and requests, such as *"What did you say?"*, *"Do you mean THIS Saturday?"*, or *"Could you please repeat that?"*, which are all response-eliciting acts, the responses to which have a functional dependence relation to their elicitations, and could also be said to have a feedback dependence relation. More precisely, the assignment of functional and feedback dependence relations can be specified as follows:

1. if the communicative function is a responsive one, then assign a functional dependence relation to the corresponding response-eliciting act;

2. if the communicative function is dimension-specific for Auto- or Allo-Feedback, assign a feedback dependence relation to the dialogue act(s) or to the dialogue segment that the feedback is about;

3. in all other cases do not assign any dependence relation.

According to this specification, no feedback dependence relation is assigned to a question like *"John WHO?"*; this can be justified by the consideration that the semantic content of such an utterance is sufficient to make clear what the feedback is about,

We may also conclude that a dialogue act can have a functional or a feedback dependence relation, but not both. This would make it possible to drop the terminological distinction and just speak of 'dependence relation'.

3.3   Annotating Rhetorical Relations

ISO 24617-2 supports the marking up of rhetorical relations between dialogue acts, without specifying any particular set of relations to be used; it only specifies *how* a rhetorical relation may be marked up as relating two dialogue acts.

In 2016 the ISO standard 24617-8 has been established for the annotation of rhetorical relations in discourse. This standard, also called "DR-Core", defines a set of 18 'core' relations that are shared by many annotation schemes. This set of relations has been used in most of the dialogues in the DialogBank. However, two problems were noted when doing so.

First, many rhetorical relations have two arguments that play different roles, for example, a Cause relation has a "Reason" (or "Cause") argument and a "Result" (or "Effect") argument. ISO 24617-2 has a provision for indicating that a Cause relation exists between two dialogue acts, but not for indicating their roles.

DR-Core annotates relations with argument roles as follows, using the reference format 'DRelML' of DR-Core:

(4) John pushed Tim. He fell on the ground.

```
<drArg xml:id="a1" target="#s1" type="event"/>
<dRel xml:id="r1" rel="cause"/>
<drArg xml:id="a2" target="#s2" type="event"/>
<implDRLink rel="r1" reason="#a1" result="#a2"/>
```

By contrast, ISO 24617-2 provides just a single slot for specifying a rhetorical relation, and has no provisions for marking up argument roles, as illustrated in (5):

(5) A: Have you seen Pete today?
    B: He didn't come in; he has the flu.

```
<dialogueAct xml:id="da1" target="#fs1" sender="#a" addressee="#b"
   dimension="task" communicativeFunction="propositionalQuestion"/>
<dialogueAct xml:id="da2" target="#fs2" sender="#b" addressee="#a" dimension="task"
   communicativeFunction="answer" functionalDependence="#da1"/>
<dialogueAct xml:id="da3" target="#fs3" sender="#b" addressee="#a"
   dimension="task" communicativeFunction="inform"/>
<rhetoricalLink dact="#da3" rhetoAntecedent="#da2" rhetoRel="cause"/>
```

This limitation could be overcome by using the <implDRLink> element of DRelML in DiAML, instead of the <rhetoricalLink>, thus replacing the last line of (5) by:

(6) <dRel xml:id="r1" rel="cause"/>
     <implDRiLink rel="r1" reason="#da3" result="#da2"/>

Second, many if not all rhetorical relations may occur either between two dialogue acts or between their semantic contents. This phenomenon is known in the literature as the 'semantic-pragmatic' distinction. Example (7) illustrates this.

(7) a. A: Have you seen Pete today?
        B: He didn't come in. He has the flu.
     b. A: Have you seen Pete today?
        B: He didn't come in. He sent me a message saying that he has the flu.

B's utterances in (7a) are causally related in the sense that the semantic content of the second utterance expresses the reason why the content of the first utterance, which answers A's question, is true. In (7b), by contrast, there is a 'pragmatic' causal relation, in the sense that the second utterance expresses why B says that Pete is not in - in this case B's utterance is causally related to the dialogue act of answering A, rather than to the content of this dialogue act.

In DR-Core this distinction is represented by indicating the types of the arguments, where 'dialogue act' is one of the possible types, and the possible types of the semantic content of a dialogue act are the other. This is illustrated in example (8), which shows the annotation of the examples in (7) represented in DRelML, the markup language of DR-Core.

(8) a. <drArg xml:id="a1" target="#fs2" type="event"/>
        <dRel xml:id="r1" rel="cause"/>
        <drArg xml:id="a2" target="#fs3" type="state"/>
        <implDRLink rel="r1" result="#a1" reason="#a2"/>

     b. <drArg xml:id="a1" target="#fs2" type="dialogueAct"/>
        <dRel xml:id="r1" rel="cause"/>
        <drArg xml:id="a2" target="#fs3" type="event"/>
        <implDRLink rel="r1" result="#a1" reason="#a2"/>

In both (8a) and (8b) a Cause relation is marked up between the arguments expressed by the markables fs2 (*"Pete did not come in today"*) and fs3 (*"He has the flu"*; *"He sent me a message saying that he has the flu"*, respectively), but in (8a) the first argument is the event of Pete not coming in which is caused by the second argument, while in (8b) it is the dialogue act of B answering A that Pete did not come in which is caused by the second argument. This distinction cannot be expressed in DiAML.

Again, a solution could be found by importing in DiAML the use of DRelML's <implDRLink> element, plus the DRelML way of identifying the event that forms the reason for the Cause relation, thus building the annotation in (9):

(9) c. <dialogueAct xml:id="da2" target="#s2" sender="#b" addressee="#a"
           dimension="task" communicativeFunction="answer"
           functionalDependence="#da1">
        <dialogueAct xml:id="da3" target="#s3" sender="#b" addressee="#a"
           dimension="task" communicativeFunction="inform" >
        <drArg xml:id="e3" target="#s3" type="event" />
        <implDRLink rel="cause" reason="#e3" result="#da2" />

The mixed DiAML/DRelML representations in (6) and (9) are perfectly well-formed as XML expressions, but from a semantic point of view it isn't clear that they make any sense, since DiAML and DRelML each have their own separate semantics. This issue, which arises more generally when annotations of different semantic phenomena is combined, is discussed in Section 4.

3.4 Additional Dimensions and Communicative Functions

The ISO 24617-2 annotation scheme has taken its nine dimensions from the DIT^{++} annotation scheme, which has an additional tenth dimension called 'Contact Management', for those dialogue acts that serve to establish and maintain contact and attention. This dimension was not included in the ISO standard because contact management does not play a significant role in every type of dialogue situation, where the other nine dimensions all do. Gilmartin et al. (2017) suggest the addition to ISO 24617-2 of communicative functions related to greeting and leavetaking in casual dialogues that may fit best in the Contact Management dimension

Another dimension that was not included in ISO 24617-2 is that of 'Task Management', which is available in DAMSL and some other annotation schemes. Task Management acts differ from dialogue acts in the Task dimension in that the latter serve to move a certain task or activity forward, whereas Task Management acts are concerned with discussing or explaining a certain task. In spontaneous conversations, task management acts hardly seem to occur, but they do occur in television debates, in parliamentary debates, and in dialogues in game situations, as for example in the DBOX dialogues. A DBOX example is the following, in which participant A explains the rules of the guessing game that they two are going to play. The 'task' in these dialogues is to play the game; the early part of the dialogue, where the game is explained, does not contribute to the task proper and contains Task Management acts (and other ones, such as feedback acts).

(10) A: First let me explain the rules. I am a very famous person.
     G: Okay.
     A: You need to guess my name.
     G: Okay.
     A: You can ask several questions except for one about my name.

The decision to not include certain common though not ubiquitous dimensions should perhaps be revisited, since one of the attractive features of the ISO scheme is that its dimensions are 'orthogonal', and there is no obligation to use *all* the dimensions in a given annotation task.

Communicative functions have been felt to be lacking in ISO 24617-2 in the Discourse Structuring dimension, in which only two functions have been defined: 'Opening' and 'Interaction Structuring', the latter functioning as a catch-all term for all forms of discourse structuring other than opening a dialogue. DIT^{++} and some other annotation schemes have other discourse structuring functions, that may be added to the ISO scheme.

It may also be useful to be more specific in the revised ISO standard document concerning the deliberate absence of any Task-specific functions, and the possibilities of adding those.

4 Including Elements from Other Annotation Schemes

In Section 3.3 we concluded that for an adequate annotation of rhetorical relations in dialogue one would like to somehow combine DiAML- and DRelML annotations. At the level of XML-based representations this is no problem, since both DiAML and DRelML representations are a compact way of using XML. However, this flexibility of XML is due to the fact that XML by itself does not have a semantics; one reason for defining DiAML and DRelML, besides the compactness of their representations, is that they both have a well-defined semantics (see

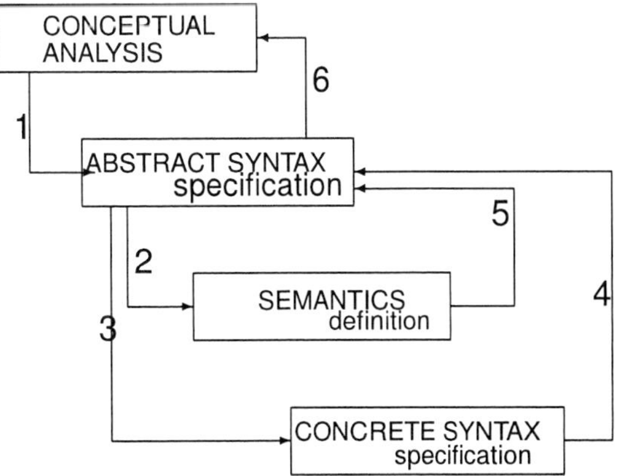

Figure 1: CASCADES design method (Bunt, 2015).

Bunt et al., 2012 and Bunt, 2014 for the semantics of DiAML, and Bunt & Prasad, 2016 for that of DRelML). Combining elements from different annotation schemes only makes sense if the semantics of the combination is well-defined.

Dealing with this issue is an interesting application of the CASCADES design method for annotation schemes (Bunt, 2015), which forms part of the ISO Principles of semantic annotation - see Figure 1 - in 'reverse engineering' mode (rather than 'top-down' mode). The reverse engineering could in this case start at the concrete syntax specification, describing the combined use of ingredients of DiAML and DRelML representations. Feedback step 4 leads to the construction of a combined abstract syntax specification, which in turn (step 6) calls for the (re-)construction of a combined metamodel. Once a stable combined metamodel has been constructed and an abstract syntax specification, step 2 (possibly iterated, via feedback step 5), calls for the specification of a semantics of the abstract annotation structures.

Appendix B shows the result of constructing a combined metamodel that combines the conceptual views underlying the ISO schemes for dialogue act annotation and discourse relation annotation. In the latter, DR-Core, a discourse relation (called a 'rhetorical relation' in ISO 24617-2) is a binary relation between two 'situations', which is a very general term that covers events, states, facts, beliefs, dialogue acts, as well as possible and negated events, facts and so on. We noted above that rhetorical relations in dialogue may occur between two dialogue acts, or between their semantic contents, or between one dialogue act and the semantic content of another. In the combined metamodel a 'semantic content' box is therefore introduced, as well as a rhetorical relation between two semantic contents, so that all three types of rhetorical relation can be annotated and can be distinguished.

Crucial in applying the CASCADES method is defining a combined semantics. The dialogue act theory that underlies the ISO scheme views a dialogue act conceptually as an 8-tuple consisiting of: (1) a sender; (2) one or more addressees; (3) a communicative function; (4) a semantic content; (5) a dimension; (6) functional dependence relations; (7) feedback dependence relations; and (8) rhetorical relations. Since an articulate annotation of the semantic content is considered to be beyond the scope of dialogue act annotation, the ISO 24617-2 annotations are, according to the abstract syntax, 7-tuples rather than 8-tuples, without a semantic content. However, the underlying theory does define the semantics of dialogue acts including their semantic content (see Bunt, 2011; 2014), namely as a mechanism for updating the dialogue participants' information states with that semantic content. Therefore, from a semantic point of view, an extension to DiAML with the semantic content of dialogue acts is well within reach. This would correspond in the concrete syntax to the introduction of a <semanticContent> element that can be used as follows (for annotating example (7a)) :

```
(11)    <dialogueAct xml:id="da2" target="#s2" sender="#b" addressee="#a"
            dimension="task" communicativeFunction="answer"
            functionalDependence="#da1">
        <dialogueAct xml:id="da3" target="#s3" sender="#b" addressee="#a"
            dimension="task" communicativeFunction="inform" >
        <event xml:id="e3" target="#s3" type="ill" />
        <semanticContent dialogAct="#da3" content="#e3"/>
        <implDRLink rel="cause" reason="#e3" result="#da2" />
```

The <event> element introduced in (11) for specifying information about the semantic content of a dialogue act could be the same as the element with the same name that is used in the ISO standards for time and events (ISO 24617-2, see also Pustejovsky et al., 2010), for annotating semantic roles (ISO 24617-4, see also Bunt & Palmer, 2013), and for spatial information (ISO 24617-7, see also Pustejovsky et al., 2013), and that has also been proposed for the annotation of modality (Lapina & Petukhova, 2017) and quantification (Bunt, 2017). This suggests that the introduction of <semanticContent> and <event> elements, with their underlying abstract syntax and semantics, may open the possibility to specify quite detailed information about the semantic content of dialogue acts.

5 Alternative Representation Formats

Developing the DialogBank, intended to be a collection of dialogues with 'gold standard' quality ISO 24617-2 annotations, involved the inspection and correction of previously annotated material. Editing annotations represented in the XML-based format of DiAML turned out to be extremely hard, since XML may be a good format for machine application, but is not fit for human consumption. Exploiting the fact that DiAML was defined following the ISO 24617-6 principles of semantic annotation, with an abstract syntax underlying the XML representations, two alternative tabular DiAML representation formats were defined and implemented that are more suitable for human use. One of these formats makes use of one column per dimension, as illustrated in Table 1; the other puts all annotations in one column, with a specification of their dimension. Both formats were proven to be complete and unambiguous, and thus semantically equivalent to the XML format, and were useful for spotting annotation errors and making improvements (Wijnhoven, 2016). Conversion programs for reformatting DiAML annotation using one format or the other, are available in the DialogBank.

In order to enhance the usefulness of the ISO 24617-2 scheme for studies of spoken discourse phenomena, the use of alternative representation formats may be made explicit in a new edition of the ISO 2461-2 standard.

funct. segment	sp	segment text	turn transcription	Task	Auto-Feedb.	Turn Man.	Time Man.	Discourse Structuring	SOM
			hello, can I help you						
TR1-f1	s	hello							da1: Initial Greeting
TR1-fs2	s	can I help you						da2: Offer	
			uhm, yes hello, maybe, I'd like to takea tanker..						
TR1-fs3	u	uhm				da3: Turn Take	da4: Stalling		
TR1-fs4	u	yes hello			da5: Positive (da1)				da6: Return Greeting (da1)
TR1-fs5	u	yes maybe						da7: Accept Offer (da2) [uncertain]	
TR1-fs6	u	I'd like to take a tanker..		da8: Inform					

Table 1: DiAML annotation of TRAINS dialogue fragment in multi-column format.
Targets of dependence relations are in parentheses; qualifiers in square brackets.

6 Conclusions and Future Work

In this paper we have discussed some deficiencies and limitations of ISO 24617-2: 2012, which may be good to tackle when this standard is considered for revision.

An incorrectness in ISO 24617-2 was noted for annotating the 'antecedent' of feedback acts that refer to a non-functional stretch of dialogue - an incorrectness that also makes an accurate annotation of speech editing acts (acts in the Own Communication Management or in the Partner Communication Management dimension) impossible. This error should be corrected, which can be done by introducing relevant non-functional segments into the dialogue segmentation.

Experiences with applying the ISO 24617-2 scheme in various annotation efforts, such as the creation of the DBOX corpus (Petukhova et al., 2014) and the ADELE corpus (Gilmartin et l., 2017), show that it may be convenient to add the DAMSL dimension of Task Management and the DIT^{++} dimension of Contact Management to the ISO annotation scheme, as well as certain communicative functions that allow more fine-grained annotation of feedback and discourse structuring acts.

Limitations of the ISO 24617-2 scheme were brought to light by the development of ISO standard

24617-6 ('DR-Core', 2016) for discourse relations, of which rhetorical relations between dialogue acts or their semantic contents are a special case. These limitations concern on the one hand the lack of a possibility to indicate the roles of the two arguments of a rhetorical relations, and on the other hand the impossibility to indicate whether a rhetorical relation applies at the level of dialogue acts or at that of their semantic content. The possibility was discussed to import elements from DR-Core into the annotation scheme for dialogue acts and to merge the underlying metamodels. Doing so could be the first step towards a more general merging of elements from annotation schemes for different semantic information, such as time and events, spatial information, semantic roles and quantification.

Acknowledgement

Research described in this paper was supported in part by grants received from City University of Hong Kong (Project nos. 9618007, 7004491, 7004755 and 7004940).

References

Allen, J. and M. Core (1997) DAMSL: Dialogue Act Markup in Several Layers. Technical Report, Multiparty Discourse Group.

Alexandersson, J., B. Buschbek-Wolf, T. Fujinami, E. Maier, N. Reithinger, B. Schmitz, and M. Siegel 1998 Dialogue acts in Verbmobil-2. Second edition. *Report 226*. DFKI Saarbrücken.

Andersson, A., M. Bader, E. Bard, E. Boyle, G. Doherty, S. Garrod, S. Isard, J. Kowtko, J. McAllister, Miller, F. Sotillo, H. Thompson, and R. Weinert (1991) The HCRC Map Task Corpus. *Language and Speech* 34, 351-366.

Bunt, H. (1994) Context and dialogue control. *Think Quarterly 3(1)*, 19-31.

Bunt H. (2009) The DIT^{++} taxonomy for functional dialogue markup. In: D. Heylen, C. Pelachaud, and D. Traum (eds) *Proceedings of EDAML/AAMAS Workshop "Towards a Standard Markup Language for Embodied Dialogue Acts"*, Budapest, pp. 13–24. Available (with updates) at http:///dit.uvt.nl

Bunt, H. (2010) A methodology for designing semantic annotation languages exploiting syntactic-semantic iso-morphisms. In Alex Chengyu Fang, Nancy Ide, and Jonathan Webster (eds.) *Proceedings of ICGL 2010, Second International Conference on Global Interoperability for Language Resources*, Hong Kong, pp. 29-45.

Bunt, H. (2011) The Semantics of Dialogue Acts. In *Proceedings 9th International Conference on Computational Semantics (IWCS 2011)*, Oxford, pp. 1-14.

Bunt, H. (2014) A Context-change Semantics for Dialogue Acts. In Harry Bunt, Johan Bos and Stephen Pulman (eds) *Computing Meaning, Vol. 4*, Berlin: Springer, pp. 177-201.

Bunt, H. (2015) On the principles of semantic annotation. In *Proceedings 11th Joint ACL-ISO Workshop on Interoperable Semantic Annotation (ISA-11)*, London, pp. 1-13.

Bunt, H. (2017) Towards Interoperable Annotation of Quantification. In *Proceedings 13th Joint ACL-ISO Workshop on Interoperable Semantic Annotation (ISA-13)*, Montpellier.

Bunt, H. and M. Palmer (2013) Conceptual and Representational Choices in Defining an ISO Standard for Semantic Role Annotation. In *Proceedings 9th Joint ACL-ISO Workshop on Interoperable Semantic Annotation (ISA-9)*, Potsdam, pp. 45-54.

Bunt, H. and R. Prasad (2016) ISO DR-Core (ISO 24617-8): Core concepts for the annotation of discourse relations. In *Proceedings 12th Joint ACL-ISO Workshop on Interoperable Semantic Annotation (ISA-12)*, Portoroz, Slovenia, pp. 45-54.

Bunt, H., Alexandersson, J., Carletta, J., Choe, J.-W., Fang, A., Hasida, K., Lee, K., Petukhova, V., Popescu-Belis, A., Romary, L., Soria, C. and Traum, D. (2010) Towards an ISO standard for dialogue act annotation. In *Proceedings 8th International Conference on Language Resources and Evaluation (LREC 2010)*, Malta, pp. 2548-2558.

Bunt, H, J. Alexandersson, J.-W. Choe, A.Fang, K. Hasida, K. Lee, V. Petukhova, A. Popescu-Belis, L. Romary, and D. Traum (2012) A semantically-based standard for dialogue annotation. In: *Proc. 8th International Conference on Language Resources and Evaluation (LREC 2012)*, Istanbul. ELRA, Paris.

Bunt, H., V. Petukhova, D. Traum, and J. Alexandersson (2016) Dialogue Act Annotation with the ISO 24617-2 Standard. In: D. Dahl (ed.) *Multimodal Interaction with W3C Standards*, Springer, Berlin, pp. 109-135.

Carletta, J., A. Isard, S. Isard, J.Kowtko and G. Doherty-Sneddon (1996) HCRC dialogue structure coding manual. *Technical Report HCRC/TR-82*, University of Edinburgh.

Dhillon, R., S. Bhagat, H. Carvey, and E. Shriberg (2004) Meeting recorder project: dialogue labelling guide, ICSI Technical Report TR-04-002.

Fang, A. and J. Cao, and H. Bunt, and X. Liu (2012) Applicability Verification of a New ISO Standard for Dialogue Act Annotation with the Switchboard Corpus, In *Proceedings of EACL 2012 Workshop on Innovative Hybrid Approaches to the Processing of Textual Data*, Avignon.

Fang, A., J. Cao, H. Bunt, and X. Liu (2012) The annotation of the Switchboard corpus with the new ISO standard for Dialogue Act Analysis. In *Proceedings 8th Joint ACL-ISO Workshop on Interoperable Semantic Annotation (ISA-8)*, Pisa, pp. 13-18.

Geertzen, J., Y. Girard, R. Morante, I. van der Sluis, H. van Dam, B. Suijkerbuijk, R. van der Werf, and H. Bunt (2004) The DIAMOND project. In *Proceedings of the 8th Workshop on the Semantics and Pragmatics of Dialogue SIGSEM 2004 (CATALOG)*, Barcelona.

Gilmartin, E., B. Spillane, M. O'Reilly, C. Saam, K. Su, B.R. Cowan, K. Levacher, A.Calvo Devesa, L. Cerrato, N. Campbell, and V. Wade (2017) Annotation of Greeting, Introduction, and Leavetaking in Text Dialogues. In *Proceedings 13th Joint ACL-ISO Workshop on Interoperable Semantic Annotation (ISA-13)*, Montpellier.

Ide, N. and L. Romary (2004) International Standard for a Linguistic Annotation Framework. *Natural Language Engineering* 10: 221-225.

ISO 24610 (2006) *Language Resource Management: Feature structures*. International Standard. International Organisation for Standardisation ISO, Geneva.

ISO 24612 (2010) *ISO 24612: Language resource management: Linguistic annotation framework (LAF)*. International Organisation for Standardisation ISO, Geneva.

ISO 24617-1 (2012) *ISO 24617-1: Language resource management – Semantic annotation framework – Part 1: Time and events*. International Organisation for Standardisation ISO, Geneva.

ISO 24617-2 (2012) *ISO 24617-2: Language resource management – Semantic annotation framework – Part 2: Dialogue acts*. International Organisation for Standardisation ISO, Geneva.

ISO 24617-4 (2014) *ISO 24617-4: Language resource management – Semantic annotation framework – Part 4: Semantic roles*. International Organisation for Standardisation ISO, Geneva.

ISO 24617-6 (2016) *ISO 24617-6: Language resource management – Semantic annotation framework – Part 6: Principles of semantic annotation*. International Standard. International Organisation for Standardisation ISO, Geneva.

ISO 24617-7 (2015) *ISO 24617-7: Language resource management – Semantic annotation framework – Part 7: Spatial information (ISOspace).* International Organisation for Standardisation ISO, Geneva.

Jurafsky, D., E. Schriberg, and D. Biasca (1997) *Switchboard SWBD-DAMSL Shallow-Discourse-Function Annotation: Coders Manual,* Draft 13. University of Colorado, Boulder.

Lapina, V. and V. Petukhova (2017) Classification of Modal Meaning in Negotiation Dialogues. In *Proceedings 13th Joint ACL-ISO Workshop on Interoperable Semantic Annotation (ISA-13)*, Montpellier.

Petukhova, V. and A. Malchanau and H. Bunt (2014) Interoperability of Dialogue Corpora through ISO 24617-2-based Querying. In *Proceedings 9th International Conference on Language Resources and Evaluation (LREC 2014*, Reykjavik, pp. 4407-4414.

Petukhova, V., Gropp, M., Klakow, D., Eigner, G., Topf, M., Srb, S., Moticek, P., Potard, B., Dines, J., Deroo, O., Egeler, R., Meinz, U., Liersch, S., Schmidt, A. (2014) The DBOX Corpus Collection of Spoken Human-Human and Human-Machine Dialogues. In *Proceedings 9th International Conference on Language Resources and Evaluation (LREC 2014*, Reykjavik.

Petukhova, V. and L. Prévot, and H. Bunt (2011) Discourse Relations in Dialogue. In: *Proceedings 6th Joint ACL-ISO Workshop on Interoperable Semantic Annotation (ISA-6)*, Oxfor, pp. 80-92.

Pustejovsky, J., J. Moszkowicz,, and M. Verhagen (2013) A linguistically grounded annotation language for spatial information. *Traitement Automatique des Langues* 53: 87-113.

Pustejovsky, J., K. Lee, H. Bunt, and L. Romary (2010) ISO-TimeML: An International Standard for Semantic Annotation. In: *Proceedings Seventh International Conference on Language Resources and Evaluation (LREC 2010)*, Malta. ELRA, Paris, pp. 394–397.

Wijnhoven, K. (2016) Annotation Representations and the Construction of the DialogBank. MA Thesis, Tilburg University.

Appendix A Dimensions and Communicative Functions in ISO 24617-2:2012

The table below lists the 56 communicative functions defined in ISO 24617-2.

Table 2: ISO 24617-2 communicative functions

General-Purpose Communicative Functions	Dimension-Specific Communicative Functions	
	Function	Dimension
Inform	AutoPositive	Auto-Feedback
Agreement	AutoNegative	
Disagreement	AlloPositive	Allo-Feedback
Correction	AlloNegative	
Answer	FeedbackElicitation	
Confirm	Staling	Time Management
Disconfirm	Pausing	
Question	Turn Take	Turn Management
Set-Question	Turn Grab	
Propositional Question	Turn Accept	
Choice-Question	Turn Keep	
Check-Question	Turn Give	
Offer	Turn Release	
Address Offer	Self-Correction	Own Communication Man.
Accept Offer	Self-Error	
Decline Offer	Retraction	
Promise	Completion	Partner Communication Man.
Request	Correct Misspeaking	
Address Request	Interaction Structuring	Discourse Structuring
Accept Request	Opening	
Decline Request	Init-Greeting	Social Obligations Man.
Suggest	Return Greeting	
Address Suggest	Init-Self-Introduction	
Accept Suggest	Return Self-Introduction	
Decline Suggest	Apology	
Instruct	Accept Apology	
	Thanking	
	Accept Thanking	
	Init-Goodbye	
	Return Goodbye	

Appendix B. Possible Extended Metamodel for ISO 24617-2

The metamodel below deviates from the one in ISO 24617-2 in the following respects:

- 'referential segments' have been introduced, and feedback dependence relations can now relate dialogue acts not only to other dialogue acts or to functional segments, but also to referential segments

- the semantic content of a dialogue act is introduced, and rhetorical relations can now relate dialogue acts not only to other dialogue acts but also to the semantic contents of other dialogue acts.

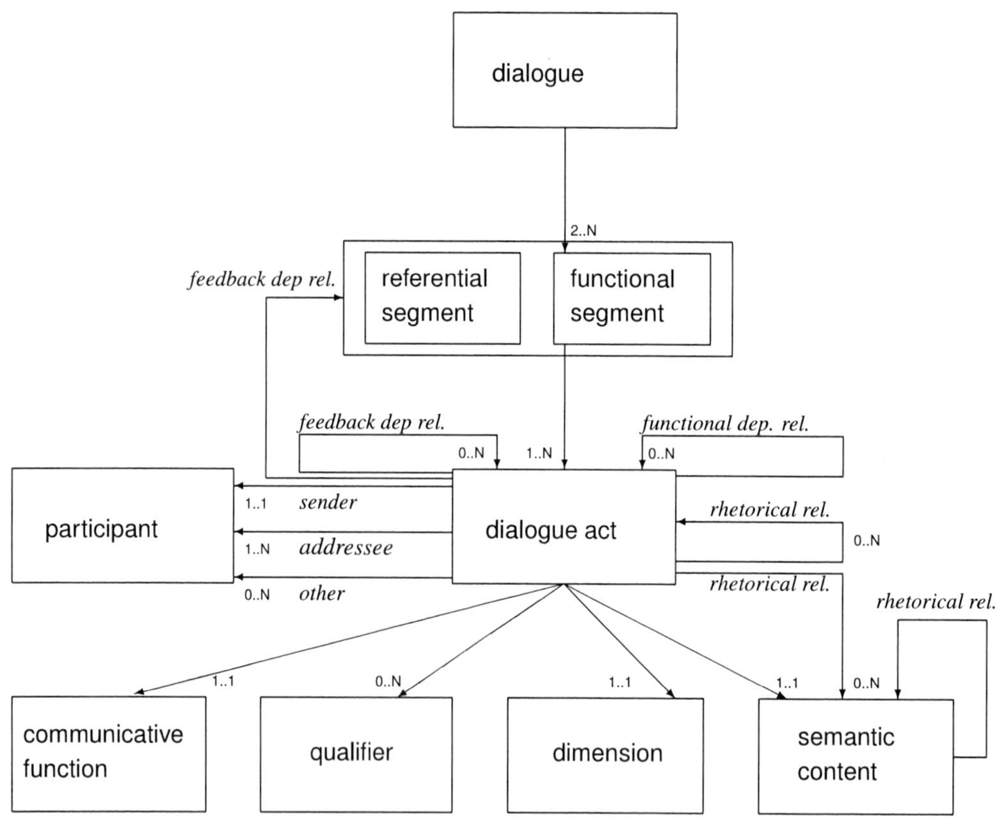

Annotation of Greeting and Leave-taking in Social Text Dialogues Using ISO 24617-2

Emer Gilmartin
ADAPT Centre, Trinity College Dublin
gilmare@tcd.ie

Brendan Spillane
ADAPT Centre, Trinity College Dublin
brendan.spillane@adaptcentre.ie

Maria O'Reilly
Trinity College Dublin
moreill2@tcd.ie

Christian Saam
ADAPT Centre, Trinity College Dublin
saamc@adaptcentre.ie

Ketong Su
ADAPT Centre, Trinity College Dublin
ketong.su@adaptcentre.ie

Killian Levacher
IBM Ireland
killian.levacher@ibm.com

Loredana Cerrato
EIT Digital
loredana.cerrato@eitdigital.eu

Benjamin R. Cowan
University College Dublin
benjamin.cowan@ucd.ie

Leigh M. H. Clark
University College Dublin
leigh.clark@ucd.ie

Arturo Calvo
ADAPT Centre, Trinity College Dublin
arturo.calvo@adaptcentre.ie

Nick Campbell
ADAPT Centre, Trinity College Dublin
nick@tcd.ie

Vincent Wade
ADAPT Centre, Trinity College Dublin
vincent.wade@adaptcentre.ie

Abstract

Dialogue act annotation aids understanding of interaction structure, and also in the design of artificial dialogue. While many dialogues can be described as task-based or instrumental, others are more interactional. These categories are not mutually exclusive; many service encounters include social talk. Much research on dialogue and particularly on description of dialogue acts for use in dialogue systems has focused on task-based dialogue. However, attention has been focusing on social aspects of spoken and text interaction, particularly in light of newer systems designed for domains such as companionship. In this paper we briefly describe social or casual talk, review how current dialogue annotation schemes, and particularly the ISO standard 24617-2 "Semantic annotation framework, Part 2: Dialogue acts", treat non-task elements of dialogue. We describe the collection and annotation using the ISO standard of a corpus of 193 text dialogues, report on a analysis of dialogue acts used in greeting, introductions and leave-taking, and propose new dialogue acts to provide coverage of these fundamental conversational sequences.

1 Introduction

It is widely accepted that dialogues proceed through dialogue moves or acts, and dialogue act annotation is very valuable in furthering understanding of the structure of interactions, particularly when such knowledge is needed in the design of artificial spoken or text dialogue. While many dialogues and indeed parts of dialogues can be described as task-based or instrumental, with clear goals, as in the case of a service encounter or business meeting, others are more interactional in nature, as in friendly chats or longer casual conversations. Indeed many service encounters include social talk from formulaic greetings and leave-taking to smalltalk. Much research on dialogue and particularly on description of dialogue acts for use in dialogue systems has focused on transactional or task-based dialogue, and often on the task itself. However, attention has been focusing on social aspects of spoken interaction, particularly in light of newer systems designed for domains such as companionship. In this paper we briefly describe social or casual talk as a model for spoken and written social interaction, reviewing how current dialogue annotation schemes and particularly the ISO standard 24617-2 Semantic annotation framework, Part 2: Dialogue acts (ISO, 2012) (henceforth ISO standard) treat non-task elements of dialogue. We then describe the collection and annotation using the ISO standard of a corpus of 193 text dialogues and report on a study of the dialogue acts used in greeting and leave-taking. From this we propose new dialogue acts to provide fuller coverage of these sequences which are fundamental to conversation.

2   Instrumental and Interactional Dialogue

With the advent of new communication technologies, text has become a medium for practically synchronous interaction. For much of history, written messages were asynchronous and did not approach the fine-grained interaction and collaboration of spoken interaction. Dialogue systems model spoken or written synchronous or near-synchronous interactions, often to fulfill a task but increasingly to create the illusion of a more social or friendly interaction, whether for casual or interactional conversation or to 'lubricate' more transactional exchanges. The text of such exchanges is closer to speech than is traditional formal written language, as has long been observed in Fairclough's ideas of 'conversationalization' of text (Fairclough, 1992) and Ong's notions of secondary orality (Ong, 1982). With live text exchange a part of everyday life we have seen an explosion of casual writing - writing which is not performed for a formal purpose but rather to fulfill social goals. It seems likely that such dialogues could be better understood with reference to spoken casual conversation, which has been the subject of study in several disciplines - we review the core notions below.

Casual social conversation includes smalltalk, gossip, and conversational narrative. Aimless social talk or 'phatic communion' has been described as an emergent activity of congregating people, and viewed as the most basic use of language (Malinowski, 1936). Researchers have theorized that such talk functions to build social bonds and avoid unfriendly or threatening silence, rather than simply to exchange information or express thought, as postulated in much linguistic theory. Instances of these views are found in the phatic component in Jakobson's model of communication (Jakobson, 1960), distinctions between interactional and instrumental language (Brown and Yule, 1983), and theories that language evolved to maintain social cohesion Dunbar (1998). Early analytic work on smalltalk focused on the 'psychologically crucial margins of interaction', conversational openings and closings in particular. This work suggests that small talk performs a lubricating or transitional function allowing talk to progress from initial silence through stages of greeting, to the business or 'meat' of the interaction, and back to closing sequences and to leave taking (Laver, 1975). The structure of casual conversation has been described in terms of distinct phases; often beginning with ritualised opening greetings, followed by approach segments of light uncontroversial small talk, and in longer conversations leading to more informative centre phases (consisting of sequential but overlapping topics), and then back to ritualised leave-takings (Ventola, 1979). Schneider (Schneider, 1988) highlighted features prevalent in casual talk which did not seem to conform to Gricean ideas of dialogue - in particular, idling sequences of repetitions of agreeing tails such as 'Yes, of course', 'MmHmm' which seem to keep the conversation going rather than add any new information. He proposed a set of maxims peculiar to this genre, concentrated on the importance of avoiding silence and maintaining politeness, and suggested that Grice's Co-operative Principle itself (Grice, 1975) remained relevant to small talk although several of the related maxims did not apply.

Syntactical, lexical, and discourse differences between (casual) conversation and more formal spoken and written genres are described in Biber and Leech's work on the Longman Corpus of Spoken and Written English (LSWE), particularly in their chapter on the grammar of conversation (Biber et al., 1999). In terms of function, Slade and Eggins view casual conversation as the space in which people form and refine their social reality (Eggins and Slade, 2004) citing gossip between workmates, where participants reaffirm their solidarity, and dinner table talk between friends. They describe the structure of social talks as segments of 'chat' (interactive exchanges involving short turns by all participants) and 'chunks' (longer uninterrupted contributions). Instrumental and interactional exchanges differ in duration; task-based conversations are bounded by task completion and tend to be short, while casual conversation can go on indefinitely. In the current work, we have started at the edges of conversations, with greetings/introductions, and leave-taking sequences. Below we review the coverage of social dimensions of talk in dialogue act annotation schemes.

3 Dialogue Act Annotation of Interactional Talk

Existing dialogue act annotation schemes are very much task-based, perhaps due to the focus on task-based dialogue for much of the history of modern dialogue systems (Allen et al., 2001). While there have been some schemes based on text conversations (Kim et al., 2010), the vast bulk of schemes have been based on spoken interaction. There have been several annotation schemes developed, often in conjunction with particular corpora or experiments, such as the schemes developed to annotate Trips and Trains, Switchboard, ICSI, and the AMI corpus(Traum, 1999; Core and Allen, 1997; Jurafsky et al., 1997; Shriberg et al., 2004; McCowan et al., 2005). More extensive domain independent schemes such as DIT++ (Bunt, 2006) have been developed culminating in the ISO standard for dialogue act annotation. The ISO standard is very useful as it (i) amalgamates contributions from pre-existing schemes, and (ii) is multifunctional and multidimensional - several acts can apply to stretches within the same contribution.

Most dialogue annotation schemes include a number of social obligation management functions. In a survey of 14 schemes, Petukova found that 10 included greeting functions, 4 included introductions, 6 had goodbyes, 5 included apology type functions, and 5 contained thanking (Petukhova, 2011). Three systems (AMI, MALTUS, and Primula) provided broader tags to reflect ideas of positivity and negativity, politeness, and positive and negative face work. The ISO standard covers more of these functions than previous schemes, although it is still largely task-based, with tags for social functions in the Social Obligations Management (SOM) dimension restricted to formalities such as greetings, apologies, or farewells. The SOM dimension of the ISO standard contains nine communicative functions - initialGreeting, initialSelfIntroduction, returnSelfIntroduction, apology, acceptApology, thanking, acceptThanking, initialGoodbye, and returnGoodbye.

Below we describe the collection and annotation of a hybrid social/task-based corpus of text dialogues which was annotated with an extended version of the ISO to more fully cover various social functions in greeting, introductions, and leave-taking.

4 ADELE Corpus - Collection

A corpus of 193 two-person text dialogues was collected and annotated with the ISO standard to provide initial training data for the ADELE project, a personalized intelligent companion capable of conversational, social dialogue. Below we briefly describe the scenario and participants and outline the interaction platform used.

4.1 Scenario

The dialogues were text-based and dyadic between English speaking adults connecting remotely via a web-based interface. Each participant was given a persona with information on home, relationships, nationality, job, hobbies and interests. The objective was to discover this information about the interlocutor and also to discover any facts or interests in common. Participants were instructed to be friendly and chatty. In order to promote friendly chat rather than 'interviewing' behaviour, one point was given for each piece of information discovered while five points were given when commonalities were discovered.

While the underlying aim of the collection was to collect dialogue acts requesting or offering information and expanding on topics, the nature of the conversations meant that the corpus also contained examples of greeting and leave-taking and casual talk for practically all of the conversations gathered.

4.2   Interaction Platform Design

The data were collected using a Dialogue Interface, which is a Google Chrome extension for the team collaboration tool Slack[1], developed in HTML5, CSS3 and JQuery. Interactions were scheduled using a Matching Engine, a RESTful API developed in Java JAX-RS and Jersey that creates new conversations between pairs of available participants and assigns each one a randomly-generated persona. All data were collected in the Dialogue Database (PostgreSQL). Through the dialogue interface, participants could converse with their match in the experiment, fill in the persona traits of the other participant and view their own.

4.3   Data Collection

The conversations were collected over two months in late 2016. There were 37 participants (26M/11F, age range 18-43), all of whom were either native English speakers or at least meeting the requirements of the IELTS International English Language Testing Service examination at level 6.5 and working/studying and living in Ireland. A total of 193 completed dialogues were collected. During the experiment, the participants interacted over the interface to discover attributes of their partner's persona. When all the attributes of a persona were discovered, participants could leave the interface. If they wished, they could be re-assigned a new fictitious persona and another anonymous participant to start a new conversation with. Thus, a participant could take part in more than one conversation over the course of the data collection, but not with a previous partner.

5   ADELE Corpus - Annotation

The conversations were annotated using a modified version of the ISO standard. A pilot annotation of a subset of the corpus was carried out by two annotators using the ISO standard to determine its suitability and whether extensions were necessary.

The dialogue act annotation of the entire conversations was to be used to train a spoken dialogue system which would be able to play the roleplaying game described above with a human partner. Therefore, lexical tags were added to the core dialogue InfoTransfer acts. These tags reflected the topic being discussed by the participants. In order to distinguish between utterances which moved the dialogue forward (by informing the interlocutor of one of the pieces of information needed to accomplish the task) and follow up (friendly comments on this information), any inform acts which were not 'first mentions' of relevant information were tagged as comments with lexical tags as above. The lexical tags took the form **[topic]** where the value for topic could be any of the persona attributes in the task, and the tags were appended to the dialogue act tags for the relevant functional segments.

During the course of the pilot annotation, annotators noted that there were recurring dialogue components in extended greeting/introductions and leave-taking (henceforth GIL) sequences which could not easily be satisfactorily annotated using the set of dialogue act tags in the Social Obligations Management (SOM) dimension of the ISO standard. An example of an extended greeting and introductions sequence is shown below to illustrate the challenges in annotation:

1. A: Hi

2. B: Hello, I'm Ann. I'm from Mexico City. Yourself?

3. A: Hi Ann, nice to meet you. I'm John.

---

[1] https://slack.com/

4. B: Hey John, nice to meet you too. How are you today?

5. A: Good, good. You? I'm from Paris, living in London now.

6. B: I'm in good form!.

In the above fragment there are four instances of **hello**, **hi**, or **hey**. The first two can be accounted for by the ISO scheme but the latter two cannot as there is not a 'generic' greet tag, but only initialGreet and returnGreet. The expression **nice to meet you** and response **nice to meet you too** in lines 3 and 4 are clearly formulaic greetings but it is unclear how to annotate them in the ISO standard. One somewhat unsatisfactory solution is to tag them as informs linked by rhetorical relations, but then the question arises of which dimension to place them in - the Task/Communicative or Social Obligations Management? A similar situation obtains with the **How are you today? – Good, good** and **You?** (ellipsis of **How are you?**) – **I'm in good form!** in lines 4-6. If the first part of these adjacency pairs are annotated as setQuestions and the second parts as informs or answers with the relevant rhetorical relations, these tags could be placed in the SOM dimension. However, these composite treatments of formulaic sequences are clumsy to implement during annotation and at odds with the specificity of other tags in SOM, and do not pinpoint the ilocutionary force of the expressions as clearly as existing tags such initalGreet and returnGreet do the **Hi** and **Hello** in lines 1 and 2.

To make annotation more efficient, additional acts were created in the SOM category to more easily mark such sequences and similarly problematic sequences in leave-taking sequences, and were added to the coding manual for the corpus. For greeting sequences, the new tags were **ntmy** and **repNtmy** to tag utterances such as 'It's nice to meet you', and responses such as 'Likewise' or 'Nice to meet you too' , **hay** and **repHay** sequences like 'How are you?' and responses such as 'Fine.', and **greet** for extra 'Hello' and 'Hi' utterances. For leave-taking, the new tags were **wntmy** and **repWntmy** for 'It was nice to meet you' and 'It was nice to meet you too'. Table 1 shows the new acts and common examples of how they occur in the corpus.

Table 1: Acts introduced for the ADELE annotation and common surface forms

Act	Common Examples	Functional Area
ntmy	Nice to meet you	Greeting
	Good to talk to you	Greeting
repNtmy	Nice to meet you too	Greeting
	Good to talk to you too	Greeting
hay	How are you?	Greeting
	How's it going?	Greeting
repHay	Fine	Greeting
greet	Hello	Greeting
	Hi	Greeting
wntmy	It was lovely to meet you	leave-taking
	Nice talking to you	leave-taking
repWntmy	It was nice to meet you too	leave-taking
	Likewise	leave-taking

The entire corpus of 193 dialogues was then annotated using this expanded scheme. Conversations were annotated using a Microsoft Excel spreadsheet adapted from those on the DialogBank website. For the purposes of the following analysis six conversations were omitted due to irregularities at the beginning or end of the conversation such as participants using their real name or confusion about the workings of the interface. The GIL sequences in the remaining 187 conversations were then analysed as described below.

6 Analysis of Greeting and leave-taking Sequences in the ADELE Corpus

While there are several areas in which attention needs to be paid to the interactional or social functions of dialogue, we are focussing on greetings and leave-taking for this study. We wish to better understand the common component utterances of these sequences and investigate if additions to the ISO scheme would help provide a clearer picture and annotation of these important elements of dialogue.

GIL sections of each conversation were marked to isolate them from the body of the conversations. Greeting sections were marked as beginning with the first utterance of the conversation, and ending with the last production of a formulaic greeting/introduction or greeting/introduction response. leave-taking sequences were marked from the first attempt to close the conversation to the final utterance of the conversation.

The annotated data set contained 40,297 words over 9231 turns or 'utterances' where a turn was defined as the text entered before a user pressed return. The vast bulk of utterances were tagged with a single label (7811 or 84.7%), 1209 (13%) had two tags, 181 (2%) had three tags, while 26 (0.3%) and 3 utterances had four and five tags respectively.

Table 2: Greeting, Introduction, and Leavetaking (GIL) Acts in ADELE corpus

Description	Count	% Corpus
All acts included in GIL sequences (GILseq)	2336	21.5
GILA: Only GIL Acts: GILseq Acts - Interloper Acts	1820	16.7
GILB: Only GIL acts without LeaveTaking Introductions: GILA - Leavetaking Introductions	1626	15
Social Obligation Management Acts (SOM) other than GIL	198	2

There were 10889 dialogue act tags of which 2336 or 21.5% were included in GIL sequences as defined above. Table 2 shows the counts for Greeting, Introduction, and Leavetaking acts in the corpus. 1329 tags related to greeting sequences and the remaining 1007 related to leave-taking sequences. It should be noted that GIL sequences sometimes contained other acts unrelated to greeting, introduction, or leave-taking, as can be seen in the above example where **I'm from Mexico City. Yourself?** in line 2 are an inform[city] and setQuestion[city] related to the task. The question is answered on line 5 near the end of the greeting/introduction sequence. The number of dialogue acts directly involved in greeting/introduction and leave-taking sequences was calculated by disregarding the 'interloping' acts related to functions other than greeting/introductions and leave-taking. Greeting/introduction alone accounted for 1034 labels, while leave-taking alone accounted for 786 labels, making a total of 1820 acts of greeting/introduction and leave-taking which account for 16.7% of all dialogue acts tagged in the corpus. The leave-taking totals include 194 instances of leave-taking Introductions – utterances which introduce the closure of the dialogue. These utterances could be included in the Discourse Structuring dimension, in which case the total for GIL drops to 1626 or 15% of all dialogue act labels. This 15% is the most conservative estimate of the proportion of GIL tags in the corpus. The total SOM acts in the corpus including SOM categories outside GIL from the ISO standard amounts to 1824 or 17%.

In terms of the prevalence of the individual greeting tags introduced during annotation, in 187 conversations there were 495 new tags – the hay (How are you?) tag appeared 68 times, the ntmy (Nice to meet you) tag appeared 101 times, and the extra greet tag appeared 66 times (each conversation contained two initialGreets). The response tags repHay and repNtmy appeared less frequently, with 49 instances of repHay and 25 of repNtmy. For the leave-taking tags, there were 139 wntmy (It was nice to meet you) tags and 47 repWntmy tags. These figures are summarized in Table 3.

Table 3: Distribution of new GIL acts

Act	Common Examples	Functional Area	Count
ntmy	Nice to meet you	Greeting	101
repNtmy	Nice to meet you too	Greeting	25
hay	How are you?	Greeting	68
repHay	Fine	Greeting	49
greet	Hello	Greeting	66
wntmy	It was lovely to meet you	leave-taking	139
repWntmy	It was nice to meet you too	leave-taking	47

7 Results and Applications to the ISO standard

The first result of interest is the high proportion of SOM acts in the ADELE corpus, and the high contribution of GIL acts to this total. To provide context, Petukova reports percentages of SOM acts in three task-based corpora (AMI, OVIS, and DIAMOND) as ranging from 0.5 to 7.8% of total dialogue acts (Petukhova, 2011). The prevalence in the ADELE corpus is much higher. This is likely due to the more sociable nature of the interactions in ADELE. It is quite interesting that the bulk of SOM in ADELE are greetings/introductions and leave-taking. It would be very interesting to see how the GIL acts added to the tags for ADELE were accounted for in other corpora as this may account for some of the variation.

Secondly, the prevalence of the new acts introduced in the ADELE annotation, over a quarter of GIL acts encountered, would provide support for extension of the range of social acts in the ISO standard to reflect longer GIL sequences in more social dialogue.

With increasing interest in friendly interfaces, there is a need for greater understanding and more accurate modelling of social as well as task-based dialogue. There are large areas of such dialogue which are not well understood or represented in dialogue annotation schemes, ranging from simple politeness formulae, such as the greeting and leave-taking acts treated here, to larger concerns of how to represent the relationship building and maintenance functions integral to casual social talk. The annotations presented above, although preliminary in nature and from a single corpus, provide evidence that it is useful to consider a greater variety of formulaic social expressions in the greetings and leave-taking functional areas. We are currently validating our annotation scheme with naïve annotators. It is hoped that the candidate acts described above will help to inform future developments of the ISO standard to allow fuller annotation of dialogues in more social as well as task-based terms, and that their use in the development of the ADELE system will be useful to other researchers in the field of casual or social dialogue system design.

8 Acknowledgments

The ADAPT Centre for Digital Content Technology is funded under the SFI Research Centres Programme (Grant 13/RC/2106) and is co-funded under the European Regional Development Fund.

References

Allen, J., G. Ferguson, and A. Stent (2001). An Architecture for More Realistic Conversational Systems. In *International Conference on Intelligent User Interfaces: Proceedings of the 6th International Conference on Intelligent User Interfaces*, Volume 14, pp. 1–8.

Biber, D., S. Johansson, G. Leech, S. Conrad, E. Finegan, and R. Quirk (1999). *Longman Grammar of Spoken and Written English*, Volume 2. Longman London.

Brown, G. and G. Yule (1983). *Teaching the Spoken Language*, Volume 2. Cambridge University Press.

Bunt, H. (2006). Dimensions in Dialogue Act Annotation. In *Proc. of LREC*, Volume 6, pp. 919–924.

Core, M. G. and J. Allen (1997). Coding Dialogs with the DAMSL Annotation Scheme. In *AAAI Fall Symposium on Communicative Action in Humans and Machines*, pp. 28–35. Boston, MA.

Dunbar, R. (1998). *Grooming, gossip, and the evolution of language*. Harvard Univ Press.

Eggins, S. and D. Slade (2004). *Analysing Casual Conversation*. Equinox Publishing Ltd.

Fairclough, N. (1992). *Discourse and social change*. Cambridge: Polity.

Grice, H. P. (1975). Logic and conversation. In J. P. Kimball, P. Cole, and J. L. Morgan (Eds.), *Syntax and semantics. Vol.3, Speech acts*. New York [etc.] ; London: Academic Press.

ISO (2012). *ISO 24617-2:2012 - Language resource management – Semantic annotation framework (SemAF) – Part 2: Dialogue acts*. Geneva, Switzerland: International Organization for Standardization.

Jakobson, R. (1960). Linguistics and poetics. In T. A. Sebeok (Ed.), *Style in language*, pp. 350–377. Cambridge: MA: MIT Press.

Jurafsky, D., C. Van Ess-dykema, et al. (1997). Switchboard Discourse Language Modeling Project (Final Report).

Kim, S. N., L. Cavedon, and T. Baldwin (2010). Classifying Dialogue Acts in One-on-One Live Chats. In *Proceedings of the 2010 Conference on Empirical Methods in Natural Language Processing*, pp. 862–871. Association for Computational Linguistics.

Laver, J. (1975). Communicative Functions of Phatic Communion. In A. Kendon, R. M. Harris, and M. R. Key (Eds.), *Organization of behavior in face-to-face interaction*, pp. 215–238. Oxford, England: Mouton.

Malinowski, B. (1936). The Problem of Meaning in Primitive Languages. In *The meaning of meaning: a study of the influence of language upon thought and of the science of symbolism* (4th ed. rev ed.)., pp. 296–336. London: Kegan Paul, Trench, Trübner.

McCowan, I., J. Carletta, W. Kraaij, S. Ashby, S. Bourban, M. Flynn, M. Guillemot, T. Hain, J. Kadlec, and V. Karaiskos (2005). The AMI Meeting Corpus. In *Proceedings of the 5th International Conference on Methods and Techniques in Behavioral Research*, Volume 88.

Ong, W. J. (1982). *Orality and literacy: the technologizing of the word*. New accents. London: Methuen.

Petukhova, V. (2011). *Multidimensional Dialogue Modelling*. Ph. D. thesis, Tilburg University, Tilburg, Netherlands.

Schneider, K. P. (1988). *Small Talk: Analysing Phatic Discourse*, Volume 1. Hitzeroth Marburg.

Shriberg, E., R. Dhillon, S. Bhagat, J. Ang, and H. Carvey (2004). The ICSI Meeting Recorder Dialog Act (MRDA) Corpus. Technical report, International Computer Science Institute, Berkeley.

Traum, D. (1999). Speech Acts for Dialogue Agents. *Foundations of Rational Agency 14*, 169–202.

Ventola, E. (1979). The Structure of Casual Conversation in English. *Journal of Pragmatics 3*(3), 267–298.

Classification of Modal Meaning in Negotiation Dialogues

Valeria Lapina[1] and Volha Petukhova[2]
Computational Linguistics[1], Spoken Language Systems[2], Saarland University, Germany
vlapina@coli.uni-saarland.de, v.petukhova@lsv.uni-saarland.de

Abstract

This paper addresses modality classification for multi-issue bargaining dialogues in order to model human-like negotiation behaviour and to efficiently compute negotiation strategies. We propose a modality annotation and classification scheme comprising semantically distinguishable categories applied reliably by humans and machines. Our classification of modality varieties is based on both the traditional dichotomy of epistemic and root modalities, and on the analysis of the available corpus data. Our modality scheme has been used for annotating human-human dialogues and training SVM-based classifiers. We built predictive models that show accuracies in the range between 73.3 and 82.6%.

1 Introduction

In any communicative situation, interlocutors communicate their beliefs, desires, expectations, interests and obligations by means of certain communicative actions, i.e. dialogue acts. These actions are used by the speaker to signal his or her intentions concerning events, objects, relations, properties involved in the communicative situation. Speaker's intentions can be rather complex, vague and ambiguous. They may also be emotionally qualified expressing particular attitudes towards their communicative partners, third parties and message content. In negotiation interactions, partners do not just negotiate through a sequence of offers. It is observed that negotiators actually rarely make concrete offers as binding commitments (Raiffa et al., 2002). Rather, participants' actions are often focused on obtaining and providing preference information. In multi-issue bargaining, a special form of negotiation, parties have the possibility to simultaneously bargain about several goods and attributes. In interest-based (win-win) bargaining, interlocutors search for integrative potential (Fisher and Ury, 1981). They have partially competitive and partially cooperative goals, conflicting, identical or partly overlapping preferences. All this allows bargainers to have a wide array of strategies. Such strategies are often communicated in natural language by means of various modal expressions. The present study addresses modality classification for multi-issue bargaining dialogues with the purpose to adequately model human-like negotiation behaviour and to efficiently compute negotiation strategies. The main objective of this study is to establish a reliable modality classification model for negotiation domain.

The paper is structured as follows. Section 2 defines modality and its types. Section 3 provides an overview of previous annotation and classification efforts. Section 4 focuses on the description of a multi-issue bargaining scenario and the role of modality in it. Section 5 addresses machine-learning data-oriented approach to modality classification by discussing experiment design, presents the obtained results and their analysis. Section 6 brings it all together by specifying the semantics of negotiation actions, extending the ISO 24617-2 dialogue act specifications with the specification of semantic content in terms of negotiation moves and their arguments. The ISO 24617-2 dialogue act metamodel is extended accordingly. Finally, we summarize our findings and outline future research directions.

2 Defining modality and its types

Linguistic modality is an omnipresent phenomenon in communication that, broadly speaking, is concerned with the speaker's subjective beliefs. Modality corresponds to the speaker's evaluation of probability of events; it concerns with what the speaker believes to be possible, necessary or desirable.

Utterances that express the speaker's subjective beliefs are modalised. A modalised utterance has a propositional and a modal content. For example, in *it must be raining* the propositional content is *it is raining*, while the modal content suggests that it is a personal perception expressing a high degree of certainty: *it must be*. If we apply a construction-centred approach (Ghia et al., 2016) to modalised utterance analysis, we may say that [It must] is a *trigger*, [be raining] is its *target*, and between the *holder* (the speaker of an utterance in this case) and the target there is a *modal relation* as depicted in Figure 1. In modal logic, a trigger corresponds to an operator, that semantically qualifies the truth of an utterance in its scope, e.g. $\Diamond$ stands for ability, $\Box$ for preference, etc. Any modalised utterance can be described in these terms. Modality triggers can be expressed verbally, prosodically, and multimodally.

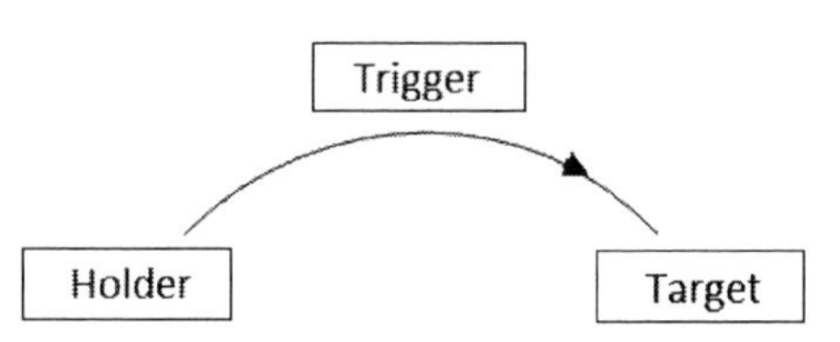

Figure 1: Modal relation between the *holder* and the *target*.

In linguistics, modality has been extensively studied by Lyons (1970), Palmer (1979), Calbert (1975), Kratzer (1981), Leech (1983), Bybee and Fleischman (1995), and many others. Previous studies distinguish between *epistemic* and *root* modalities.

Epistemics deal with possibilities that follow from the speaker's knowledge, whereas roots deal with possibilities that follow from the circumstances surrounding the main event and its participants; epistemics are taken to be speaker-oriented, roots subject-oriented, see Bybee et al. (1994). An epistemic modality (Lyons, 1970; Palmer, 1979; Nuyts, 2001) is generally understood as a weak commitment of the speaker to the truth of the proposition based on evidence or personal beliefs.

There are several types of root modalities distinguished. For instance, a *deontic* (Palmer, 1979; Peters et al., 2009; Nuyts, 2001) modality is concerned with rules, norms, and principles of either ethical or legal nature and it often expresses permissions or obligations. Scholars commonly distinguish between deontic and *dynamic* modalities (Palmer, 1979). Dynamic modality corresponds to expression of possibility that does not depend on rules, but either on the laws of nature (for example, physics) or personal abilities of the modality holder. Dynamic and deontic modal meanings may share common triggers, such as *can* and *possible*.

Modality that is concerned with expressing liking or disliking an event is called *bouletic* (Rubinstein et al., 2013) or *boulomaic* (Kratzer, 1981; Nuyts, 2001). The modal meaning that corresponds to expressing one's goals is referred to as *teleological* modality. In practice, it can be challenging to distinguish between boulomaic and teleological modalities, that is why some scholars (Portner, 2009; Rubinstein et al., 2013) propose to treat modal meanings that generally express speaker's priorities (both goals and preferences) as *prioritizing* modality. In addition, *volitive* modality indicates the desires and intentions of the speaker.

To sum up, most modality classification approaches account for *epistemic, deontic, dynamic, prioritizing (boulomaic, teleological)*, and *volitive* modal meanings.

3 Modality classification

To be practically useful, modality taxonomies need to facilitate reliable human and machine annotations. Existing automatic modality classification approaches rely on classification schemes of different granularity and complexity levels, with specific domain properties and constraints. For example, Nirenburg and Raskin (2004) proposed modality taxonomy to classify attitudinal propositional meaning. Their classification includes seven classes: epistemic, deontic, volitive, potential, epiteuctic (describing success of an event), evaluative, and saliency (highlighting important information).

	Nirenburg & Raskin (2004)	Medlock & Biscoe (2007)	Kilicoglu & Bergler (2007)	Baker et al. (2010)	Rubinstein et al. (2013)	Kobayakawa et al. (2009)	Lavid et al. (2016)
Epistemic	v	v	v	v	v	v	v
Deontic	v			v	v	v	v
Dynamic				v	v	v	v
Volitive	v			v		v	v
Bouletic				v	v	v	
Teleological					v		
Epiteuctic	v			v			
Evaluative	v						
Saliency	v						
Circumstantial					v		

Table 1: Overview of modality categories defined in various annotation schemes.

Medlock and Briscoe (2007) developed an annotation scheme for automatic classification of hedging (i.e. speculative language) in scientific texts. This annotation comprises two categories: speculative and non-speculative. The authors admit that even for human annotators it is a challenge to distinguish speculative from non-speculative sentences. The annotation scheme was applied to automatic modality classification using weakly supervised learning methods, achieving 75% accuracy.

Kilicoglu and Bergler (2008) designed a modality classification scheme to analyse biomedical texts. Their classification included the epistemic modality and its subcategories following Palmer: speculatives (uncertainty), deductives (inference), assumptives (inference from what is generally known). The highest accuracy of 93% was achieved based on syntactic features.

Kobayakawa et al. (2009) used a fine-grained annotation scheme and trained an SVM-based classifier to predict modality classes. Their classification includes 18 categories, some of which correspond to sub-categories of epistemic, deontic and dynamic modalities such as request, recommendation, will, wish, judgment, unnecessary, permission, possible. Other categories are more language and domain specific, e.g. unexpected, meaningless, hearsay, emphasis, admiration, duty, properness, qualifiedness, tentative, and natural occurrence. The classifier showed an accuracy of 78% on this multi-class classification task.

The scheme for modality annotation proposed by Baker et al. (2010) includes eight main categories: permissive, success, effort, intention, ability, want and belief. A string-matching tagger enriched with syntactic patterns has been implemented and showed a reasonable performance result in terms of precision (86%).

Rubinstein et al. (2013) proposed a hierarchical taxonomy inspired by Kratzer (Kratzer, 1981). The scheme defines three main coarse-grained categories (*epistemic, ability, priority*) and seven fine-grained classes: epistemic, circumstantial, ability, deontic, bouletic, teleological, and bouletic/ teleological. It has been observed that annotation was challenging for human annotators due to the ambiguity of modal verbs. The measured inter-annotated agreement was rather moderate in terms of Krippendoff's α .49.

Lavid et al. (2016) propose a linguistically-motivated annotation model of modality in English and Spanish. Their annotation scheme is hierarchical and comprises a core tagset (epistemic, deontic, dynamic, and volitional modal meanings) and a two-tiered extended tagset that specifies each core modality. The epistemic modality is subdivided into evidential (perception, cognition, and communication) and non-evidential (possibility, probability, certainty, doubt, apprehension). The deontic modality in the extended tagset is divided into obligation, recommendation, permission, prohibition, and absence of obligation. The dynamic modality is represented as necessity, tendency, and possibility which may mean either ability or situational possibility. The volitional modality in the extended tagset can either mean willingness or acceptance. The authors report having achieved a high inter-annotator agreement (the Cohen's kappa coefficient is 0.854).

The proposed schemes differ with respect to the number, level and nature of the defined concepts (see Table 1). However, most manual and automatic classification efforts showed that annotation success does not depend so much on the scheme complexity and granularity, but rather on the clarity and semantic distinctiveness of the defined concepts. Well-defined categories facilitate effective human and machine classification process, the annotation should fulfill certain criteria.

The design of an annotation scheme should be based on the principle of *semantic adequacy*, which

Linguistic modality	Annotation	Definition	Example
Prioritizing	Preference	agent A expresses that he is in favour of action α[1]	I *like* anti-smoking television advertisements
Prioritizing	Dislike	agent A expresses that he is not in favour of action α	This is even *worse* for me
Prioritizing	Necessity	agent A expresses that action α is necessary for him	I *have to* have at least all outdoor smoking allowed
Dynamic/Deontic[2]	Ability	agent A expresses that action α is possible for him	We *can* go for no change in tobacco taxes
Dynamic/Deontic	Inability	agent A expresses that action α is not possible for him	It's *impossible* for me to accept no smoking in public transportation
Volitional	Acquiesce	agent A expresses that action α is possible, but not favourable for him	*$In-breath* okay, it is still possible

Table 2: Defined modality categories with definitions and examples. The modality triggers are marked *italic*.

requires that semantic annotations should have a well-defined semantics (Bunt and Romary, 2002). We based our modality annotation scheme on the following criteria (Bunt, 2014; Petukhova, 2014): (1) compatibility: it incorporates categories of existing schemes, see (Sections 2 and 3; (2) theoretical and empirical validity: each category is semantically defined and observed in the corpus, Section 4; (3) completeness: the scheme provides good coverage of the phenomena in question, Section 4.2; (4) distinctiveness: each category is clearly distinct; and (5) effective usability: both humans and machines can understand and distinguish the categories, Section 5. It has been demonstrated in the past that the fulfillment of these criteria supports well-founded decisions when designing the conceptual content and structure of an annotation scheme (Petukhova, 2011).

4 Modality expressions in negotiations

Modality is an important tool in negotiations that structures the interaction and enables participants to interpret each others' intentions and to evaluate their dynamically changing goals and strategies efficiently. In negotiation, participants introduce their options. When establishing jointly possible values, a bargaining range, the participants' actions are focused on obtaining and providing information about preferences and abilities. Parties also tend to mention the least desirable events. Apart from preferences and dislikes, a negotiator has certain goals to achieve, those are signalled by teleological modal expressions. Thus, the use of prioritizing modality is frequent.

Cooperative negotiators adjust their offers taking the partner's priorities into consideration, non-cooperative ones prefer to stick to their initial offers. Cooperative behaviour may be characterized by acknowledging other parties' preferences and making concessions where possible. Verbally, it can be communicated by utterances expressing acquiescence (see Table 2). Non-cooperative (adversarial, competitive) behaviour, by contrast, may be articulated by expressing inability and dislike.

4.1 Data collection

The data used in our modality classification experiments is referred to as the Metalogue Multi-Issue Bargaining (MIB) corpus (Petukhova et al., 2016). The data was collected in simulated negotiations in which two participants (City Councilor and Business Representative) negotiate the city's 'smoking-ban' policy based on a list of negotiation preferences that have been randomly assigned to them. Each participant in the experiment received a background story and instructions, as well as a preference profile. Their task was to negotiate an agreement which assigns exactly one value to each issue, exchanging and eliciting offers concerning $\langle ISSUE; VALUE \rangle$ options. The participants were randomly assigned their roles. They were advised to start with the highest possible values according to their preference

---

[1]In negotiation domain, action α mostly corresponds to *offers* expressed in the semantic content of an utterance.

[2]In our scenario, it is not always possible to distinguish between expressions of agent's personal physical abilities (dynamic) and possibilities imposed by norm and conventions including those related to the agent's membership in a certain professional group or political party (deontic).

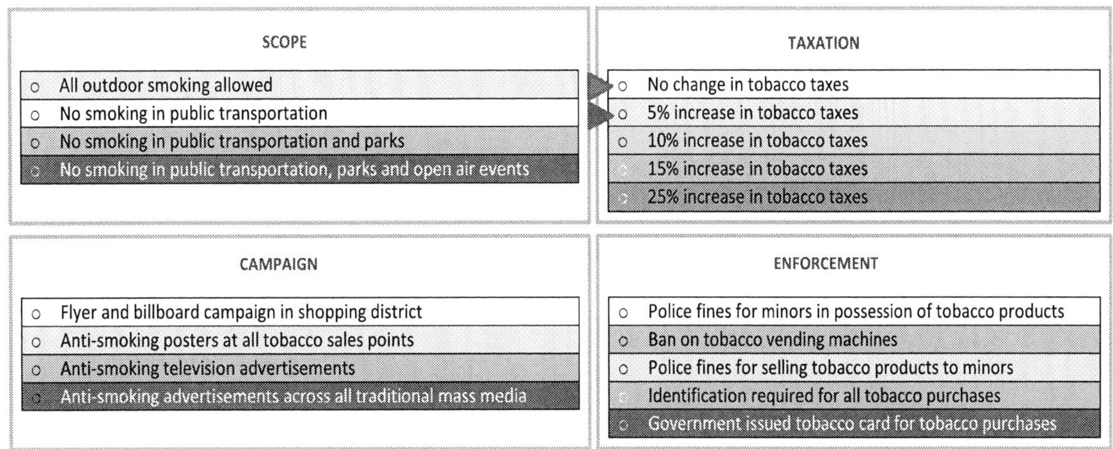

Figure 2: Example of preferences in four issues presented to participants as a colour.

information. The participants were not allowed to show their preference cards to each other. No further rules on the negotiation process, order of discussing issues, or time constraints were imposed. They were allowed to withdraw or re-negotiate previously made agreements within one session, or terminate a negotiation.

The anti-smoking regulations were concerned with four main *issues*: (1) smoke-free public areas (smoking ban scope); (2) tobacco taxes (taxation); (3) effective anti-smoking campaign (campaign); and (4) enforcement policy and police involvement (enforcement), see Figure 2. Each of these issues involves four to five most important negotiation *values* with preferences assigned representing parties negotiation positions, i.e. preference profiles. Nine cases with different preference profile were designed. The preferences strength was communicated to the negotiators through colours. Brighter orange colours indicated increasingly negative options; brighter blue colours increasingly positive options.

The collected corpus consists of 24 dialogues with 8 participants involved, of a total duration of about 2.5 hours, comprising approximately 2.000 speaking turns (about 10.000 tokens). To study modality we extracted 1145 task-related utterances.

4.2   Data annotations

The recorded data was transcribed, segmented and annotated with dialogue act information following the ISO standard. The ISO 24617-2 taxonomy ISO (2012) distinguishes 9 dimensions, addressing information about a certain *Task*; the processing of utterances by the speaker (*Auto-feedback*) or by the addressee (*Allo-feedback*); the management of difficulties in the speaker's contributions (*Own-Communication Management*) or that of the addressee (*Partner Communication Management*); the speaker's need for time to continue the dialogue (*Time Management*); the allocation of the speaker role (*Turn Management*); the structuring of the dialogue (*Dialogue Structuring*); and the management of social obligations (*Social Obligations Management*). Additionally, to capture the negotiation task structure, *Task Management* acts are introduced. These dialogue acts explicitly address the negotiation process and procedure. This includes utterances for coordinating the negotiators' activities (e.g., "Let's go issue by issue") or asking about the status of the process (e.g., "Are we done with the agenda?"). Task Management acts are specific for a particular task and are often similar in form but different in meaning from Discourse Structuring acts, which address the management and monitoring of the interaction. Examples of the later are utterances like "To sum up", and "Let's move to a next round".

With respect to modality, three main types of utterances are observed in the corpus: non-modalised utterances (41%), utterances containing triggers of prioritizing modality (preference - 30%, necessity - 2%, dislike - 3.1%, and acquiescence - 3%), and dynamic (ability - 19% and inability- 1.2%), see Table 2 for examples. The developed modality scheme has these seven modality categories. They were

Feature type	Training set			
	Original data		+Simulated Data	
	Baseline	SVM	Baseline	SVM
	(MNB accuracy, in %)	accuracy, in %	(MNB, accuracy, in %)	accuracy, in %
unigrams	67.6	74.3	65.8	79.5
TFIDF unigrams	69.5	79.0	66.9	77.0
bigrams	69.5	80.0	67.9	82.6
TFIDF bigrams	69.5	75.2	71.4	79.7
1-skip-bigrams	73.3	73.3	68.0	79.8

Table 3: Classification results in terms of accuracy (in %) obtained on collected 'original' human-human and when adding artificially 'simulated' utterances.

chosen after studying the existing modality annotation schemes (see Section 3), the domain of multi-issue bargaining (see Section 4), and the corpus.

The modality types were annotated by two independent annotators using audio recordings and manually produced transcriptions. The annotators were instructed to look only at utterances expressing task-related acts and assign to them one of the seven modality categories. A list of verbal and paralinguistic triggers was provided for each category. A near perfect inter-annotator agreement on average was reached in terms of Cohen's kappa of 0.91 (Cohen, 1960).

5   Assessing automatic modality classification and learnability

To classify modal meanings in multi-issue bargaining dialogues, SVM-based learning experiments were conducted in stratified ten-fold cross-validation setting. Support Vector Machines (SVM) are known to generalize well when applied to small training samples sets and show a rather robust multi-class performance when using (Gaussian) radial basis function kernel (RBF kernel), see Chang et al. (2010).The obtained performance has been compared to the previously undertaken efforts reported in the literature (Section 3) and to the baseline system built on the training data using different features. As the baseline, Multinomial Naive Bayes (MNB) classifier was trained to predict modality classes. The MNB algorithm assumes conditional independence between features which makes it suitable to be used as a strong baseline. Moreover, MNB is robust, fast, and easy to implement.

Features were computed from speech transcriptions, such as token unigrams and bigrams, 1-skip bigrams of lemmas, tf-idf weights for unigrams and bigrams, and various combinations of those. We measured the trained classifier's accuracy assessing its performance on different types of features and a set of tuned default exhaustive grid search parameters. Additionally, error analysis was performed by studying the confusion matrices.

Our feature selection experiments showed that the classifier's accuracy ranges between 72 and 82.6%, and does not differ significantly when features are varied (see Table 3). It should be noticed, however, that the use of bigrams resulted in the highest accuracy scores.

The collected human-human data set was rather small to train robust predictive models in data-oriented way. To extend a training set with more data, *user simulation* is often used and is efficient when domain and task structure are well-defined, and the user model truly reflects what real users are likely to do (Paek, 2006). Applied to our domain and tasks, we based the generation of simulated modalised/non-modalised utterances on trigger patterns extracted from transcribed human-human dialogues and changing possible targets. For example, the originally recorded utterance was I prefer *a smoking ban* resulted in the generated one I prefer *a discount*, substituting the value *a smoking ban* by *a discount*. The larger training set comprises 6145 utterances. All trained models were tested on original human-human data.

When training on the data extended with simulated utterances, the results in terms of accuracy are consistent with those obtained on the original data: the use of unigrams and bigrams of tokens results in the highest accuracy scores, and SVM clearly outperforms the baseline Multinomial Naive Bayes classifier.

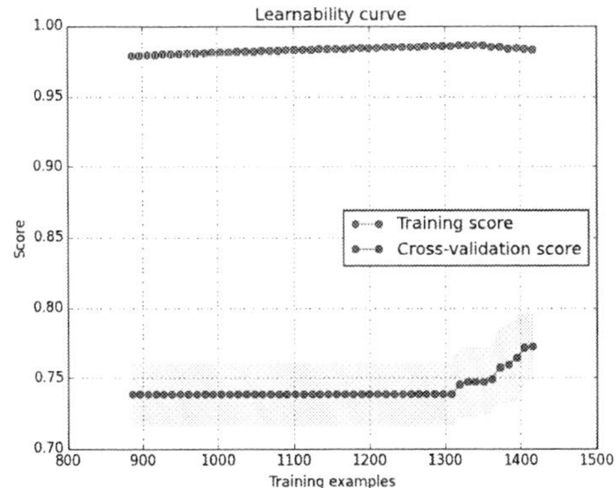

Figure 3: Learnability curved using original human-human data.

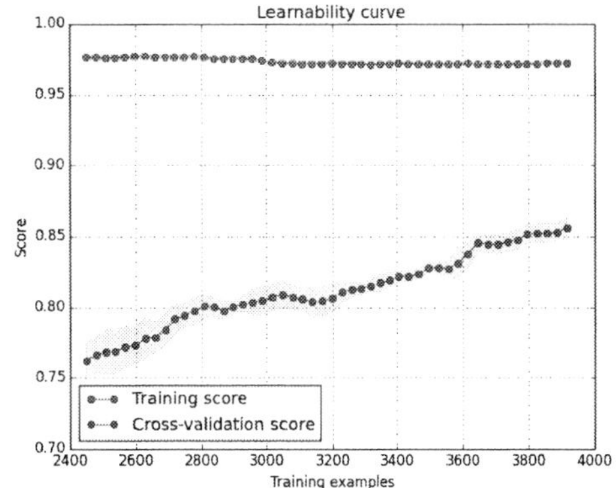

Figure 4: Learnability curved using all available data.

Error analysis was performed by a detailed study of the confusion matrices, as well as assessing classifier precision for each class. The analysis of the confusion matrices showed that generally there are not many classification errors, and some errors were expected. For instance, discrimination between non-modalised utterances and those expressing preference presented the biggest problem to the classifier. This may be attributed to the absence of a verbal modality trigger in many 'preference' utterances. Elliptical forms are quite common as speakers rely heavily on the context and paralinguistics, e.g. intonation, and other prosodic features. In other cases an utterance has a verbal modality trigger, however, its meaning is ambiguous and can be disambiguated when certain contextual parameters are known. For example, *I think public transport and parks*, where *I think* indicates preference expressing boulomaic modality rather than being a trigger of epistemic modality.

Collecting and annotating data is costly. Knowing the minimal amount of data needed for training a robust predictive model will save efforts. Therefore, we conducted a series of learnability experiments and plotted learnability curve, see Figures 3 and 4. The experiments show that when training on all available data (original and simulated) the curve does not level off. This suggests that the classifier performance will further benefit from adding more training data.

6 Modal negotiation semantics

Negotiations are commonly analysed in terms of certain actions, such as offers, counter-offers, and concessions, scc Watkins (2003), Hindriks et al. (2007). We considered two possible ways of using such actions, also referred to as 'negotiation moves', to compute the semantic meaning of partners' contributions in negotiation dialogues. One is to treat negotiation moves as task-specific dialogue acts. Due to its domain-independent character, the ISO 24617-2 standard does not define any communicative functions that are specific for a particular kind of task or domain, but the standard invites the addition of such functions, and includes guidelines for how to do so. For example, a negotiation-specific kind of $Offer_N$ function could be introduced for the expression of commitments concerning a negotiation value.[3] Another possibility is to use negotiation moves as the semantic content of general-purpose dialogue acts. For example, a negotiator's statements concerning his preference to a certain option can be represented as $Inform(A, B, \Box offer(X; Y))$.

We specified 8 basic negotiation moves: offer, counterOffer, exchange, concession, bargainIn, bargainDown, deal and withdraw, see Petukhova et al. (2017).

Negotiators often communicate their cooperativity by using modal utterances that express preference and ability. Non-cooperative behaviour, by contrast, may be articulated by expressing inability and dislike. Modality expressions are mainly observed in *Inform* and *Answer* acts.

According to ISO 24617-2, the representation of a dialogue act annotation with the ISO Dialogue

---

[3]Negotiation 'Offers' may have a more domain-specific name, e.g. *Bid* for selling-buying bargaining.

Act Markup Language (DiAML) makes use of the XML element `<dialogueAct>`. This element has the following attributes:

- `@target`, whose value is a functional segment identified at the second level;
- `@sender, @addressee, @otherParticipant`;
- `@communicativeFunction, @dimension`;
- `@certainty, @conditionality`, and `@sentiment` qualifiers;
- `@functionalDependence` and `@feedbackDependence`, which have `<dialogueAct>` elements and `<functionalSegments>` as values.

Additionally, rhetorical relations among dialogue acts are represented by means of `<rhetoLink>` elements.

`<NegotiationSemantics>` element has been added to DiAML to represent the semantic content of a dialogue act. A shallow negotiation semantics is defined in terms of `<NegotiationMove>` with attributes defined for different types of such moves. For example:

```
<dialogueAct xml:id="dap1TSK38" sender="#p1" addressee="#p2"
   dimension="task" communicativeFunction="inform"
   target="#fsp1TSKCV38">
     <NegotiationSemantics>
       <NegotiationMove type="counterOffer"/>
     </NegotiationSemantics>
   <rhetoricalLink rhetoAntecedent="#dap2TSK37"
   rhetoRel="substitution"/>
 </dialogueAct>
```

Additionally, dependent on annotation goals, approach, granularity and type of semantic processing, `<NegotiationSemantics>` elements are extended with `<Arg>` elements for negotiated issues and values, and `<Operators>` for logical operators between arguments. Modal relations can be represented by `<modalLink>` linking the holder (e.g. speaker) and target (semantic content) with values describing the speaker's attitudes to the necessity or probability of the events, and the speaker's abilities. Consider Figure 5 for the ISO 24617-2 meta-model extended with a modality relation between one or more participants (i.e. holder or actor) and one or more targets that mainly consist of an event and its arguments forming a semantic content (a negotiation move).

The full proposed DiAML representation of utterance *P1: I prefer all outdoor smoking allowed* produced by the sender P1 addressed to P2 is a task-related Inform act with the semantic content $\Box offer(1A)$ is as follows:

```
<dialogueAct xml:id="da1" sender="#p1" addressee="#p2"
dimension="task" communicativeFunction="inform"
target="#fsp1TSKCV38 qualifier="certain">
    <NegotiationSemantics>
    <NegotiationMove xml:id="nm1" type="offer"/>
        <Arg>issue-1; option-A</Arg>
        <modalLink holder="#p1" target="#nm1" modalRel="preference"/>
    </NegotiationSemantics>
</dialogueAct>
```


7   Conclusion and future work

There have been numerous attempts to automatically classify modal meanings in written, mostly scientific discourse. The objective of our study required designing a modality classification approach that can be applied to the modelling of spoken (multi-modal) negotiation dialogues. The present negotiation

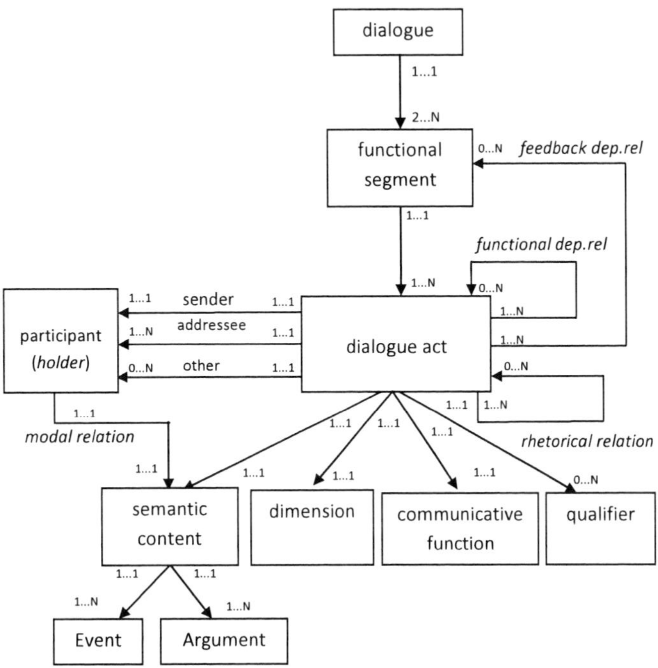

Figure 5: ISO 24617-2 metamodel for dialogue act annotation extended with modality elements.

modality annotation scheme includes categories related to expressions of speaker's *necessity, preferences, acquiescence* and *abilities*. The categories have been proven to be observable in data, semantically distinguishable and self-explanatory, which facilitated efficient human annotation and machine classification process.

The trained SVM classifier has generally showed good results in terms of accuracy. When it was trained only on the original data, accuracy ranged between 72% and 78%, outperforming a baseline multinomial Naive Bayes classifier in most cases. After extending the training set with artificially simulated utterances, we achieved accuracy range between 77% and 82.6%.

In future, we will test our predictive models within other negotiation domains and settings in order to assess their generalisability. We also plan to include multi-modal triggers as features to the classifier input space.

Acknowledgments

This research is partly funded by the EU FP7 Metalogue project, under grant agreement number: 611073. We are also very thankful to anonymous reviewers for their valuable comments.

References

Baker, K., M. Bloodgood, B. J. Dorr, N. W. Filardo, L. Levin, and C. Piatko (2010). A modality lexicon and its use in automatic tagging. In *Proceedings of the Seventh International Conference on Language Resources and Evaluation (LREC10)*, pp. 1402–1407. European Language Resources Association.

Bunt, H. (2014). Annotations that effectively contribute to semantic interpretation. In H. Bunt, J. Bos, and S. Pulman (Eds.), *Computing Meaning*, Volume 4, pp. 49–69. Springer.

Bunt, H. and L. Romary (2002). Towards multimodal content representation. In K. S. Choi (Ed.), *Proceedings of LREC 2002, Workshop on International Standards of Terminology and Language Resources Management*, pp. 54–60. ELRA.

Bybee, J. and S. Fleischman (1995). *Modality in Grammar and Discourse*. Typological studies in language. J. Benjamins.

Bybee, J. L., R. D. Perkins, and W. Pagliuca (1994). *The evolution of grammar: Tense, aspect, and modality in the languages of the world*, Volume 196. University of Chicago Press Chicago.

Calbert, J. (1975). Toward the semantics of modality. In J. Calbert and H. Vater (Eds.), *Aspekte der Modalitt*, pp. 2–70. Gunter Narr.

Chang, Y.-W., C.-J. Hsieh, K.-W. Chang, M. Ringgaard, and C.-J. Lin (2010). Training and testing low-degree polynomial data mappings via linear SVM. *Journal of Machine Learning Research 11*(Apr), 1471–1490.

Cohen, J. (1960). A coefficient of agreement for nominal scales. *Education and Psychological Measurement 20*, 37–46.

Fisher, R., W. L. Ury, and B. Patton (2011). *Getting to yes: Negotiating agreement without giving in*. Penguin.

Ghia, E., L. Kloppenburg, M. Nissim, P. Pietrandrea, and V. Cervoni (2016). A construction-centered approach to the annotation of modality. In *Proceedings of the 12th ISO Workshop on Interoperable Semantic Annotation*, pp. 67–74.

Hindriks, K., C. M. Jonker, and D. Tykhonov (2007). Analysis of negotiation dynamics. In M. Klusch, K. V. Hindriks, M. P. Papazoglou, and L. Sterling (Eds.), *Cooperative Information Agents XI: 11th International Workshop, CIA 2007, Delft, The Netherlands, September 19-21, 2007. Proceedings*, pp. 27–35. Berlin, Heidelberg: Springer Berlin Heidelberg.

ISO (2012). *Language resource management – Semantic annotation framework – Part 2: Dialogue acts. ISO 24617-2*. Geneva: ISO Central Secretariat.

Kilicoglu, H. and S. Bergler (2008). Recognizing speculative language in biomedical research articles: a linguistically motivated perspective. *BMC bioinformatics 9*(11), 1.

Kobayakawa, T. S., T. Kumano, H. Tanaka, N. Okazaki, J.-D. Kim, and J. Tsujii (2009). Opinion classification with tree kernel SVM using linguistic modality analysis. In *Proceedings of the 18th ACM conference on Information and knowledge management*, pp. 1791–1794. ACM.

Kratzer, A. (1981). The notional category of modality. In H. Eikmeyer and H. R. (eds.) (Eds.), *Words, worlds, and contexts: New approaches in word semantics*, pp. 38–74. Berlin: de Gruyter.

Lavid, J., M. Carretero, and R. J. Zamorano-Mansilla (2016). A linguistically-motivated annotation model of modality in English and Spanish: insights from MULTINOT. *LiLT (Linguistic Issues in Language Technology), Special Issue on Modality in Natural Language Understanding 14*, 1–33.

Leech, G. (1983). *Principles of Pragmatics*. Longman linguistics library ; title no. 30. Longman.

Lyons, J. (1970). *New horizons in linguistics*. Number v. 1 in A Pelican original. Penguin.

Medlock, B. and T. Briscoe (2007, June). Weakly supervised learning for hedge classification in scientific literature. In *Proceedings of the 45th Annual Meeting of the Association of Computational Linguistics*, Prague, Czech Republic, pp. 992–999. Association for Computational Linguistics.

Nirenburg, S. and V. Raskin (2004). *Ontological semantics*. MIT Press.

Nuyts, J. (2001). *Epistemic Modality, Language, and Conceptualization: A cognitive-pragmatic perspective*. Human Cognitive Processing. John Benjamins Publishing Company.

Paek, T. (2006). Reinforcement learning for spoken dialogue systems: Comparing strengths and weaknesses for practical deployment. In *Proceedings of the Interspeech-06 Workshop on Dialogue on Dialogues - Multidisciplinary Evaluation of Advanced Speech-based Interactive Systems*, Pittsburgh, Pennsylvania. International Speech Communication Association (ISCA).

Palmer, F. (1979). *Modality and the English modals*. Longman linguistics library. Longman.

Peters, P., P. Collins, and A. Smith (2009). *Comparative Studies in Australian and New Zealand English: Grammar and beyond*. Varieties of English Around the World. John Benjamins Publishing Company.

Petukhova, V. (2011). *Multidimensional dialogue modelling*. doctoral thesis, Tilburg University.

Petukhova, V. (2014). Understanding questions and finding answers: semantic relation annotation to compute the expected answer type. In *In Proceedings of the Tenth Joint ISO - ACL SIGSEM Workshop on Interoperable Semantic Annotation (ISA-10)*.

Petukhova, V., H. Bunt, and A. Malchanau (2017). Computing negotiation update semantics in multi-issue bargaining dialogues. In *Proceedings of the 21stWorkshop on the Semantics and Pragmatics of Dialogue (SemDial 2017 - SaarDial)*, Saarbrücken, Germany, pp. 114–124.

Petukhova, V., C. Stevens, H. de Weerd, N. Taatgen, F. Cnossen, and A. Malchanau (2016). Modelling multi-issue bargaining dialogues: Data collection, annotation design and corpus. In N. Calzolari, K. Choukri, T. Declerck, S. Goggi, M. Grobelnik, B. Maegaard, J. Mariani, H. Mazo, A. Moreno, J. Odijk, and S. Piperidis (Eds.), *Proceedings of the Tenth International Conference on Language Resources and Evaluation*, pp. 31–33. European Language Resources Association (ELRA).

Portner, P. (2009). *Modality*. Oxford Surveys in Semantics & Pragmatics. OUP Oxford.

Raiffa, H., J. Richardson, and D. Metcalfe (2002). *Negotiation analysis: The science and art of collaborative decision making*. Harvard University Press.

Rubinstein, A., H. Harner, E. Krawczyk, D. Simonson, G. Katz, and P. Portner (2013). Toward fine-grained annotation of modality in text. In *Proceedings of IWCS 2013 Workshop on Annotation of Modal Meanings in Natural Language (WAMM), Potsdam, Germany*, pp. 38–46.

Watkins, M. (2003). Analysing complex negotiations. *Harvard Business Review 9-903-088*, 1–22.

Project notes on building a conversation parser on top of a text parser: Towards a causal language tagger for spoken Chinese

Andreas Liesenfeld
Nanyang Technological University, Singapore
Heinrich-Heine Universitaet Duesseldorf, Germany
`lies0002@ntu.edu.sg`

Abstract

This ongoing doctoral study examines cause and effect relationships in Chinese spoken language corpora and aims to build a tagger (Cause-Chi) that automatically annotates linguistic patterns used to express these relationships. Drawing on insights from Construction Grammar (CxG), Cause-Chi is a tool to detect explicit causal language and automatically parse constructions of causation and their slot-fillers for Chinese conversational corpus data. Built on top of an existing tagger for text corpora, Cause-Chi is designed to not only detect lexical constructions but also conversation-specific causal language such as multi-segment causal expressions and the usage of temporal constructions to express causal relation. Cause-Chi is currently under development and will be released in 2018 together with MYCanCor, a small corpus of spoken Chinese, and a mini-constructicon of causal constructions based on the corpus.

1 Project outline

Cause-Chi is a causal language tagger for spoken Chinese born out of the idea to build a system that can extend shallow semantic parsing beyond lexical triggers on the sentence level. Even when limiting the scope of the project to explicitly stated relationships of cause-effect, this has proven to be a particularly difficult task considering the wide variety of linguistic and other behavioral patterns that we use to express cause-effect relationships in conversation (Wolff et al., 2005).

This paper focuses on several issues that were encountered in the process of building a conversation parser on top of a text parser. Most available CxG-based semantic parsers are designed for text data, not conversational data (e.g. most FrameNet parsers such as SEMAFOR and among others Das et al., 2014; Roth and Lapata, 2015; Taeckstroem et al., 2015). Since the semantic annotation and parsing community already has mature, well-studied tools for parsing expressions of causal relationships in texts, a common approach is to build on top of an existing tool for text data analysis instead of building a new spoken language parser from scratch. This from-text-to-speech approach might be of interest to the dialog annotation community because it describes how existing text parsing systems can be extended to conversation data. In the remainder of this paper, we outline some of the problems (and solutions) that were encountered in the process of rebuilding the annotation scheme of a text tagger to take conversational data as input.

2 Annotating Chinese lexical constructions of causality

The core of the existing system is the text tagger "Causeway" for lexical constructions of causality designed on New York Times corpus data (Dunietz et al., 2015; 2017). This tagger uses supervised approaches to learn causal relationships and to identify slot-fillers of the constructions in the corpus based on a list of around 170 lexical cues of constructions of causal language (Dunietz et al., 2015). It is only concerned with explicit causal language within the boundaries of a sentence. The tagger only annotates complete tuples consisting of three elements: a **causal connective**, a **cause** phrase or clause expressing an event or state, and an **effect** event or state.

Cause-Chi not only redesigned this existing system for lexical cues of Chinese (not English) but also extended it to take functional segments in dialog acts as input. To this end, the existing annotation framework was converted to align with the ISO 24617-8 core annotation scheme, following the mapping guidelines laid out in Bunt et al. (2016). ISO DR-Core was chosen because it offers a theory-neural standard to map semantic information that can be integrated with CxG frameworks. Cause-Chi tags causal connectives in functional segments using the DiAML markup language in order to identify causal relationships ("**ISO DRel 1: Cause**"). This relation can be stated using a large variety of possible expressions of causality including verbs, conjunctions, adjectives and MWEs (see Table 1).

Type of construction	Example (from the MYCanCor corpus)
Verb	ling6 ('make, to let'), gaau2 dou3 ('make, cause')
Conjunction	so2 ji5 ('so, therefore), jan1 wai6 ('because')
Adjective	zung6 jiu3 ('important'), jim4 zung6 ('serious, grave')
MWE	bat1 dak1 liu5 ('extremely')
Nominal	git3 gwo2 ('result'), hau6 gwo2 ('consequence')
Preposition	bing6 ('furthermore'), dou3 ('to, until')
Complex	jyut6 loi4 jyut6 ('more and more'
Other	jyun4 ('completion marker'), gam3 ('so')
(Temporal)	jin4 hau6 ('after'), gan1 zyu6 ('and then')

Table 1: Examples of explicit constructions of causal language from the MYCanCor Spoken Chinese corpus in Jyutping romanization for Cantonese.

Preliminary tests show that Cause-Chi achieves relatively good results for tuples (causal connective, cause, effect) that are located within one turn. As soon as this is not the case, however, the detection rate drops dramatically. These results are in line with previous studies that have shown that connective detection in speech is a more challenging task than in text (Riccardi et al., 2016).

We aim to incorporate additional ways of how causal relationships are expressed in conversation by gradually taking more complex and multi-segment constructions of causality into account. Two phenomena will be described here. Manual annotation of causal language in the MYCanCor corpus of spoken Chinese revealed two frequently used patterns of expressing causality that the above lexical-item based tagging approach does not capture: **(1) the establishment of causal relationships using more than one functional segment in more than one turn** and **(2) the usage of temporal constructions to express causal relationships**.

3   Multi-segment constructions of causality

Multi-segment causal expressions refer to cause-connective-effect tuples that are either interrupted by dialog acts or span over more than two turns. These causal relations are not identified by the vanilla tagger because the cause-effect elements are not directly preceding or following the causal connective. In Example (1) the stated expressed causal relation is "I don't join, so I don't go." using the connective "jan1 wai6" (because). Here, only the cause "don't join" is in proximity to the connective. The annotation of the full connective-cause-effect tuple fails because a number of dialog acts precede the effect. This causes the tagger to dismiss the incomplete tuple instead of correctly identifying the effect "not going". The problem can in some cases be solved by increasing the parsing range to detect a complete tuple or by correctly annotating the dimension and coherence relation of the functional elements in question (Example 1.1).

(1)   P1: Yinwei wo bu   canjia. Zhidao ma.
      P2: Wo   zai ting.

P1: Jiu bu qu le.
(This is a Chinese example in Pinyin romanization from the MYCanCor corpus)

'P1: Because I don't participate. You Know.'
'P2: I'm listening.'
'P1: I'm just not going.'

(1.1) DiAML Representation:

```
<dialogAct id="a1" target="#s1" sender="#p1"
addressee="#p2"\" dimension="task"
  communicativeFunction="inform" />
<dialogAct id="a2" target="#s2" sender="#p2"
addressee="#p1" dimension="autoFeedback" />
  <dialogAct id="a1" target="#s1" sender="#p1"
addressee="#p2"\" dimension="task"
communicativeFunction="inform" /> <dRel xml:id="r1"
  target="#s2" rel="cause"/> <drArg xml:id="e2" target="#s4" />
  <explDRLink rel="#r1" result="#da1"reason="#e2"/>
```

4   The use of temporal language to express causality

Manual annotation of the MYCanCor corpus has shown that temporal constructions such as the completion marker "wan" (after, finished) are frequently used to express causal relationships in conversation. Since temporal constructions are not identified by Cause-Chi as causal connectives, the tagger does not identify a causal relationship in these cases. Correct tagging of the use of temporal language to express causality has proven to be a rather challenging task because the tagger has to somehow disambiguate between the "regular" use of temporal constructions and the use of these constructions for the purpose of causality. In Example (2), P2 uses the "wan" construction to express a causal relationship between "seeing the doctor" and "feeling much better". Cause-Chi does not identify this causal relationship because no causal connective is used.

A possible way to solve this problem is to test whether the used temporal (or completion) construction can be replaced by a causal construction (such as "because") by learning possible slot-fillers in the preceding and following functional segments. This way, P2's dialog act "After I saw the doctor, I feel much better" could be restated as "Because I saw the doctor, I feel much better", given that the "seeing a doctor" and "feeling better" constructions appear often enough with the "because" connective in the corpus. Alternatively, causal relationships could also be inferred between events (or states) by learning pairs of related predicates ("see doctor" - "feel better") (Hu et al. 2017). These methods, however, deal with implicit causal relationships and go beyond the scope of this project in its current state.

(2)   P1: Ni   jintian zenmeyang?
       P2: Kan wan   yisheng   ganjue hao duo le.
       (This is a Chinese example in Pinyin romanization from the MYCanCor corpus)

       'P1: How are you today?'
       'P2: After I saw the doctor, I feel much better.'

(2.1) DiAML Representation:

```
<dialogAct id="a1" target="#s1" sender="#p1"
```

```
addressee="#p2"\" dimension="task"
   communicativeFunction="inform" />
 <dialogAct id="a2" target="#s2" sender="#p2"
addressee="#p1" dimension="task" />
communicativeFunction="inform" /> <dRel xml:id="r1"
   target="#s2" rel="cause"/> <drArg xml:id="e2" target="#s4" />
   <explDRLink rel="#r1" result="#da1"reason="#e2"/>
```

5 Discussion and future work

An enhanced version of Cause-Chi that captures the above stated two phenomena is currently in development. Cause-Chi's modular design allows to add features that are able to capture additional ways of how causal relationships are expressed in Chinese, building on the core lexical-trigger parser. Two of such modules are designed to deal with the above mentioned multi-segment and temporal constructions of causality. Possible additional modules could deal with the distinction between degrees and types of causation, addressing a shortcoming of the current tagger that threats causality as binary.
Cause-Chi is expected to be released in 2018 together with MYCanCor, a small corpus of spoken Chinese, and a mini-constructicon of causal constructions based on the corpus.

References

[1] BUNT, Harry; PRASAD, Rashmi. ISO DR-Core (ISO 24617-8): Core Concepts for the Annotation of Discourse Relations. In: Proceedings 12th Joint ACL-ISO Workshop on Interoperable Semantic Annotation (ISA-12). 2016. p. 45-54.

[2] DAS, Dipanjan, et al. Frame-semantic parsing. Computational linguistics, 2014, 40.1: 9-56.

[3] DUNIETZ, Jesse; LEVIN, Lori S.; CARBONELL, Jaime G. Annotating Causal Language Using Corpus Lexicography of Constructions. In: LAW@ NAACL-HLT. 2015. p. 188-196.

[4] DUNIETZ, Jesse; LEVIN, Lori; CARBONELL, Jaime. Automatically Tagging Constructions of Causation and Their Slot-Fillers. Transactions of the Association for Computational Linguistics, 2017, 5: 117-133.

[5] HU, Zhichao; WALKER, Marilyn A. Inferring Narrative Causality between Event Pairs in Films. In: Proceedings of the 18th Annual SIGdial Meeting on Discourse and Dialogue, Saarbruecken. 2017.

[6] RICCARDI, Giuseppe; STEPANOV, Evgeny A.; CHOWDHURY, Shammur Absar. Discourse connective detection in spoken conversations. In: Acoustics, Speech and Signal Processing (ICASSP), 2016 IEEE International Conference on. IEEE, 2016. p. 6095-6099.

[7] ROTH, Michael; LAPATA, Mirella. Context-aware frame-semantic role labeling. Transactions of the Association for Computational Linguistics, 2015, 3: 449-460.

[8] TAECKSTROEM, Oscar; GANCHEV, Kuzman; DAS, Dipanjan. Efficient inference and structured learning for semantic role labeling. Transactions of the Association for Computational Linguistics, 2015, 3: 29-41.

[9] WOLFF, Phillip, et al. Expressing Causation in English and Other Languages. 2005.

The Representation and Extraction of Quantitative Information

Tianyong Hao
Guangdong University of Foreign Studies
haoty@gdufs.edu.cn

Yunyan Wei
Guangdong University of Foreign Studies
yunyan_wei@126.com

Jiaqi Qiang
Guangdong University of Foreign Studies
qiangjiaqi@yeah.net

Haitao Wang
China National Institute of Standardization
wanght@cnis.gov.cn

Kiyong Lee
Korea University
ikiyong@gmail.com

Abstract

Quantitative expressions are abundant in various domain texts. They, however, require metadata information to be understood properly. Especially in the current big data era, both industrial and academic demands for a precise and standardized processing of datasets that carry quantitative information have drastically increased. This paper makes a summary report on a recent proposal for standardizing the annotation, representation, and extraction of *quantitative information* as part of an ISO standard on semantic annotation framework (SemAF). This proposal aims at specifying a markup language, QML, grounded on a construct-based model, for representing quantitative information in text across languages. As is shown, the general framework of this language consists of six main procedures that include a step for extending its extraction method to the processing of specific domain texts in application. The paper focuses on the application of a QML-running engine to medical resources, while checking its performance for some concrete cases.

Keywords: annotation, extraction, information, quantitative, QML, representation

1 Introduction

With the current advances in Artificial Intelligence (AI) technologies, a growing number of applications, such as question answering, automatic speech translation, and intelligent assistant system, in Information Retrieval (IR) and Natural Language Processing (NLP) have been developed to require the extraction of metadata information from unstructured texts as a core module (Nadkarni et al., 2011). In processing such texts, a very large number of quantitative expressions, e.g., *HbA1c superior or equal to 7.5%*, are found requiring essential metadata information across languages and domains for their understanding, while being geared to information extraction and data analysis in general (Hao et al., 2016). Particularly in both industry and academia, the demand for a precise acquisition of quantitative information has surged since big data was made available. Business investment companies, for instance, often need to obtain quantitatively specific and statistically valid information of target companies by analyzing a large amount of data in quantitative terms from their annual reports, e.g., net sales, gross profit, operating expenses, operating profit, interest expenses, net profit before taxes, net income, etc. The increasingly expanding medical informatics research requires a larger number of medical reports, articles, and abstracts to be processed in order to analyze the dose of medicine, the eligibility criteria of clinical trials, the phenotype characteristics of patients, the lab tests in clinical records, etc. that all carry quantitative information (Thadani et al., 2009; Miotto and Weng, 2015; Weng et al., 2014; He et al., 2015). All of the demands, whether in business industry or in academic research, claim for the accurate identification and extraction of textual fragments that convey quantitative information for automated processing, computation and exchange (Hao et al., 2016).

For illustration, consider the following passage in a medical abstract (Ahmed et al., 2008):[1]

(1) Among 100 patients with type 2 diabetes forty two had *HbA1c more than 7.5%*, while seventy had fasting *blood glucose more than 120 mg/dl*. All patients with *HbA1c more than 7.5%* had increased fasting blood glucose. While thirty out of seventy patients with *fasting blood glucose more than 120 mg/dl* had *HbA1c less than 7.5%*. None of the patients with *fasting blood glucose less than 120 mg/dl* had *HbA1c more than 7.5%*.

This is part of a medical report on the result of examining type 2 diabetes mellitus. In order to understand the whole passage, especially the summarizing sentence (2a), for instance, it is necessary to analyze the two interrelated pairs, (2b) and (2c), of quantitative expressions in an explicit way:

(2) a. All patients with HbA1c more than 7.5% had *increased* fasting blood glucose.

    b. HbA1c more than or less than 7.5%

    c. blood glucose more than or less than 120 mg/dl

By an *explicit* way it is meant that at least two requirements are satisfied: normalization and machine learnability. The way of providing quantitative expressions, for instance, with metadata information, which we call *annotation*, should be standardized as a means of normalizing its whole process. However, in the IR and NLP areas, as claimed by Damen et al. (2013), there is no such standardized way of annotating quantitative expressions. When a new system is developed, a new annotation method will have to be developed from scratch. In most cases, the newly developed method cannot meet the need for information extraction so that human labors have to involve in the whole procedure, thus resulting to the increase of the overall cost (Murata et al., 2008). To employ machines for such a task, the process of annotation should be made learnable by machines. In short, a generally acceptable standard for the computational processing of quantitative expressions in natural language texts is in urgent need for IR and NLP applications.

To that end, this paper presents our current efforts to propose a normalized and machine learnable annotation scheme for representing and extracting quantitative information as an international standard under ISO (International Organization for Standardization). Two proposals were formally recommended as ISO preliminary working items in an ISO working group meeting held during COLING,[2] and another ISO meeting held in Vienna last June. The proposal is based on Bunt (2015) and Lee (2015) that discuss the annotation of measure expressions within the framework of ISO standards on semantic annotation.

The representation scheme for quantitative information is generally based on XML with an annotation scheme specified in abstract terms, called *abstract syntax*, listing the types of basic entities referred to by markables in a target source material and also of various relations among these entities. Our proposed construct-based modeling, in a sense, carries the same role of an abstract syntax by listing *constructs* for an annotation scheme. Our proposed construct-based specification of ways of annotating quantitative information in language is supplemented by a set of extraction guidelines for the purposes of practical applications such as the extraction of quantitative information from medical abstracts. The set of guidelines consists of six sequential procedures:

(3) Extraction Guidelines

    1. text pre-processing

    2. numeric, unit, and comparison operator identification

    3. variable identification

---

[1]Taken from https://www.ncbi.nlm.nih.gov/pubmed/19999209.

[2]https://sites.google.com/site/alr12coling2016/

4. variable-measure association

5. measurement unit normalization

6. filtering and verification

The proposed construct-based model with specific extraction procedures aims to provide a clear, simple, and explicit way of processing quantitative information. If it is accepted as a standard, it is expected to unify various representations of data such as medical abstracts that involve quantitative information and calculations in an interoperable format and ultimately to assist machines to carry out computational performances effectively in dealing with quantities expressed in natural language.

2 Basic Concepts and Construct-based Modeling

Linguistic expressions of either phrasal or sentential categories that are represented in either textual, visual or any other viable forms carry various types of information. We define the type of information, called *quantitative information* (QI), to be a set of pieces of information that can be analyzed in numerical and unit-based terms involving measurement. This definition narrows down the scope of computationally processable texts in language to a manageable set of markables and a small set of relations over entities referred to by these markables, especially for our proposed QML. Non-numerical information involving distances such as *very far* is, for instance, excluded, whereas expressions such as *250 km* are chosen as markables that carry quantitative information as defined. Quantified phrases such as *all men*, several women or *15 dogs and 5 cats* are also excluded from the set of markables either because they carry no numeric information or because they have no units mentioned.

QML is a specification language for quantitative information obtainable from language. It has two levels, abstract and concrete. In the abstract modeling level, it lists a finite non-empty set of basic entities, called *constructs*.[1] Ideally speaking, a set of representation schemes can be developed to be isomorphic to such a construct-based model proposed, while keeping the principle of meaning preservation at both levels (see Bunt (2010, 2015), Lee (2015), and ISO (2016)). An XML-based QML is one of such representation schemes to be discussed in the following section.

The construct-based model of QML consists of the following non-empty finite sets of constructs:

(4) a. a set V of variables ranging over the set of discourse entities,

b. a set N of reals represented by numerals including decimals,

c. a set U of (scientific) units, either standardized or normalized to standards, and

d. a set R of (comparative) relations over N x U, called *measures*.

This model constitutes a tuple $<V, N, U, R>$, with its substructure $<V, N, U>$ satisfying a function q for quantitative information that maps V to N x U. This function q is then understood as linking a measure m in N x U to some discourse entity x in V. A comparative relation r in R such as $\leq$ (*less than or equal to*) or $>$ (*more than*) can also be understood as linking a measure in the measure set N x U to a target variable.[2]

Here is an illustration. Consider:

(5) BMI (Body Mass Index) must between 20-40 kg/m^2

---

[1]This level is called *abstract syntax* and the concrete level with a representation scheme, *concrete syntax*.

[2]Pure mathematical equations or formulas for scientific calculations like *1+1=2* and *1 plus 1 equals 2* are not considered as quantitative expressions, for the set R does not contain mathematical operators such as *addition (+)* or *multiplication* x.

BMI is a quantitative variable in V, *20-40* a value range specified by two numerals in N, kg/m^2 a measurement unit in U, and the relation *between*, which is expressible by two comparison relations *greater than or equal to* and *less than or equal to*, in R.

Consider another example taken from a medical abstract on abnormal liver chemistries (Kwo et al., 2017):[3]

(6) A true healthy normal ALT level ranges from 29 to 33IU/l for males, 19 to 25IU/l for females and levels above this should be assessed.

This text contains two complex pieces of quantitative information that link the two discourse entities in a medical domain, *healthy normal ALT level for males* and *healthy normal ALT level for females*, to their two respective measure ranges with their lower and upper limit measures specified. The representation scheme based on this construct-based model of QML makes it clear how such information is captured and represented.

3   XML-based QML

We propose QML, an XML-based markup language for the annotation and representation of quantitative information. It is grounded on the construct-based model of QML just introduced. Two of the constructs of QML, V and N x U, are tagged with $<qVariable>$ for variables and $<qMeasure>$ for quantitative information (measures), respectively. Each of the XML elements tagged as such carry attribute specifications, as shown in Table 1:

Table 1: XML-based Representation Scheme QML

Annotation	Inline Representation
Variables	`<qVariable Normalized="A" Source="B">C</qVariable>`
Measures	`<qMeasure Target="#C" Relation="D" Unit="E">F</qMeasure>`

For the purpose of simple illustration, we have here adopted an inline format for representation, although a standoff format is a standard for ISO semantic annotation frameworks (see ISO (2012)). Each of the XML elements represented inline can easily be converted into a standoff format by introducing an attribute like `@target` for the construct-type elements.

In QML as a representation scheme as specified above, the element, tagged `<qVariable>`, for variables is characterized by one required attribute `@Normalized` as an identifier with a normalized value `"A"` for `"C"`, the identified variable mentioned. The attribute `@Source` is implied or optional with its value `"B"` referring to the source for normalization. The element, tagged `<qMeasure>`, represents quantitative information. `"F"` is a numeric expression in text referring to a construct of the type *real* in the set N, while `"E"` is a unit for `F"`. `"F"` and `"E"` together as a pair represent a measure. Hence, the attribute `@Unit` is a required attribute for `<qMeasure>`.

The element `<qMeasure>` represents more than a measure, represented by a pair `"F"` and `"E"`. It represents two types of relations in R. With the attribute `Relation` it modifies the value of a measure with the attribute `@Relation="D"`, where `"D"` is the normalized value of `@Relation` such as `greater than`. Then the attribute `@Target` links this modified value to the target variable `"#C"` that occurs in `<qVariable>`, where the sign # indicates that it occurs elsewhere in the annotation.

With just two elements `<qVariable>` and `<qMeasure>` specified with a short list of attributes, QML thus provides a simple and yet flexible method to annotate quantitative information in text by marking up various constructs constituting each piece of quantitative information. QML can adapt to unstructured texts in different domains and different languages. As shown in Table 2, texts in English,

---

[3]Taken from http://www.nature.com/ajg/journal/v112/n1/abs/ajg2016517a.html?foxtrotcallback=true. See.

Chinese, Japanese, and Korean from medical, business, history, and military domains, are annotated precisely in QML.

Table 2: Multi-lingual Texts from Different Domains Annotated with QML

Language	Original Texts	Annotated Texts
English	hba1c value between 7.5-9%	<qVariable Normalized="HBA1c" Source="UMLS">hba1c</qVariable> value <qMeasure Target="hba1c" Relation="greater_equal" Unit="%">7.5</qMeasure> - <qMeasure Target="hba1c" Relation="lower_equal" Unit="%">9</qMeasure>
	hba1c at the beginning of the trial between 8.5% and 10%	<qVariable Normalized="HBA1c" Source="UMLS">hba1c</qVariable> at the beginning of the trial <qMeasure Target="hba1c" Relation="greater_equal" Unit ="%">8.5</qMeasure> - <qMeasure Target="hba1c" Relation="lower_equal" Unit ="%">10</qMeasure>
Chinese	出口产品超过 324.8 亿美元	<qVariable Normalized="出口产品" Source="NA">出口产品</qVariable> <qMeasure Target="出口产品" Relation="greater_equal" Unit="美元">324.8 亿</qMeasure>
	不合格进出口产品 10.87 万批，超过 290.1 亿美元	<qVariable Normalized="不合格进出口产品" Source="NA">不合格进出口产品</qVariable> <qMeasure Target="不合格进出口产品" Relation="equal" Unit ="批">10.87 万</qMeasure> <qMeasure Target="不合格进出口产品" Relation="greater_equal" Unit ="美元">290.1 亿</qMeasure>
Japanese	日本の総人口は 2015 年（平成 27 年）の国勢調査によると 127,094,745 人	<qVariable Normalized="日本の総人口" Source="NA">日本の総人口</qVariable>は 2015 年（平成 27 年）の国勢調査によると <qMeasure Target="日本の総人口" Relation="equal" Unit="人">127,094,745</qMeasure>
	2010 年（平成 22 年）には出生数が約 107 万人	2010 年（平成 22 年）には<qVariable Normalized="出生数" Source="NA">出生数</qVariable>が <qMeasure Target="出生数" Relation="around" Unit="人">107 万</qMeasure>
Korean	전투기 820 여대	<qVariable Normalized="전투기" Source="NA">전투기</qVariable> <qMeasure Target="전투기" Relation="greater_equal" Unit="대">820</qMeasure>
	정찰기(감시통제기) 30 여대	<qVariable Normalized="정찰기" Source="NA">정찰기(감시통제기)</qVariable> <qMeasure Target="정찰기(감시통제기)" Relation="greater_equal" Unit="대">30</qMeasure>

By encoding all the link information into <qMeasure>, the representation scheme of QML fails to be totally isomorphic to the abstract modeling of constructs for quantitative information, specified in Section 2. The introduction of an additional element such as <qLink> may be able to preserve the isomorphism, while deleting the attribute @Target for the link of quantitative information, from <qMeasure>. Nevertheless, the current specification of QML can be converted into a representation format similar to the ones proposed by Bunt (2015) and Lee (2015). Here is an illustration of representing the annotation of *HbA1c value between 7.5-9%*:

Illustration for Conversion

```
<qInformation>
   <entity xml:id="x1" target="HbA1c" normalization="HbA1c"
     type="medicalConcept" />
   <measure xml:id="me0" target="" />
   <measure xml:id="me1" target="7.5%" value="7.5" unit="%" />
   <measure xml:id="me2" target="9%" value="9" unit="%" />
   <meLink xml:id="ml1" entityID="#x1" measureID="#me0" relType="value" />
   <comLink xml:id="cl1" measureID1="#me0" measureID2="#me1"
     relType="≥(greaterThanOrEqualTo)" /> (* lower limit *)
   <comLink xml:id="cl2" measureID1="#me0" measureID2="#me2"
     relType="≤(lowerThanOrEqualTo)" /> (* upper limit *)
</qInformation>
```

Here, the element <entity> stands for <qVariable> and the element <measure> for <qMeasure> in QML. The element <meLink> defines the link of a measure <measureID> to the entity <entityID> as the value attribute of the entity (relType="value"). The element <qMeasure> is a complex element which combines quantitative information represented by <measure> with the link element <meLink>s. The element <qMeasure> can also represent the type of association, corresponding to @relType in <comLink> such as "greaterThanOrEqualTo", "lowerThanOrEqualTo", "equalTo", "greaterThan", etc. In this illustration, the medical concept "HbA1c" is associated with two quantitative boundaries, upper and lower limits, in percentages which are represented by two <comLink>s.

This representation scheme is theoretically elegant, preserving isomorphism to its abstract specification. We do, however, find a certain degree of redundancy. For practical reasons, we thus claim that our QML is simpler and flexible in the sense that it is easy to introduce normalization-related non-textual information into the representation scheme. The normalization of variable and measure expressions is required to allow uniform calculations. The numeric expression such as *fifty-five* and the unit expression such as *feet*, for instance, should be normalized to *55* and *m*, based on a metric system that allows conversions.

4 Extraction of Quantitative Information

We also aim at proposing extraction guidelines for quantitative information as an ISO technical specification. The extraction guidelines are comprised of six main procedures: 1) text pre-processing, 2) numeric, unit, and comparison operator identification, 3) variable identification, 4) variable-measure association, 5) measurement unit normalization, and 6) filtering and verification. The general framework of the guidelines is shown in Fig. 1 with each of the procedures described as follows:

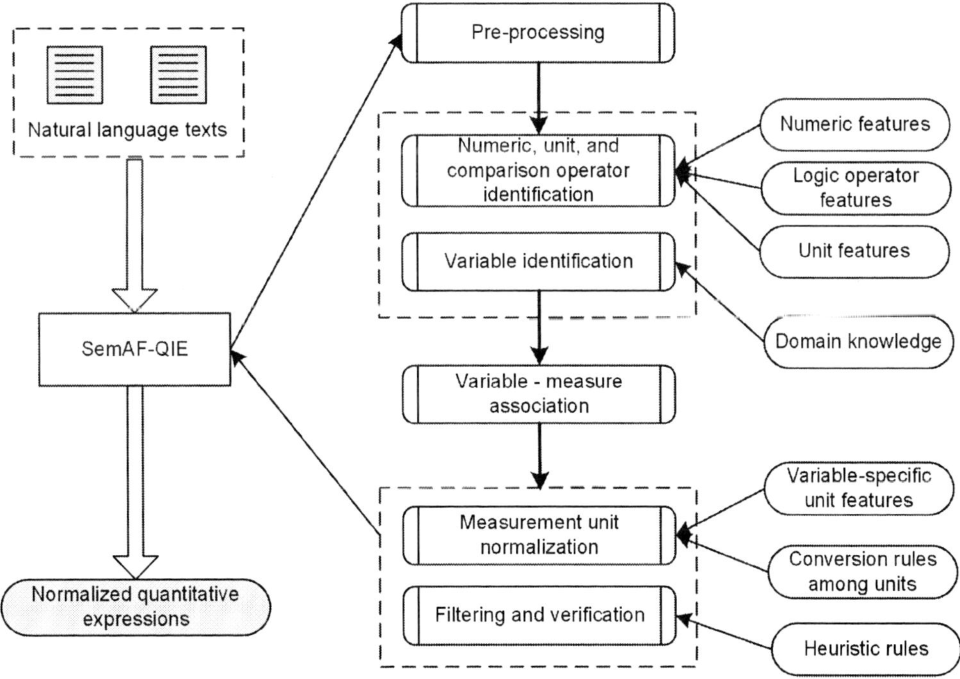

Figure 1: General Guidelines for the Extraction of Quantitative Information

1) **Pre-processing of Raw Texts:** Raw texts commonly contain noise content and thus need to be cleaned. The procedure mainly removes inconsistent character coding, replaces special symbols with normalized ones (e.g. replacing *cm3* by using cm^3), cleans redundant blank spaces, and rectifies typos

in numeric representations (e.g. replacing *18,5* in *BMI less than 18,5 kg/m^2* with *18.5*). Numbers in character type then need to be detected and transformed into Arabic digits (e.g., *two weeks* is converted to *2 weeks*). All the changes are marked with labels, while the original text is kept intact at the same time. Each of the texts is then parsed into sentences in order to match each of the sentences with a set of regular expressions while checking whether it contains numbers as candidates.

2) **Extraction of Numerics, Units, and Relations:** A set of regular expressions is pre-defined to identify numeric expressions around numbers so as to skip certain cases that are not quantitative expressions, e.g., ICD 9/10 codes referring certain diseases commonly exist in medical texts and should be skipped. In order to allow mathematical calculations explicitly in numeric terms only, non-quantifiable expressions such as *a couple of*, *some*, *a little* are ignored. For the extraction of units, training datasets are set up, consisting of a good number of meta units (e.g. *mg* rather than *mg/dl*) and special units (e.g. *ml/min 1.73 m^2*). Some rules are then defined to detect unknown and incomplete units by extending meta units with their context. With some pre-defined features, comparison relations over measures are extracted: for example, $\geq$ and $\leq$ are extracted from *between 6.5–10%*.

3) **Identification of Variables:** In order to detect both known and unknown variables with which quantitative information is associated, a list of identification methods can be provided. As a general guideline, four pieces of information can be made use of: (1) domain dictionary, (2) domain knowledge, (3) contextual information, and (4) n-Gram co-occurrence information. The first two can be utilized to identify known variables and the last two to identify unknown variables.

4) **Association of Measures with Variables:** Two general methods can apply to the association of measures with variables: a structure-based method and a sequence-based method. The first method detects certain pre-defined structures and associates measures and related variables by associative rules. The second method utilizes word sequences to associate measures with variables by processing a sentence word by word. These methods also work when a sentence contains more than one variable-measure pairs.

5) **Normalization of Measurement Units:** Variable-specific units have certain features that constitute a knowledge base in each specific domain and these features can be used to correct some obvious errors. For example, *kg* is a unit which is exclusively used for the variable *HbA1C*. Units that are missing can also be recovered by the context of their use or with some pre-defined unit features that are provided in the knowledge base. Conversion rules also apply to units in order to replace them with more preferred units and also to normalize them according to a set of predefined rules: for example, *250 mg/dl* is normalized to *13.89 mmol/l*.

6) **Filtering and Verification:** Various errors need to be filtered out or corrected. Measure values may occur with no units specified. There may be default cases that need to be made explicit. Some special units may be missing and need to be recovered. There may also be wrong associations between variables and measure values. Errors may occur in the process of extending the range of measure values or averaging them. To verify and filter out such errors, a list of heuristic rules are to be introduced.

5 Evaluation & Discussion

In order to test the effectiveness of the proposed QML and the general extraction guideline, three human annotators were employed to manually annotate 7,714 clinical trials from US National Institute of Health (NIH) [2] for diabetes disease as reference standard with a Kappa value 0.86. The annotations included 3,466 quantitative expressions for HbA1c and 1,142 expressions for glucose. Using the widely used evaluation metrics: precision, recall, and F1 score, the performance of our method as Valx against the human annotations is presented in Table 3.

For variable HbA1c, Valx achieved 2054 correct extractions for type 2 diabetes with an overall precision of 98.8%, a recall of 96.9%, and an F1 of 97.8%. Similarly, for type 1 diabetes datasets, Valx achieved an overall precision of 99.6%, a recall of 98.1%, and an F1 of 98.8%. The F1 scores for both

---

[2]http://www.ClinicalTrials.gov/

type 2 and type 1 diabetes datasets were higher than 97%. Moreover, we also tested Valx for other variables. For variable glucose, Valx obtained an F1 of 96.1% on type 2 diabetes and an F1 of 95.6% on type 1. These experiments demonstrated the effectiveness of the proposed QML and the guideline framework.

Table 3: Performance of Valx on Diabetes Clinical Trial Texts for the Variable HbA1c

Dataset	# by human	# by Valx	# Correct	Precision	Recall	F1
Diabetes Type 2	2120	2079	2054	98.8%	96.9%	97.8%
Diabetes Type 1	469	462	460	99.6%	98.1%	98.8%
Both	2589	2541	2514	98.9%	97.1%	98.0%

During the manual annotation procedure, there were some special cases of difficulty arising from the complexity of medical texts. We identified 7 types of complexity, *semantic*, *context*, *association*, *parsing*, *variable*, *numeric*, and *coding* types, which were considered as possible causes of the system errors in following the extraction procedures. As shown in Table 4, human annotators were able to correctly label the quantitative expressions, for instance, by rectifying the typos *egal* and *HbA 1c* to *equal* and *HbA1c*d, respectively. These cases, however, caused difficulties that the Valx system failed to resolve.

Table 4: Types of Special Difficulties in the Process of Annotation

Type	Example text	Clinical trial ID
Semantic	*HbA1c = 7.5% and = 10%*	NCT00117780
Context	*HbA1c <=130% of **upper limit of normal of local hospital lab***	NCT00223574
Association	*The proportion of subjects who are randomized with an **HbA1c** <7.5% will be limited to be no more than **20%***	NCT00495469
Parsing	*HbA1c superior or **egal** to 7.5%*	NCT01144728
Variable	*Glycosylated haemoglobin (**HbA 1c**) < 10%.*	NCT00274118
Numeric	*HbA1c between **45** and **94***	NCT01513798
Coding	*6.5% ≦HbA1c ≦9% at screening visit*	NCT00541437

For the cases of processing quantitative information that changes over time or is associated with embedded subordinate constructions, our proposed extract system allowed users to extract such information or annotate associated measure values by introducing necessary annotation labels with the specification of finer-grained features. In addition, we built a system using Valx, as reported in our previous work (Hao et al., 2016), on the basis of our proposed extraction guideline framework. Valx is now open source and can be publicly downloaded from *www.OHNLP.org* and *GitHub*. An online demo is available at *http://202.116.195.64:9000/valx*.

6 Summary

In this paper, we have presented two preliminary work items on quantitative information (QI) in text. One is to be proposed as an ISO international standard on the annotation and representation of quantitative information in language, and the other is to be developed as a technical specification (TS) on a set of specific guidelines for the extraction of QI in text. For these two related work items, we have proposed a specification language QML, grounded on a construct-based model, which identifies various basic entity types, called *constructs*, that constitute quantitative information. We have claimed that QML is a simple and flexible markup language applicable across languages in various domains including the medical domain. To make QML more applicable in concrete terms, we have outlined the general procedure of following QML-based extraction guidelines for quantitative information. We have also mentioned a certain degree of complexity that may arise in actual applications or system running.

7 Acknowledgments

This work was supported by National Natural Science Foundation of China (No. 61772146 & No. 61403088), National Key R&D Program of China (2016YFF0204205) and China National Institute of Standardization (522016Y-4681 & 712016Y-4941).We are also grateful to very detailed comments by four anonymous reviewers.

References

Ahmed, N., S. Jadoon, M.-U.-D. Khan RM, and M. Javed (2008). Type 2 diabetes mellitus: how well controlled in our patients? *J Ayub Med Coll Abbottabad 20*(4), 70–72.

Bunt, H. (2010). A methodology for designing semantic annotation languages exploring semanticsyntactic iso-morphisms. In *Proceedings of the Second International Conference on Global Interoperability for Language Resources (ICGL 2010), Hong Kong*, pp. 29–46.

Bunt, H. (2015). On the principles of interoperable semantic annotation. In *Proceedings of the 11th Joint ACL-ISO Workshop on Interoperable Semantic Annotation*, pp. 1–13.

Damen, D., K. Luyckx, G. Hellebaut, and T. Van den Bulcke (2013). Pastel: A semantic platform for assisted clinical trial patient recruitment. In *Healthcare Informatics (ICHI), 2013 IEEE International Conference on*, pp. 269–276. IEEE.

Hao, T., H. Liu, and C. Weng (2016). Valx: A system for extracting and structuring numeric lab test comparison statements from text. *Methods of Information in Medicine 55*(3), 266–275.

He, Z., S. Carini, I. Sim, and C. Weng (2015). Visual aggregate analysis of eligibility features of clinical trials. *Journal of Biomedical Informatics 54*, 241–255.

ISO (2012). *ISO 24612 Language resource management - Linguistic annotation framework (LAF)*. International Organisation for Standardisation, Geneva.

ISO (2016). *ISO 24617-6 Language resource management - Semantic annotation framework – Part 6: Principles of semantic annotation (SemAF Principles*. International Organisation for Standardisation, Geneva.

Kwo, P. Y., S. M. Cohen, and J. K. Lim (2017). Acg clinical guideline: Evaluation of abnormal liver chemistries. *The American Journal of Gastroenterology 112*, 18–35.

Lee, K. (2015). The annotation of measure expressions in iso standards. In *Proceedings 11th Joint ACL-ISO Workshop on Interoperable Semantic Annotation (isa-11)*, pp. 55–56.

Miotto, R. and C. Weng (2015). Case-based reasoning using electronic health records efficiently identifies eligible patients for clinical trials. *Journal of the American Medical Informatics Association 22*(e1), e141–e150.

Murata, M., T. Shirado, K. Torisawa, M. Iwatate, K. Ichii, Q. Ma, and T. Kanamaru (2008). Sophisticated text mining system for extracting and visualizing numerical and named entity information from a large number of documents. In *NTCIR*.

Nadkarni, P. M., L. Ohnomachado, and W. W. Chapman (2011). Natural language processing: an introduction. *Journal of the American Medical Informatics Association 18*(5), 544–551.

Thadani, S. R., C. Weng, J. T. Bigger, J. F. Ennever, and D. Wajngurt (2009). Electronic screening improves efficiency in clinical trial recruitment. *Journal of the American Medical Informatics Association 16*(6), 869–873.

Weng, C., Y. Li, P. B. Ryan, Y. Zhang, F. Liu, J. Gao, J. T. Bigger, and G. Hripcsak (2014). A distribution-based method for assessing the differences between clinical trial target populations and patient populations in electronic health records. *Applied Clinical Informatics 5*(2), 463–479.

Towards Interoperable Annotation of Quantification

Harry Bunt

TiCC, Tilburg Center for Cognition and Communication
Tilburg University, The Netherlands
`harry.bunt@uvt.nl`

Abstract

This paper presents an approach to the annotation of quantification that is under development in the context of an effort of the International Organisation for Standardisation ISO to define interoperable formalisms for semantic annotation. The paper focuses on the theoretical background and requirements for an ISO standard annotation scheme in this area.

1　Introduction

Quantification occurs when a predicate is applied to one or more sets of individual objects, as in example sentence (1):

(1)　Santa gave the children a present.

A singular noun phrase like *a present* may seem to refer to a single object, but this sentence most likely does not mean that a single present was given to all the children, but rather that each one of a certain set of children was given a different present, so in this predication two sets of individuals are involved: a set of children and a set of presents (plus the set consisting of Santa, and a set of give-events).[1] In technical terms, the quantification over the children has wider scope than the one over presents. Relative scope is one of the most studied aspects of quantification in natural language (see e.g. Montague, 1971; Cooper, 1983; Kamp & Reyle, 1993; Szabolcsi, 2010; Ruys & Winter, 2011).

Another aspect is the 'distributivity' of a quantification, i.e. the question how a predicate is 'distributed' over a set of arguments, as exemplified by sentence (2), which is most likely intended to express that *"the piano"* was lifted collectively by *"the two men"*, rather than by each of the men individually.

(2)　The two men lifted the piano.

Quantification occurs in almost every sentence in natural language, because of the occurrence of plural noun phrases that refer to sets of individual objects, and of singular noun phrases like *"a present"* in (1) that occur within the scope of other noun phrases.

The International Organisation for Standardisation ISO has in recent years established a number of standards for linguistic annotation in general, and semantic annotation in particular, in order to support the development of interoperable annotated corpora that are useful both for linguistic research and for language technology applications. In order to be applicable across theories and approaches, annotation standards should on the one hand be theory-neutral, but on the other hand take theoretical insights into account. This paper outlines an ISO standard annotation scheme under development for quantification, which builds on logical and linguistic theories of quantification, notably on the theory of generalized quantifiers and on the event-based semantics that is widely adopted in semantic theories and that underlies several other ISO schemes for semantic annotation.

---

[1]We do not consider mass noun quantification in this paper. See Bunt (1985) for how the notion of a set can be extended to cover non-discrete collections denoted by mass nouns, and what this means for mass noun quantification.

2 Theoretical Background

2.1 Generalized Quantifier Theory

Quantification has been studied extensively in logic (Frege, 1879; Tarski, 1936; Mostowski, 1957; Lindström, 1966); in linguistics (Higginbotham & May, 1981: Keenan & Stavi, 1986; Zwarts, 1984; Partee, 1988; Szabolcsi, 2010; Ruys & Winter, 2011), in formal semantics (Montague, 1974; Barwise & Cooper, 1981; van Benthem, 1984; Westerstahl, 1985; Kamp & Reyle, 1993), and in computational semantics (Alshawi, 1990; Bos, 1995; Pulman, 2000; Robaldo, 2014). In logic, the study of quantification and its role in formal reasoning has long (from Aristotle to Tarski) been restricted to the use of the universal ($\forall$, *"for all"*) and existential ($\exists$, *"for some"*) quantifiers. Relatively recently (Mostowski, 1957; Lindström, 1966), it was noted that the universal and the existential quantifier can both be viewed as expressing a property of the involvement in a predication of sets of individual objects: the universal quantifier expresses that all the elements of a given domain are involved; the existential quantifier that at least one of them is involved. This notion of a quantifier has been generalized to other properties such as those expressed in English by *"most, less than half of, three"*, or *"more than 200"*. The concepts in this broader class of quantifiers are called *generalized quantifiers*.

According to the theory of generalized quantifiers (GQT), words like *all* and *some* in English, as well as their equivalents in other languages, do not form the counterparts of the universal and existential quantifiers of formal logic, and neither do words like *three*, and *most*, which have been called 'cardinal quantifiers' and 'proportional quantifiers' (Partee, 1988), form the counterparts of certain generalized quantifiers. In formal logic, quantifications are expressions like $\forall x.p$ and $\exists x.p$, which say that p is true of all individual objects in the universe of discourse and of at least one such object, respectively. In natural languages, by contrast, it is not possible to say in a similar way that something is true for all objects or for some object. The English expressions that are closest to the universal and existential quantifiers of formal logic are *"everything, something"*, and *"everybody, somebody"* (and similarly in other languages), but these expressions do not quantify over all entities, but only over things and persons, respectively. Instead, natural languages have quantifying expressions like *"all politicians, a present, some people"*, and *"more than five sonatas"*, which indicate a certain domain that the quantification refers to. GQT therefore views noun phrases as quantifiers in natural language, rather than determiners (Barwise and Cooper, 1981). Determiners, instead, denote mappings from sets of entities to logical quantifiers (properties of sets of individual objects).

2.2 Event-based semantics

Some aspects of sentence meaning can be accounted for only if verbs are viewed as introducing events (in a broad sense of 'event', that includes states, facts, processes, and their negations), rather than predicates. Adverbial modifications are prime examples of this, and have prompted Davidson (1989) to introduce events as individual objects into the semantic of natural language, notably as additional arguments of predicates that correspond to verbs, as illustrated in (3a). Parsons (1990) has proposed a variation of this approach which does not increase the number of arguments of a verb-related predicate, but instead uses one-place predicates applied to existentially quantified event variables, and thematic roles, a.k.a. semantic roles, to represent the roles of the participants in events, as illustrated in (3b). This approach, known as 'neo-Davidsonian', has been widely adopted in modern semantics, and has been the basis of the ISO standard 24617-4 for the annotation of semantic roles.

(3) a. $\exists x.\exists y.\exists e.[present(x) \land child(y) \land give(e,santa,x,y)]$

 b. $\exists x.\exists y.\exists e.[\, present(x) \land child(y) \land give(e) \land agent(e, santa) \land theme(e,x) \land beneficiary(e,y)]$

The latter representation makes the roles explicit of the participants in an event and has the advantage that it allows the representation of certain quantification aspects, such as the collective/individual distinction, as a property of the way in which a certain set of participants is involved in an event. The ISO 24617-4 annotation of (1) would look as in (4):

(4) <event xml:id="e1" target="#m2" pred="give"/>
    <entity xml:id="x1" target="#m1" entityType="santa"/>
    <srLink event="#e1" participant="#x1" semRole="agent">
    <entity xml:id="x2" target="#m3" entityType="child"/>
    <srLink event="#e1" participant="#x2" semRole="beneficiary"/>
    <entity xml:id="x3" target="#m4" entityType="present"/>
    <srLink event="#e1" participant="#x3" semRole="theme"/>

Quantifying expressions such as *"twice"* and *"more than five times"*, as in *"I called you twice"*, also necessitate the introduction of sets of events, since these expressions count the number of elements in a set of events of a certain type. Similarly for expressions of frequency, as in *"I will call you twice every day"*.

For an annotation schema for quantification, this paper proposes an approach that combines GQT with the neo-Davidsonian view on predicate-argument relations, including the use of semantic roles (as defined in ISO 24617-4) for characterizing event participation. This is brought out most clearly in the semantics of the annotations, which makes use of Discourse Representation Structures (DRSs) that involve sets of events with sets of participants. For example, the annotation of the NP *"Two men"* is interpreted as the DRS in (5a), which can be read as follows: *There is a set X of cardinality 2 that consists of men.* A semantic role link, like the one for the agent role with collective distributivity, is interpreted as the DRS in (5b), and the sentence *"Two men lifted a piano"* is interpreted as the DRS (6), obtained by combining the DRSs for the NPs, the verb, and the semantic role relations.

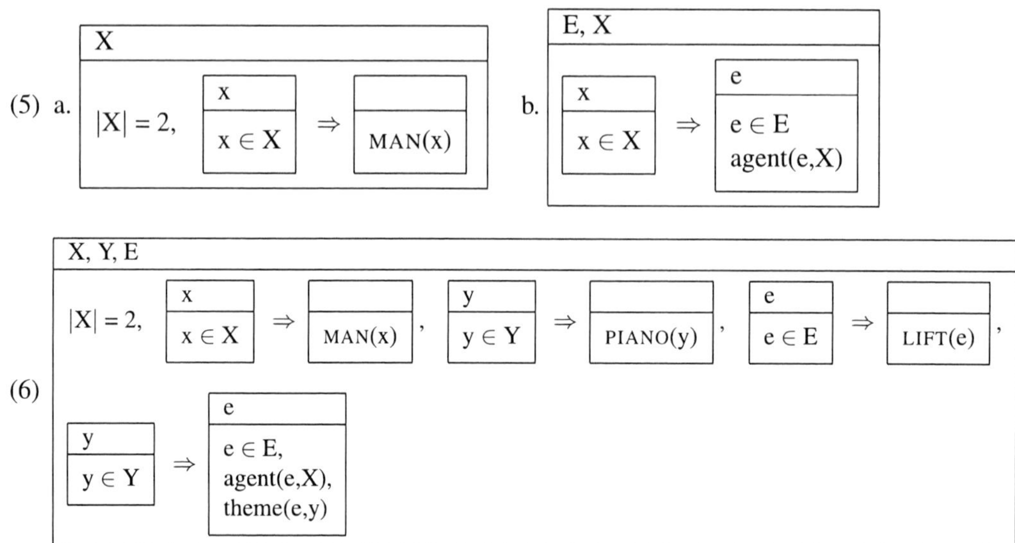

3   Related Work

Some work on the annotation of quantification has been going into ISO-TimeML (ISO 24617-1), which has certain limited provisions for dealing with time-related quantification. For example, a temporal quantifier like *"daily"* is represented as follows, where "P1D" stands for "period of one day":

(7) <TIMEX3 xml:id="t5" target="#token0" type="SET" value="P1D" quant="EVERY"/>

The attribute @quant is used as one of the attributes of temporal entities, in order to indicate that the entity is involved in a quantification. ISOspace (ISO 24617-7) makes use of the same @quant attribute, but now applied to spatial entities, and in addition uses the attribute @scopes to specify a scoping relation. If the @scopes attribute for a <spatialEntity> tag with its ID being X is filled with the value Y, this relation means that the quantifier for X has scope over the quantifier for Y. The following example illustrates this:

(8) a. There's a computer$_{se1}$ on$_{ss1}$ every desk$_{se2}$.

    b. <spatialEntity id="se1" target"#token2" form="nom" countable="true" quant="1",
       scopes="∅"/>
      <spatialEntity id="se2" target="#token5" form="nom" countable="true" quant="every"
       scopes="#se1"/>
      <spatialSignal id="ss1" target="#token3" type="dirTop" />
      <qsLink id="qsl1" relType="EC" figure="#se1" ground="#se2" trigger="#ss1"/>
      <oLink id="ol1" relType="above" figure="#se1" ground="#se2" trigger="#ss1"
       frameType="intrinsic" referencePt="#se2" projective="false" />

('EC' designating the spatial relation 'externally connected'.) This is intended to correspond to the following formula in predicate logic, which says that on every desk there is a computer (rather than that a certain computer is setting on every desk):

(9) $\forall se2\ \exists se1\ [[DESK(se2) \wedge COMPUTER(se1)] \leftrightarrow [EC(se2,se1) \wedge ABOVE(se2,se1)]])$

The limitations of this approach for annotating temporal quantification have been discussed by Bunt & Pustejovsky (2010), and improvements have been suggested by Lee & Bunt (2012).

Indirectly related to the definition of an annotation scheme for quantification is the Groningen Meaning Bank project (Bos et al., 2017) at the University of Groningen, which is developing a resource consisting of sentences paired with DRSs that represent their meanings. This work cannot be compared directly with the usual kind of annotation work, which associates pieces of semantic information with individual words and small stretches of text like phrases and clauses, whereas in the Groningen Meaning Bank DRSs are associated with full sentences. It may however be interesting to compare these DRSs with those that come out of the compositional interpretation of annotations as pursued here.

4 Quantification Information to be Annotated

4.1 Quantification domains

NPs, expressing generalized quantifiers in natural language, consist of two parts: (1) a prenominal expression, including determiners such as *"all"*, *"some"*, *"the"*, *"a"*, *"most"*, *"all five"*, and *"less than 200"*, and (2) a noun or nominal complex. This second part, called the *restrictor*, indicates a certain domain that is considered in the quantification. We use the term *'source domain'* to refer to this set of entities (or, alternatively, to the characteristic property of these entities; cf. Gawron, 1996). The fundamental difference between quantification in logic and quantification in natural language, mentioned in Section 2.1, is reflected in the fact that natural language quantifiers have this restrictor component.

Quantification in natural language is very often restricted to a contextually determined part of the source domain, the *'reference domain'*, also called 'context set' (Westerstahl, 1985; Partee et al., 1990). For example, the quantifier *"everybody"* in (10a) does not apply to every person, but only to the reference domain consisting of the students in a particular class, and in (10b) the quantifier *"all the twenty-seven countries"* refers to a contextually determined set of 27 countries (rather than to the source domain of all countries). The occurrence of a definite NP in general indicates that the domain of a quantification is restricted to a certain reference domain, rather than to its source domain; therefore the definiteness of an NP is an item of quantification information to be annotated.

(10) a. Everybody must hand in the essay before next Thursday, the 20th.

    b. The proposal was accepted by all the twenty-seven countries

The prenominal part of a full-fledged NP may be a sequence of different types of determiners. Grammars commonly distinguish different classes of determiners, with different possible sequencing and co-occurrence restrictions. For example, in English grammar it is customary to make a distinction between predeterminers, central determiners, and postdeterminers (e.g. Quirk et al., 1972; Leech and Svartvik, 1975; Bennett, 1974). This classification can be made in such a way that the determiners in each class have a different function:

- predeterminers express the (absolute or proportional) quantitative involvement of the reference domain, and may, additionally, provide information about the distribution of a quantification over the reference domain;
- central determiners determine the definiteness of the NP, and thus co-determine a reference domain;
- postdeterminers contain information about the cardinality of the reference domain.

This is illustrated by the NP *"All my nine grandchildren"* in (11), where *"all"* is a predeterminer, *"my"* a central determiner, and *"nine"* a postdeterminer. The information carried by the various kinds of determiners is to be captured in the annotation of quantifications.

(11) All my nine grandchildren are boys.

4.2 Scope and Distributivity

Scope and distributivity, briefly mentioned in the introduction, are two important aspects of quantification in natural language to be taken into account in annotations. Studies of scope in quantifying expressions have focused almost exclusively on the relative scopes of sets of participants, as in the classical example *"Everybody in this room speaks two languages"*. In logic it is customary to assume that the relative scopes of sets of participants are linearly ordered (but see Hintikka, 1973 and Sher, 1990 on 'branching quantifiers'), but in natural language there are clear cases where none of the quantifications has wider scope than another. An example is provided by (12):

(12) Three breweries supplied five inns

The intended reading here is not that each one of three breweries supplied each one of five inns (wide scope of *"three breweries"*), nor that each one of five inns was supplied by each of three breweries (wide scope of *"five inns"*), but that in total three breweries supplied in total five inns. In this total-total, or *cumulative* reading (Scha, 1981) the two quantifications have equal scope; the two cardinal determiners both indicate the amount of involvement of the respective reference domains in the predication.

Not only the relative scoping of sets of quantified *participants* is a semantically important issue, but also the relative scoping of participants and *events*. This is illustrated by the two possible readings of the sentence in (13):

(13) Everyone will die.

Besides the reading according to which everyone is mortal, there is also a reading which predicts an apocalyptic future event in which everyone will die. (Note that the latter interpretation involves the consideration of events in which multiple participants occupy the same role. Several approaches, such as those of the VerbNet and PropBank frameworks allow only a single occupant for each semantic role; the ISO approach to semantic role annotation (ISO 24617-4), does allow multiple participants in the same semantic role.) There is no way to represent this second reading without explicitly introducing events; (14a) and (14b) show how the two readings can be represented in first-order logic by assigning alternative relative scopes to the quantifications over events and participants:

(14) a. $\forall x. \text{ person}(x) \rightarrow \exists e. [\text{die}(e) \wedge \text{future}(e) \wedge \text{theme}(e,x)]$

  b. $\exists e. \text{ die}(e) \wedge \text{future}(e) \wedge \forall x. [\text{person}(x) \rightarrow \text{theme}(e,x)]$

In the annotation in (15) the relative scope of events and participants is marked up by means of the attribute 'eventScope' that has been added to the XML element <srLink> from ISO 24617-4. There is a tendency in natural language that quantification over events has narrow scope, so this attribute has the default value "narrow".

(15) <entity xml:id="x1" target="#m1" entityType="passenger"/>
    <event xml:id="e1" target="#m2" pred="die" time-"fut"/>
    <srLink event="#e1" participant="#x1" semRole="theme" eventScope="wide"/>

The annotation of scope will thus make use of two relations: one between the sets of participants involved and one between each set of participants and the events in which they participate.

Distributivity comes in an obvious form in the distinction between individual (or 'distributive') and collective participation, but other cases must be distinguished as well. In example sentence (16) the three boys involved did not necessarily do all the carrying either collectively or individually, but where they may have carried some heavy boxes collectively and some other, less heavy boxes individually:

(16) The boys carried all the boxes upstairs

The quantifications in this sentence have 'unspecific' distributivity (Bunt, 1985); the sentence just says that all the boxes were somehow carried upstairs by the boys, Following Kamp & Reyle (1993), we use the notation X^* to designate the set consisting of the members of X and the subsets of X, and the predicate P^* to designate the characteristic function of the set X^*, where P is the characteristic function of X. Using moreover the notation R_0 to indicate the characteristic function of a reference domain that forms a subset of a source domain with characteristic function R, the interpretation of (16) can be represented in second-order predicate logic as follows:

(17) $\forall x.[\text{box}_0(x) \rightarrow \exists y.\exists e.[\text{boy}_0{}^*(y) \wedge \text{carry-up}(e) \wedge \text{agent}(e,y) \wedge \exists z.[\text{box}_0{}^*(z) \wedge [x{=}z \vee x{\in}z] \wedge$
$$\text{theme}(e,z)]]]$$

The distributivity of a quantification is not a property of the set of participants in a set of events, but a property of the way of participating. This is illustrated by example (18), assuming that *"the men"* individually had a beer, and collectively carried the piano upstairs.

(18) The men had a beer before carrying the piano upstairs.

Distributivity should thus be marked up on the participation relation in the drinking and carrying events, as in the annotation fragment shown in (19), where the XML element <srLink> from ISO 24617-4 has been enriched with the attribute 'distr':

(19) <entity xml:id="x1" target="#m1" cntityType="man"/>
    <event xml:id="e1" target="#m2" pred="drink"/>
    <event xml:id="e2" target="#m3" pred="carry"/>
    <srLink event="#e1" participant="#x1" semRole="agent" distr="individual"/>
    <srLink event="#e2" participant="#x1" semRole="agent" distr="collective"/>

4.3   Quantification and Modification

The restrictor part in a full-fledged NP is in the simplest case just a noun, but in general may contain adjectives and other expressions that modify the noun, such as other nouns (in noun-noun combinations in English, like *"bread crumbs"*, or as composite nouns in other languages, like *"broodkruimels"* in Dutch), prepositional phrases, and relative clauses. Moreover, conjunctions of nouns (possibly with modifications) may further add complexity to restrictors.

Modifications bring certain issues of quantification, such as scope and distributivity, e.g. the restrictor *"heavy books"* in the sentence *"Peter carried some heavy books"* may be interpreted as referring to certain books that are heavy each (distributive reading) or to a heavy pile of books (collective reading).

Scope issues arise in particular when a noun is modified by a PP, as in (20), where a quantification inside the PP takes scope over the one of the head noun. This phenomenon is known as 'inverse linking' (May, 1977; May and Bale, 2007; Ruys and Winter, 2011; Barker, 2014). The phenomenon of inverse linking with PP modification is widespread; especially the case of an universally quantified main NP and existentially quantified PP is quite common.

(20) Mr Kay met with a council member from every town that expressed an interest in the proposal.

It has been claimed in the literature that in the case of inverse linking the quantifier of the embedded NP always takes maximal scope, but this has been challenged by Szabolcsi (2010), who provides counterexamples.

To capture the relevant information related to quantification within a complex restrictor, the annotation of complex restrictors needs to be articulated in marking up the head noun that is central to the restrictor, and the various possible modifiers, with indications of their distributivity and of the scope inversion that may occur with PPs as well as (though less commonly) with relative clauses (Barker, 2014; Szabolsi, 2010).

5   Towards an ISO Standard Annotation Scheme

An ISO standard annotation scheme for the annotation of quantification should fit within the series of semantic annotation standards known collectively as the Semantic Annotation Framework (SemAF), ISO 24617. It should as such be compatible with the existing parts of SemAF: Part 1, Time and events; Part 2, Dialogue acts; Part 4: Semantic roles; Part 7: Spatial information, and Part 8: Discourse relations. Moreover, it should be defined according to the ISO Principles for semantic annotation (ISO 24617-6; see also Bunt, 2015, and Pustejovsky et al., 2017), which means that it should have a 3-part definition consisting of (1) an abstract syntax; (2) a concrete syntax; (3) a semantics. This formal definition should be supported by a metamodel that captures the fundamental concepts used in annotations and the way they are related. Appendix A contains the specification of such a metamodel for quantification.

For reasons of space, we leave any consideration of the abstract syntax of quantification annotations out of this paper. It may be noted, though, that following the ISO principles, the semantics of the annotations is specified for the abstract syntax, and *a fortiori* applies to any rendering of the abstract annotation structures. In particular, the ISO principles require every representation format for semantic annotations to be defined by a so-called 'ideal' concrete syntax, i.e. a syntax that is (1) complete, in the sense of defining a representation for every annotation structure defined by the abstract syntax; (2) unambiguous, i.e. every representation defined by the concrete syntax is a rendering of one annotation structure defined by the abstract syntax (see Bunt, 2010). Organizing the definition of annotations according to this 3-part setup with a semantics defined for abstract annotation structures and using only ideal representation formats has the advantage that alternative representations of the abstract annotation structures inherit the semantics of the abstract syntax, and the representations in any ideal format can be converted to any other ideal format in a meaning-preserving way. In other words, all ideal representation formats are semantically equivalent. A benefit of this approach is that it supports the design of user-friendly representations. While XML representations are convenient for automatic processing, they are not suitable for human use, but they can be automatically converted to other formats that are more convenient for use by human annotators and dialogue researchers.

As a simple example, the natural language quantifier expressed by the NP *"two men"* corresponds to an abstract annotation structure that pairs the markable for an occurrence of the expression *"two men"* with a quadruple of concepts as shown in (21a); a concrete representation in XML may look as in (21b); and the semantic interpretation as shown in (21c), obtained by applying the interpretation rule (22). Rules of this kind, where 'P' stands for the characteristic predicate of a source domain, as defined by the lexical semantics of an NP head noun, and C is a predicate that expresses quantitative involvement, as defined by the semantics of a determiner, form the specification of the compositional semantics of annotation structures.

(21) a. $\langle \text{man}, \text{some}, \text{indef}, \lambda z.|z| = 2 \rangle$

    b. <entity xml:id="x1" target="#m1" entityType="man" involvement="2"/>

c.
$$
\boxed{\begin{array}{l} \text{X} \\[4pt] |\text{X}| = 2, \ \boxed{\begin{array}{c} \text{x} \\ \hline \text{x} \in \text{X} \end{array}} \Rightarrow \boxed{\begin{array}{c} \ \\ \hline \text{MAN(x)} \end{array}} \end{array}}
$$

(22) $V(\langle \text{P}, \text{some}, \text{indef}, C \rangle) =$
$$
\boxed{\begin{array}{l} \text{X} \\[4pt] C(|\text{X}|), \ \boxed{\begin{array}{c} \text{x} \\ \hline \text{x} \in \text{X} \end{array}} \Rightarrow \boxed{\begin{array}{c} \ \\ \hline \text{P(x)} \end{array}} \end{array}}
$$

6   Concluding Remarks

In this paper we have indicated some of the most important requirements for the specification of an ISO standard annotation scheme for quantification, focusing on the theoretical foundations provided by (1) the theory of generalized quantifiers; (2) a neo-Davidsonian approach to events and their participants; (3) the separation of the abstract and concrete syntax of annotations, following the distinction between annotations and their representations as made in the ISO Linguistic Annotation Framework (ISO 24612; cf. Ide and Romary, 2004) and elaborated in the ISO Principles of semantic information, with (4) its way of associating a semantics (using higher-order Discourse Representation Structures) with abstract annotation structures, abstracting away from representation formats.

We have identified a number of properties of quantification in natural language that have to be taken into account in a semantically adequate annotation scheme, including those that occur in noun modification structures with quantifier restrictors, such as the distributivity of adjectival modification and inverse linking in modification by preposition phrases.

The specification of an annotation scheme following the theoretical directions indicated in this paper is in preparation as a new part of the ISO Semantic Annotation Framework (SemAF, ISO 24617).

Bibliography

Alshawi, H. (1990) Resolving Quasi Logical Form. *Computational Linguistics* 16: 133-144.

Barker, C. (2014) Scope. In: S. Lappin and C. Fox (eds) *The Handbook of Contemporary Semantic Theory*, John Wiley, Chapter 2, pp. 40-76.

Barwise, J. (1979) On Branching Quantifiers in English. *Journal of Philosophical Logic* 8: 47-80.

Barwise, J. and R. Cooper (1981) Generalized Quantifiers and Natural Language. *Linguistics and Philosophy* 4, pp. 159-219.

Bennett, M. (1974) *Some extensions of a Montague fragment of English*. Ph. D. Dissertation, University of California, Los Angeles.

Benthem, J. van (1984) Questions about Quantifiers. *Journal of Symbolic Logic* 49: 443-466.

Bos, J. (1995) Predicate Logic Unplugged. In *Proceedings 10th Amsterdam Colloquium*, Amsterdam: ILLC, pp. 133-142.

Bos, J.,V. Basile, K. Evang, N. Venhuizen, and J. Bjerva (2017): The Groningen Meaning Bank. In: Nancy Ide and James Pustejovsky (eds): *Handbook of Linguistic Annotation*, pp 463-496, Berlin: Springer.

Bunt, H. (1985) *Mass terms and model-theoretic semantics.* Cambridge, UK: Cambridge University Press.

Bunt, H. (2010) A methodology for designing semantic annotation languages exploiting syntactic-semantic iso-morphisms. In Fang, A., Ide, N. and Jonathan Webster (eds.) *Proceedings of ICGL 2010, Second International Conference on Global Interoperability for Language Resources*, City University of Hong Kong, pp. 29-45.

Bunt, H. and J. Pustejovsky (2010) Annotating Temporal and Event Quantification. In *Proceedings of ISA-5, Fifth International Workshop on Interoperable Semantic Annotation*, Harry Bunt and Ernest Lam (eds), City University of Hong Kong, pp. 15-22.

Bunt, H. (2015) On the principles of semantic annotation. In *Proceedings 11th Joint ACL-ISO Workshop on Interoperable Semantic Annotation (ISA-11)*, London, pp. 1-13.

Choe, J.-W. (1987) *Anti-quantifiers and A Theory of Distributivity.* Ph.D. Dissertation, MIT.

Cooper, R. (1983) *Quantification and syntactic theory.* Dordrecht: Reidel.

Davidson, D. (1967) The logical form of action sentences. In N. Rescher (ed.) *The Logic of Decision and Action.* Chapter 3. University of Pittsburgh Press.

Frege, G. (1879). *Begriffsschrift, eine der arithmetischen nachgebildete Formelsprache des reinen Denkens.* Halle: Nebert.

Gawron, J.M. (1996) Quantification, quantificational domains, and dynamic logic. In *Handbook of Contemporary Semantic Theory*, edited by Shalom Lappin, Oxford: Blackwell, pp. 247-267.

Higginbottom, J.and R. May (1981) Questions, quantifiers and crossing. *The Linguistic Review* 1, 41-80.

Hintikka, J. (1973) Quantifiers vs. Quantification Theory. *Dialectica* 27: 329-358.

Ide, N. and Romary, L. (2004) International Standard for a Linguistic Annotation Framework. *Natural Language Engineering* 10: 221-225.

Ide, N. and H. Bunt (2010) Anatomy of Annotation Schemes: Mappings to GrAF. In *Proceedings 4th Linguistic Annotation Workshop (LAW IV)*, Uppsala, Sweden, pp. 115-124.

ISO 24612 (2010) *ISO 24612: Language resource management: Linguistic annotation framework (LAF).* International Organisation for Standardisation ISO, Geneva.

ISO 24617-1 (2012) *ISO 24617-1: Language resource management – Semantic annotation framework – Part 1: Time and events.* International Organisation for Standardisation ISO, Geneva.

ISO 24617-2 (2012) *ISO 24617-2: Language resource management – Semantic annotation framework – Part 2: Dialogue acts.* International Organisation for Standardisation ISO, Geneva.

ISO 24617-4 (2014) *ISO 24617-4: Language resource management – Semantic annotation framework – Part 4: Semantic roles.* International Organisation for Standardisation ISO, Geneva.

ISO 24617-6 (2016) *ISO 24617-6: Language resource management – Semantic annotation framework – Part 6: Principles of semantic annotation.* International Standard. International Organisation for Standardisation ISO, Geneva.

ISO 24617-7 (2015) *ISO 24617-7: Language resource management – Semantic annotation framework – Part 7: ISOspace.* International Organisation for Standardisation ISO, Geneva.

Kamp, H. and U. Reyle (1993) *From Discourse to Logic.* Dordrecht: Kluwer Academic Publishers.

Keenan, E. (1987) Unreducible n-ary Quantification in Natural language. In P. Gardenfors (ed.) Generalized Quantifiers, *Linguistic and Logical Approaches.* Dordrecht: Reidel.

Keenan, E. and Stavi, J. (1986) A semantic characterization of natural language determiners, *Linguistics and Philosophy*, 9: 253-326.

Keenan, E. and Westerstahl, D., (1997) Generalized quantifiers in Linguistics and Logic, in J. van Benthem and A. ter Meulen (eds.), *Generalized quantifiers in Natural Language*, Dordrecht: Foris, pp. 837-993.

Lee, K. and H. Bunt (2012) Counting time and events. In *Proceedings 8th Joint ISO-ACL SIGSEM Workshop on Interoperable Semantic Annotation (ISA-8)*, ILC-CNR, Pisa.

Leech, G. and J. Svartvik (1975) *A communicative grammar of English.* London: Longman.

Lindström, P. (1966) First Order Predicate Logic with Generalized Quantifiers. *Theoria* 32, 186-195.

May, R. (1977) *The Grammar of Quantification.* Ph.D. Dissertation, MIT.

May, R. and A. Bale (2005) Inverse linking. In M. Everaert and H. van Riemsdijk (eds.) *The Blackwell Companion to syntax, Vol. 2.* Oxford: Blackwell, Chapter 6, pp. 639-667.

Montague, R. (1971) The proper treatment of quantification in ordinary language In *Formal Philosophy*, edited by R. Thomason New Haven: Yale University Press 1974,

Mostovski, A. (1957) On a Generalization of Quantifiers. *Fundamentae Mathematicae* 44, 12-36.

Parsons, T. (1990) *Events in the Semantics of English: A Study in Subatomic Semantics.* Cambridge (MA): MIT Press, .

Partee, B. (1988) Many Quantifiers. In *ESCOL 89: Proceedings of the Eastern States Conference on Linguistics.* Reprinted in *Compositionality in Formal Semantics: Selected Papers by Barbara Partee*, Oxford: Blackwell 2004, pp. 241-158.

Partee, B., Ter Meulen, A. and Wall, R. (1990) *Mathematical Models in Linguistics.* Springer, Berlin.
Pulman, S. (2000) Bidirectional contextual resolution. *Computational Linguistics* 26: 497-538.

Pustejovsky, J., H. Bunt, and A. Zaenen (2017) Designing Annotation Schemes: From Theory to Model.' In: Nancy Ide and James Pustejovsky (eds): *Handbook of Linguistic Annotation*, Springer, Berlin

Quirk, R., S. Greenbaum, G. Leech, and J. Svartvik (1972) *A grammar of contemporary English.* London: Longman.

Robaldo, L. (2014) On the identification of quantifiers' witness sets: a study of multi-quantifier sentences. *Journal of Logic, Language and Information* 23 (1).

Ruys, E. and Y. Winter, Y. (2011) Scope Ambiguities in Formal Linguistics. In D. Gabbay and F. Guenthner (eds.) *Handbook of Philosophical Logic* 16, Dordrecht: Foris.

Szabolcsi, A. (2010) *Quantification.* Cambridge, UK: Cambridge University Press.

Scha, R. (1981) Collective, Distributive and Cumulative Quantification. In J. Groenendijk and M. Stokhof (eds.) *Formal Methods in the Study of Language.* Amsterdam: Mathematisch Centrum, pp. 483-512.

Sher, G.(1990) Partially-ordered (branching) quantifiers: a general definition. *Linguistics and Philosophy* 14: 393-422.

Tarski, A. (1936) Das Wahrheitsbegriff in den formalisierten Sprachen. *Studia Philosophica* 1, 261-405. *Natural Language Engineering* 10: 221-225.

Westerstahl, D. (1985) Determiners and context sets. In *Generalized Quantifiers in Natural Language*, edited by Johan van Benthem and Alice ter Meulen, Dordrecht: Foris, pp. 45-71.

Zwarts, F. (1984) Determiners: a relational perspective. In A. ter Meulen (ed.) *Studies in Model-theoretic Semantics*, Dordrecht: Foris, pp. 37-63.

Appendix A. Specification of a metamodel for quantification annotation

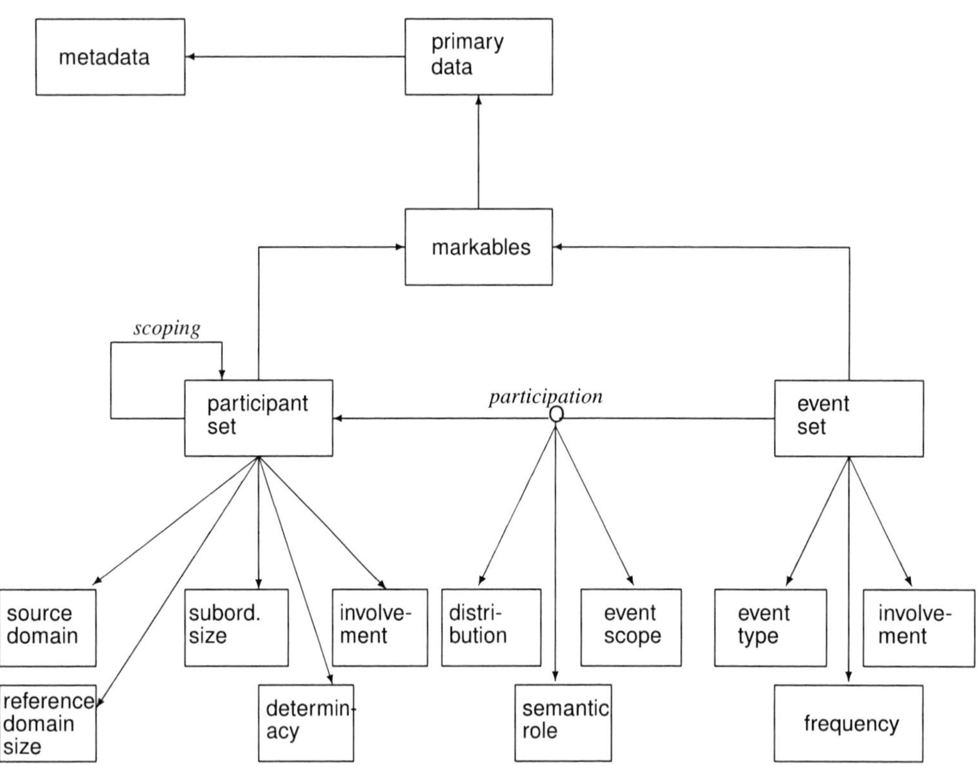

Figure 1: Metamodel for the annotation of quantification

PACTE : a collaborative platform for textual annotation

Pierre André Ménard, Caroline Barrière
Centre de recherche informatique de Montréal
`pierre-andre.menard@crim.ca, caroline.barriere@crim.ca`

Abstract

In this article, we provide an overview of a web-based text annotation platform, called PACTE. We highlight the various features contributing to making PACTE an ideal platform for research projects involving textual annotation of large corpora performed by geographically distributed teams.

1 Introduction

With the availability of large amount of textual data on the web, or from legacy documents, various text analysis projects emerge to study, analyze and understand the content of these texts. Projects arise from various disciplines, such as psychological studies (e.g. detecting language patterns related to particular mental states) or literary studies (e.g. studying patterns used by particular authors), or criminology studies (e.g. analyzing crime-related locations). Text analysis projects of large scale often involve multiple actors, in a distributed spatial setting, with collaborators all over the world.

While their perspectives are different and their goals are varied, most text analysis projects require some common functionalities: document selection (to gather a proper corpus for pattern analysis), text annotation (to mark actual metadata about documents, paragraphs, sentences, words or word segments) and annotation search (to search the annotated segments for the ones of interest). Furthermore, many projects would benefit from basic automatic annotation of textual components (sentences, nominal compounds, named entities, etc). Yet, each project would likely also have its particularities as to what are the important text patterns to study, and perhaps such patterns are best annotated by human experts.

We are in the process of developing a text project management and annotation platform, called PACTE (`http://pacte.crim.ca`), to support such large-scale distributed text analysis. A key component of PACTE is to not only allow for easy annotation (whether manual or automatic), but to also provide the very essential search component, to retrieve through the mass of texts, segments of information containing specific annotations (e.g. retrieving all documents mentioning a particular city). In its final state, PACTE will contain the common required project management functionalities, as well as common annotation services, but also allow for particularities (e.g. specialized schema definition).

The platform also aims at encouraging interdisciplinary collaborations, as much automatic textual analysis in the recent years is data-driven, using machine learning models which require a lot of annotated data. A known bottleneck to these supervised models is the lack of availability of annotated data. By providing a platform which makes it easy to annotate using user-defined schemas, we hope to encourage various users from various disciplines to perform annotation.

In the remaining of this demonstration note, we will show (Section 2) an example of an annotation project with definitions of the various terms used when discussing annotation projects (e.g. types, schemas, features, groups, etc). We will then highlight (section 3) the distinctive features of PACTE, mainly focusing on eight important aspects of PACTE, that it (1) is web-based, (2) handles large volumes of text for both annotation and search, (3) allows easy project management, (4) allows collaborative annotation, (5) provides some automatic annotation services, (6) allows users to define specific schemas for targeted manual annotation, (7) provides text search capabilities, (8) offers management of custom lexicon. Then, we compare PACTE to other platforms (Section 4) and we give the current state and future development of PACTE (Section 5).

2   Example of an annotation project

To give a sense of the conceptual framework underlying the development of PACTE as to provide a useful platform for large-scale text annotation projects, we choose to describe a particular use case. Let's assume a research project involving the annotation of temporal expressions (numeric or nominal expressions denoting a period or point in time) on court decision documents, which often detail the timeline of a court case. The original format of the documents (pdf, doc, rtf, txt, etc) makes up the *source corpus* while the raw text document extracted from the source would make up the *imported corpus* (also referred to as *corpus*). The researcher might also have, hopefully, research assistants available which will act as *annotators* for the project.

The researcher leading this project might choose to use the TimeML specification which includes several data structures to specify different temporal information. Let's take two of them : Timex3 for tagging explicit temporal expressions (e.g. "three months ago", "January 3rd in the morning"), and Event for expressions describing elements being positioned in time (e.g. "M. X bought his car"). Each of them, Timex3 and Event, can be viewed as an *annotation type* defined by a specific data structure, or *schema*, containing attributes and types. For example, the TimeML specification indicates that the Event annotation type includes three attributes : a unique identifier of type integer, a comment of type string (free text) and a class as an enumeration (occurrence, perception, reporting, etc.). These information would be declared as *attributes*, with their associated *data types*, in the Event schema.

PACTE would allow the definition of particular schemas such as Event or Timex3, at the start of a research project annotation task. Users would be assigned to this task in order to peruse the documents and create *annotation instances* (referred as *annotations*) for each expression they deem relevant for the Event or Timex3 type. As the researcher might want to check the agreement between annotators, *groups* of annotation instances can be created and given access to only one annotator at a time, thus preventing unwanted interactions. Schemas can also be defined at the group level, therefore allowing the same instances to be annotated by different users using different schemas. For example, one annotator might annotate using the standard Event schema in one group while another annotator in a different group would use an enriched schema with more attributes to define events. The researcher can then have access to both groups to compare annotation spans and attributes values. While all researchers will not use every aspects of these concepts (types, schemas, groups, etc.), they are an integral part of PACTE as to give a lot of flexibility to address the needs of many projects.

3   PACTE features overview

While some annotation platforms, both open-source and proprietary, already exist with a variety of features, our experience has shown some limitations when using them for large scale, multi-user annotation projects. PACTE is our humble addition to the group of available platforms in the hope to give researchers the possibility of seamlessly managing large-scale multi-user projects with minimal effort, giving them time to focus on the actual research aspects of their research. Following are some features of PACTE relevant to this goal.

Web-based applications such as the PACTE platform provide easy access to any user with internet access, regardless of their location, which is useful for project collaborations between research teams from different institutions. PACTE thus enables users to upload source corpora, define schemas, manage projects and annotate documents via its web interface with-

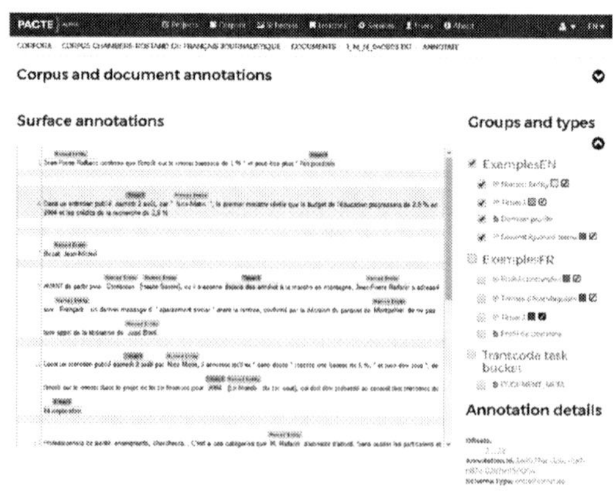

Figure 1: PACTE's main annotation window

out any additional software installation or access rights

other than being able to run a web browser. The user interface is designed to easily and quickly be changed from one language to another depending on the user preference (currently in French and English, but can be expanded). In addition to the user interface, PACTE also features a secured web service (a programmatic interface) through which users, using their own credentials, can access their own raw data (documents, annotations). Following the example from Section 2, a researcher could download, using the secured web service, the Event and Timex3 annotations created by annotators on his project, train a machine-learning algorithm to link the two types of annotations (using TLINK type of annotation from TimeML standard), upload the new annotations back into the corpus using the secured web service and view the result in-situ using the user interface of PACTE.

Large corpora are often used in projects involving web-crawled documents as a source corpus or when dealing with crowd created resources like Wikipedia. PACTE architecture offers an expandable storage component in order to cope with the high volume needed by these kind of projects. Features across the platform are designed to balance the need for high volume of documents, both in the back end and front end of the platform. Furthermore, a document-level language identification service is activated at the time of corpus creation, automatically assigning a language to each document. A user can then decide to work with a multilingual corpus and keep all the documents tagged with various languages, or alternatively, the user can declare a corpus monolingual and ask the platform to discard all documents not identified with that particular language.

Easy project management is enabled in PACTE with multistep project workflow definition and management, letting the researchers plan simple or complex annotation projects with their team. For each step, the researcher can decide which corpus, annotators and schemas are used and which preexisting annotations should be seen as read-only by the annotators in order to help them with their current task (e.g. ordinals could be preannotated to help the annotation with Timex3). Projects working with large corpora will also benefit from various user-assignment strategies in order to quickly distribute multiple documents between multiple users participating in a project's step. A strategy could purposely include overlap of documents among annotators to later allow for calculating inter-annotator agreement (an important measure to be considered when annotated data is used for machine learning projects). Curation steps can also be included to validate, manipulate and prepare annotations before and after any annotation step.

Collaborative annotation is mainly done with Brat rapid annotation tool (BRAT) (Pontus Stenetorp et al. (2012)) as it contains many features desirable for PACTE. As BRAT is a complete and standalone system, the user interface[1] was unhooked from the storage backend in order to evolve with PACTE's needs. It was integrated in PACTE as part of the manual annotation window (see Figure 1) to allow the user to both easily select which annotation types to display and which annotation types to use for the current annotation task. For each annotation instance, a pop-up window is presented to the user to enter or modify values for each attribute defined in the schema.

As shown on the right section of Figure 1, PACTE features annotation groups which act as containers to manage annotations. Each single annotation must be in exactly one group and respect a schema definition dedicated to this group. These groups are used during annotation project in order to isolate the work of each annotators, simplifying management and enforcing a more rigorous annotation protocol.

Automatic annotation services are integrated into the platform in order to simplify the annotation of large corpora for researchers needing to quickly enrich text documents with various informational features. These services are provided for multiple aspects of text analysis for both French and English documents.

A first set of *linguistic* annotation services is in place to provide information on word tokens such as stem, lemma, number, genre, part-of-speech tags, or on chunked phrases (verbal, nominal, etc). These types of annotations are useful for analysis of linguistic phenomenon as well as providing character and word level information to train machine learning models.

A second set of *lexico-semantic* annotation services is designed to interact with PACTE lexicon

---

[1] BRAT is available at : `https://github.com/crim-ca/brat-frontend-editor`

module to tag usage of terms in a corpus. Simple string match strategies allow to tag terms' surface forms, but more complex disambiguation algorithms are included to highlight terms contextual senses as found in a multidomain lexicon (Bernier-Colborne et al., 2017). When no lexicon is available, some discovery tools can be called to extract, through statistical measures, important keywords of a document.

A third set of *semantic* annotation services targets the challenging tasks of named entity tagging, temporal expression tagging, named entity linking (wikification), to mention some of them. These services can process both English and French documents encoded in UTF-8 format.

As highlighted above, one important aspect of PACTE is to handle large corpora. As some of these services are cpu intensive, PACTE services are executed on a service gateway which manages parallel execution and load balancing. In a more advanced setup, PACTE supports process elasticity by dynamic instantiation of new processing units, enabling the system to cope with high demand, traffic or larger resources. Each service is wrapped in a container, thus easily integrating tools using different languages or technologies.

Schema definition tools will help users define schemas corresponding to their specific information needs. Each schema is split in two parts: the target and the attributes. The user first defines which entity the schema will target: a corpus, an entire document or parts of the document's textual content. Regardless of the target, a list of attributes can then be specified, each attribute being assigned a label, a data type and a description to help annotators understand the attribute's goal. Data types can be numeric, boolean, or string, either in free text or taken from an enumeration of literals, and can be declared as a single entry or an array of one of the predefined data types. This gives the user much flexibility to adapt to different types of annotation tasks. A subset of Json schemas is used internally to define each schema, providing a simple and fast format for importing, exporting and processing annotations. As this format is easy to process by both human and machine, it is an ideal balance between interoperability and operational needs. Conversion modules can be developed to adapt the contained information to other more standardized formats, like converting a text with its Timex3, Event and Tlink annotations into TimeML xml-based format.

Text search capabilities are essential when dealing with large quantities of text documents. PACTE allows for both searches on the actual text content of documents, and on their annotations (either automatically or manually generated). Although text content search is available in many text editing platforms, text annotation search is a more unique and valuable function of PACTE. For example, a user might require the list of documents containing annotations of type Timex3 with a subtype of *time*.

Lexicon management is another important module in PACTE enabling the user to define and manage a lexical resource. A lexical resource contains concepts described minimally by their concurrent terms. But each concept can be further described by a definition, usage examples, its terms genre, number, part-of-speech type, etc. Each concept can be linked to one or more user-defined domains. These domains can be defined as child or parent of other domains, thus enabling the creation of multilevel lexicons. These lexicons are made available to annotation services by snapshots in order to insure integrity of the lexical resources.

4 Platform comparison

The closest comparable project available is probably the WebAnno platform (Eckart de Castilho, R. et al. (2016)). PACTE and WebAnno share many similar features, being both web platforms, using Brat user interface as the main manual annotation tool and enabling the management of annotation projects with users, documents and annotation schemas (or layers in WebAnno).

The most discriminative aspect of PACTE is the focus on the processing of large corpora, either manually or automatically, as an annotation target. In WebAnno, corpora are managed as integral parts of projects, being stored in a SQL database on a per-project basis. Annotators select which documents they wish to annotate from the list of the project's corpus. Data is exported at the end of the project in order to be processed or aggregated offline with other annotations. Alternatively, corpora are standalone entities in PACTE as they can exist outside the lifespan of a project. Users can thus apply multiple annotation projects (or a multistage project) on the same corpus, limiting costly manipulations over a large scale resource. Large corpora also require different selection methods of documents for the annotation tasks in order to adapt to the goal of the project, like in-depth validation or larger coverage of the resource. PACTE offers a random distribution mode to assign a specific number of documents taken from a corpus to specific users. In this mode, the project manager can also add a parameter to require that a specific number of documents should be processed by a number of annotators in order to assess their agreement. PACTE also provides a manual distribution mode to fine-tune the list of documents for each annotators, providing sort and search functions to browse through the documents of a large corpus.

Large corpora also require special consideration when applying automatic annotation tools. While WebAnno provides an automation tool that helps users annotate more efficiently, it does not offer automated annotation tools like those described for PACTE in the Section 3. Users in PACTE run these automated tools and store the resulting annotations in containers called annotation groups to keep them separate from user annotations. Access to these annotation groups can be controlled during projects to either hide or offer them as read-only resources to help the annotators. PACTE also uses a service gateway which relays processing requests on a message queue to annotation services. The service gateway manages the parallelism of multiple workers per annotation service as well as elasticity during peak periods, creating new workers to help process new requests. A scalable annotation storage service also enables the input of large quantities of automatically generated annotations.

5   Current state and road map

PACTE is currently under active development and a first partial alpha release is being tested in order to provide insights and feedback on real-world annotation projects. Some key features are being fine-tuned to improve the ease and speed at which annotators can do their work, thus improving their experience with the platform. The alpha version contains the main login page, basic corpus management (e.g. view/delete of documents), a manual annotation interface for the creation, modification and deletion of annotations. A lexicon management module is also included, as it is needed for some automatic annotation services. The next version of PACTE will include custom schema design and annotation project management, as well as automatic annotation services, as defined in section 3.

Once fully functional, PACTE will be released as an open-source project, thus enabling research groups to either host their own projects or collaborate with others on a centralized installation. Long-term plans include adding several extensions and services, such as semi-automatic annotation using active learning, corpus analysis tools, dynamic service subscription and other semantic annotation services.

Acknowledgments : This project was supported in part by Canarie grant RS-10 for Software Research Platform and the Ministère de l'Économie, de la Science et de l'Innovation (MESI) of the Government of Québec.

References

Bernier-Colborne, G., C. Barrière, and P. A. Ménard (2017). Fine-grained domain clasification of text using TERMIUM Plus. In *IWCS Workshop on Language, Ontology, Terminology and Knowledge Structures*.

Eckart de Castilho, R., Mújdricza-Maydt, É., H. Yimam, S.M., Gurevych, I., Frank, A., and Biemann, C. (2016). A Web-based Tool for the Integrated Annotation of Semantic and Syntactic Structures. In *Proceedings of the LT4DH workshop at COLING 2016, Osaka, Japan*.

Pontus Stenetorp, S. Pyysalo, G. Topić, T. Ohta, and S. A. J. Tsujii (2012). brat: a Web-based Tool for NLP-Assisted Text Annotation. In *Demonstrations Session at EACL 2012*.

Interoperable annotation of (co)references in the Democrat project

Loïc Grobol[1,2], Frédéric Landragin[1], Serge Heiden[3]

(1) Lattice, CNRS, ENS Paris, Université Sorbonne Nouvelle,
PSL Research University, USPC, 1 rue Maurice Arnoux, 92120 Montrouge, France
(2) ALMAnaCH, Inria, 2 rue Simone Iff, 75589 Paris, France
(3) IHRIM, ENS Lyon, CNRS, University of Lyon, 15 parvis René Descartes 69342 Lyon, France
`{loic.grobol, frederic.landragin}@ens.fr`; `slh@ens-lyon.fr`

Abstract

This paper proposes XML-TEI-URS, a generic TEI-based format for the annotation of coreferences in arbitrary corpora. This proposal is made in the context of Democrat, a French *Agence Nationale de la Recherche* project that aims to produce a large corpus of written French with coreference annotations, in an attempt to design a corpus that is usable both by humans and automated tools and as compatible as possible with future concurrent annotations.

1 Introduction

In this paper we propose XML-TEI-URS, a TEI-compliant format for coreference annotation inspired by Glozz' URS (Unit-Relation-Schema) metamodel (Widlöcher and Mathet 2012). Our main goal is to provide a standard that is easy to process for automated tools, compatible with other types of annotations and stays as human-readable as possible, in order to improve the interoperability of annotated corpora.

This proposal is formulated in the context of the Democrat project (Landragin 2016), which aims to produce a large corpus of written French with coreference annotations. It also takes inspiration from the MC4 projet (Mélanie-Becquet and Landragin 2014) —which has served as a proof-of-concept for the Democrat project—, the ANCOR (Muzerelle et al. 2014) and PCC (Polish Coreference Corpus (Ogrodniczuk et al. 2015)) corpora, which fulfilled similar objectives, respectively for oral French and written Polish and previous standardisation initiatives, such as Bruneseaux and Romary (1997).

We first give a rough description of the existing formats for coreference-annotated corpora, then go on to look at the tools available in the TEI for coreference annotation, and finally describe how we plan to implement coreference annotation in the Democrat corpus and in a TEI-compliant version of the ANCOR corpus.

2 Context

Historically, the first corpus with coreference annotations was the MUC corpus (Grishman and Sundheim 1996) released in 1995 in the occasion of the 6th Message Understanding Conference and annotated using simple inline SGML. Its natural successor, ACE (Doddington et al. 2004), which was dedicated to the related Entity Detection and Tracking task and released in 2003 used a similar format, but with stand-off annotations to replace some of the inline ones used in the MUC corpus.

In 1999, in the context of the MATE project Poesio, Bruneseaux, and Romary (1999) proposed a generic scheme for annotating coreference in the MATE workbench (Isard et al. 2000), both in terms of representation format and annotation conventions. The MATE project and its follow up (Poesio 2004) inspired the format of several subsequent corpora, most notably the GNOME (Poesio 2000) and AnCora (Taulé, Martí, and Recasens 2008) corpora and directly influenced the markup scheme used by the MMAX2 annotation format in which several corpora have been annotated. Among them were ARRAU (Poesio and Artstein 2008), LiveMemories (Rodríguez et al. 2010) and EPEC-KORREF (Soraluze et al. 2012). To our knowledge, this was the first effort of standardization of coreference annotations. These formats were XML-based, using elements similar —but not identical— to those proposed by the TEI for stand-off annotation. While being similar, they were not generally compatible, and not necessarily easy to reuse.

A major event for coreference-annotated corpora was the release in 2007 of the first edition of the OntoNotes corpus (S. S. Pradhan et al. 2007), followed by several other editions. It is to this day the largest coreference-annotated corpus, with nearly 3M words in three languages –Arabic, English and Chinese. Its format was inspired from those of the MUC and ACE corpora, with inline SGML annotations for coreference (and other

"

types of annotation, most notably for parsing in independent files and formats) and with a methodology inspired in part by the MATE guidelines. The use of the OntoNotes corpus in the CoNLL-2011 and CoNLL-2012 (S. Pradhan et al. 2012) shared tasks made it the standard evaluation ground for coreference detection systems, but in that case, the compatibility of the corpus and its ease of reuse in other contexts was far from being evident.

An example of a coreference corpus that followed a TEI-format is the PCC, developed by Ogrodniczuk et al. (2015). Its format is an extension of the one used by its base, the NKJP corpus (Adam Przepiórkowski and Łaziński 2008), and coreference annotations are implemented as stand-off annotations in separate files.

Regarding French, for now, the only publicly available[1] large-scale coreference-annotated corpus is ANCOR (Muzerelle et al. 2014), a 418k words corpus of transcribed oral. This transcription imposed the base of its format, as the source corpora were in the Transcriber's (Barras et al. 1998) TRS format. As for the coreference annotations, they started as stand-off Glozz annotations in separate files, that were later integrated into the original Transcriber files. The resulting corpus has thus an non-standard format that is importable neither in Transcriber nor in Glozz and can be cumbersome to parse for other applications. Another corpus of importance for our reflexions is MC4, a diachronic corpus of written French, annotated for the MC4 project as a proof-of-concept. Its format, XML-TEI-Analec, is the base of our reflexion here, presenting TEI-compliant stand-off coreference annotations in self-contained files.

The Democrat project, started in 2015, aims at creating and using a large-scale coreference-annotated diachronic corpus of written French by 2019. To that aim, it plans to leverage the experience gathered in the similar but smaller-scaled MC4 project. The manual annotation of this corpus is planned to be done with Analec (Landragin, Poibeau, and Victorri 2012) at first, while phasing it out for appropriate tools implemented for the TXM platform (Heiden 2010). For now, this annotation procedure yields native Analec files, with optional conversion to the XML-TEI-Analec format.

3 Linguistic annotations and coreference in the TEI

The description of an annotation in any kind of representation is made of two parts: a way of marking the element (markable) that is being annotated (unitizing) and a way of stating the annotations you are giving about it (categorizing).

For coreference (as for most linguistic annotations), the markables are usually contiguous spans of text. Unitizing is thus easily done using TEI's <span> element (or possibly <seg> as in the PCC). The main point of divergence is on how to specify the boundaries of those spans. Following Bański et al. (2016), we can identify three main pointing mechanisms in the TEI for stand-off annotations:

- Offset-based mechanisms such as TEI pointers (see Cayless (2013) for details and perspectives)
  - Used by the PCC and NKJP corpora through TEI's `string-range` and separate files.
  - Does not require source text alteration, but has to refer to a specific version of it.
- In-source <anchor> or similar markers
  - Used by Analec to denote markable (e.g. mentions) boundaries.
  - Requires minimal source text alteration and does not limit concurrent annotations.
  - Considerable source text clutter (particularly with concurrent annotations).
- Referring to <w> words/tokens
  - Used by TXM to mark words (tokens) for lemmatisation and POS-tagging.
  - Requires source text alteration and the non-trivial choice of a segmentation
  - Does not ease character-level boundaries encoding.
  - Considerably eases the aggregation of e.g. syntactic and coreference annotations.

As for categorizing, the TEI offers the <fs> structure, that can support a variety of annotations, including recursive structures, multivalued features, free-text features… This mostly solves the issue of annotating mention features — such as definiteness or syntactical type — but also cluster-level features — such as associativity or agreement — that have no support in the source text.

Finally, it is of course crucial for coreference annotation to be able to denote relations between mentions. There are usually two types of relations that have to be annotated: coreference relation between pairs of entity,

---

1. Tutin et al. (2000) presents another large-scale corpus with anaphoric links annotations, which is not publicly available. It uses a close derivative of the MATE format.

which can be directed (from a source to a target) in the case of anaphora ; and coreference of a set of mentions (usually called a *coreference chain*). While there is no explicit way of specifying this kind of relation in the TEI, one can be designed with existing elements. Since mentions are already annotated, these relations can simply be annotated as references to them. There are mechanisms for this usage in the TEI, under the *linking* and *aggregating* categories (TEI consortium 2016). Analec uses `<join>` elements to that purpose, which is arguably non-conform with the stated purpose of these elements. The PCC corpus uses the more generic `<ptr>`, which is more relevant, but makes the association between elements of a coreference chain harder, as it then requires to look for siblings of a given `<ptr>`. A third possibility exists in the form of the `<link>` element, which "defines an association [...] among elements". This last alternative seems to be the most standard way of marking both URS relations and URS schema in the TEI, the only inconvenient being the necessity of relying on the order of `xml:id` in the `target` attribute to mark the direction of directed relations. It is also coherent with the recommendations of (Bruneseaux and Romary 1997).

4 XML-TEI-URS: a format for coreference annotation

In this section, we describe the XML-TEI-URS format: a lightweight format for the annotation of coreferences. This format is heavily inspired from the XML-TEI-Analec format described in Mélanie-Becquet and Landragin (2014), with an effort to improve its compliance with the spirit of the TEI guidelines and its integration in various types of TEI-formatted documents. The core of the format is the implementation in TEI elements of the URS metamodel introduced by Widlöcher and Mathet (2012).

- Mentions are *units* in the Glozz sense, i.e. contiguous[2] spans of the source text. They are represented by `<span>` elements with `type="unit"`.
- Coreference relations between mentions are represented by `<link>` elements with `type="relation"` whose `target` attributes are, in that order, the `xml:id` of the source mention and the `xml:id` of the target mention.
- Coreference chains are represented by `<link>` elements with `type="schema"` whose `target` attributes are the `xml:id` of their member mentions, in no particular order.
- All of these might point to a `<fs>` using `ana` attributes to encode further linguistic annotations.

While they may seem redundant in the context of coreference, relations and schema are both needed for the annotation of more sophisticated concepts — for example bridging anaphora — that are naturally represented as directed relations between coreferences chains. This justify their inclusion here, however close the concepts and their concrete representations may seem.

Note that none of theses requirements specify where those elements should be located. This is due to the lack of a dedicated place in TEI documents for stand-off annotations. In our experiments with ANCOR, we follow Romary (2017) and use the `<standOff>` element, which has not yet made its way into the official TEI guideline. If full compliance with the current TEI guidelines is required, however we see two main strategies: either place coreference annotation in the `<back>` of the document (as in Analec), possibly in a dedicated `<div>` or place them in the `<body>` of an external file (as in the PCC corpus). Either way, we encourage the use of `<spanGrp>` and `<linkGrp>` to avoid redundancy in the annotation. In the same way, to ensure a better hierarchy of annotations, we suggest that `<fs>` elements be grouped together in dedicated `<div>` elements, thus separating different types of annotations. These do not allow factoring out informations as do e.g. `<spanGrp>`, but they should provide easier information retrieval for corpus users. See example 1 for an application to the ANCOR corpus.

Example 1: XML-TEI-URS for the ANCOR corpus

```
<text>
<body>
    <div type="section" xml:id="s2">
        <timeline>
            <when absolute="3.531" xml:id="t2.0"/>
            [...]
            <when absolute="25.924" xml:id="t7.0"/>
            [...]
        </timeline>
        <u start="#t2.0" who="#spk1" xml:id="u2" end="#t2.1">
```

---

2. Contiguity is actually not required for `<span>`, so this could be easily extended to non-contiguous units.

```
          [...]
        </u>
        [...]
        <u start="#t7.0" who="#spk2" xml:id="u7" end="#t7.19">
            [...]
            <w xml:id="u7-w20">en</w>
            <w xml:id="u7-w21">octobre</w>
            <w xml:id="u7-w22">mille</w>
            <w xml:id="u7-w23">neuf</w>
            <w xml:id="u7-w24">cent</w>
            <w xml:id="u7-w25">soixante</w>
            <anchor synch="#t7.6" type="time"/>
            [...]
            <w xml:id="u7-w36">à</w>
            <w xml:id="u7-w37">ce</w>
            <w xml:id="u7-w38">moment-là</w>
            <w xml:id="u7-w39">après</w>
            [...]
        </u>
        [...]
    </div>
    [...]
</body>
</text>
<standOff>
    <div type="coreference">
        <spanGrp type="unit">
            [...]
            <span ana="#m2713-fs" from="#u7-w21" to="#u1-w25" xml:id="m2713"/>
            <span ana="#m2714-fs" from="#u7-w37" to="#u1-w38" xml:id="m2714"/>
            [...]
        </spanGrp>
        <div type="unit-fs">
            [...]
            <fs xml:id="#m2713-fs">
                <f name="type">
                  <string>DATE</string>
                </f>
                [...]
            </fs>
            [...]
        </div>
        <linkGrp type="relation">
            [...]
            <link ana="#r212-fs" target="#m2713 #m2714" xml:id="r212"/>
            [...]
        </linkGrp>
        [...]
        <linkGrp type="schema">
            [...]
            <link target="#m2713 #m2714 #m2731" xml:id="s150"/>
            [...]
        </linkGrp>
    </div>
</standOff>
```

The format described above does not impose a particular pointing mechanism from those listed in section 3. However, in the specific context of the Democrat project, mentions boundaries may not occur inside of words, which relieves us from the burden of supporting character-level annotation. In addition to this, the TXM platform that is planned to support the final corpus already allows orthographic tokenisation as a support for its own internal annotations. This considerations lead us to recommend the use of the third solution, namely annotating mentions as spans anchored to <w> elements as shown in example 1.

As a support for the development and test of our proposed format, we used it to convert the ANCOR corpus to a fully TEI-compliant format. This involved both converting its original transcription-related annotation to their TEI equivalents and converting its coreference annotations to the format described above, example 1 shows an example of this. This shows the capacity of our format to adapt to different corpus paradigms, and bodes well for further applications, including to documents with more complex TEI representations. It also eases the access to the annotations of ANCOR for the automated annotation tools we are developing in the Democrat project (which was part of our initial motivation) compared to both the original ANCOR format and MC4's XML-TEI-Analec format.

It should also be noted that this format, while designed for coreference annotation, is not restricted to this application. Indeed, Glozz' URS metamodel has been shown to be suitable for a variety of applications such as analysis of opinion or discourse structures, which gives us hopes for the adoption of our format for other kinds of annotations, thus increasing the general interoperability of annotated corpora.

5   Conclusion and perspectives

In this paper, we presented a quick overview of the formats used for existing coreference-annotated corpora. While some efforts of standardization exist, it is our beliefs that those do not fulfill our goals of simplicity and interoperability for the annotation of the Democrat corpus. The XML-TEI-URS format we propose is TEI-compliant and plays well with other types of linguistic annotations, including transcription annotations for oral corpora. At the same time, it offers some leeway, particularly regarding pointing mechanisms, in order to accommodate different exigences for corpus makers and users. This proposal is also intentionally agnostic regarding the theoretical framework used for the actual annotation of (co)reference. In that sense, it is complementary to of e.g. the future recommendations of ISO (2017) and potentially any other paradigm.

We worked within the limits of the TEI, which already provides suitable tools for reference annotation. However, we deplore the lack of dedicated mechanisms to attach stand-off annotations to documents, and it is our hope that the integration of the `<standOff>` element in the TEI guidelines would fulfill that lack.

Our next steps should be the release of both an explicit TEI XML schema for our format, and the release of the whole ANCOR corpus in this format as a proof-of-concept. In the context of the Democrat project, we will also have to refine the actual features we use for the annotation of coreference phenomena, features that could then make their way into our recommendations for the annotation of coreference in other projects.

6   Acknowledgements

This work is part of the "Investissements d'Avenir" overseen by the French National Research Agency ANR-10-LABX-0083 (Labex EFL).

This work has been supported by the ANR DEMOCRAT (Description et modélisation des chaînes de référence: outils pour l'annotation de corpus et le traitement automatique) project ANR-15-CE38-0008.

References

Adam Przepiórkowski, Barbara Lewandowska-Tomaszyk, Rafał L. Górski, and Marek Łaziński. 2008. "Towards the National Corpus of Polish." In *Proceedings of the Sixth International Conference on Language Resources and Evaluation (LREC'08)*. Http://www.lrec-conf.org/proceedings/lrec2008/. Marrakech, Morroco: European Language Resources Association (ELRA), May.

Bański, Piotr, Bertrand Gaiffe, Patrice Lopez, Simon Meoni, Laurent Romary, Thomas Schmidt, Peter Stadler, and Andreas Witt. 2016. *Wake up, standOff!* TEI Conference 2016. Wien, Austria, September.

Barras, Claude, Edouard Geoffrois, Zhibiao Wu, and Mark Liberman. 1998. "Transcriber: a Free Tool for Segmenting, Labeling and Transcribing Speech." In *Proceedings of the First International Conference on Language Resources and Evaluation (LREC)*. Granada, España: European Language Resources Association (ELRA), May.

Bruneseaux, Florence, and Laurent Romary. 1997. "Codage des références et coréférences dans les DHM." In *ACH-ALLC'97*. Kingston, Canada.

Cayless, Hugh A. 2013. "Rebooting TEI Pointers." *Journal of the Text Encoding Initiative* (6).

Doddington, George, Alexis Mitchell, Mark Przybocki, Lance Ramshaw, Stephanie Strassel, and Ralph Weischedel. 2004. "The Automatic Content Extraction (ACE) Program : Tasks, Data, and Evaluation." In *Proceedings of the Fourth International Conference on Language Resources and Evaluation (LREC-2004).* ACL Anthology Identifier: L04-1011. Lisboa, Portugal: European Language Resources Association (ELRA), May.

Grishman, Ralph, and Beth Sundheim. 1996. "Message Understanding Conference-6: A Brief History." In *Proceedings of the 16th Conference on Computational Linguistics - Volume 1,* 466–471. COLING '96. København, Danmark: Association for Computational Linguistics.

Heiden, Serge. 2010. "The TXM Platform: Building Open-Source Textual Analysis Software Compatible with the TEI Encoding Scheme." In *24th Pacific Asia Conference on Language, Information and Computation (PACLIC),* 389–398. Sendai, Japan: Institute for Digital Enhancement of Cognitive Development, Waseda University, November.

Isard, Amy, David McKelvie, Andreas Mengel, and Morten Baun Møller. 2000. "The MATE Workbench: A Tool for Annotating XML Corpora." In *Content-Based Multimedia Information Access - Volume 1,* 411–425. RIAO '00. Paris, France: Centre de hautes études internationales d'informatique documentaire.

ISO/TC 37/SC 4/WG 2. 2017. *ISO AWI 24617-9 Language resource management – Part 9 Semantic annotation framework (SemAF).* Reference. Geneva, CH: International Organization for Standardization.

Landragin, Frédéric. 2016. "Description, modélisation et détection automatique des chaînes de référence (DEMOCRAT)." *Bulletin de l'AFIA* 92:11–15.

Landragin, Frédéric, Thierry Poibeau, and Bernard Victorri. 2012. "ANALEC: a New Tool for the Dynamic Annotation of Textual Data." In *International Conference on Language Resources and Evaluation (LREC 2012),* edited by European Language Resources Association (ELRA), 357–362. İstanbul, Türkiye, May.

Mélanie-Becquet, Frédérique, and Frédéric Landragin. 2014. "Linguistique outillée pour l'étude des chaînes de référence questions méthodologiques et solutions techniques." *Langages,* no. 195 (September): 117–137.

Muzerelle, Judith, Anaïs Lefeuvre, Emmanuel Schang, Jean-Yves Antoine, Aurore Pelletier, Denis Maurel, Iris Eshkol, and Jeanne Villaneau. 2014. "ANCOR Centre, a Large Free Spoken French Coreference Corpus: Description of the Resource and Reliability Measures." In *Proceedings of the Ninth International Conference on Language Resources and Evaluation (LREC'14).* Reykjavík, Ísland: European Language Resources Association (ELRA), May.

Ogrodniczuk, Maciej, Katarzyna Głowińska, Mateusz Kopeć, Agata Savary, and Magdalena Zawisławska. 2015. *Coreference in Polish: Annotation, Resolution and Evaluation.* Walter De Gruyter.

Poesio, Massimo. 2000. "Annotating a Corpus to Develop and Evaluate Discourse Entity Realization Algorithms: Issues and Preliminary Results." In *Proceedings of the Second International Conference on Language Resources and Evaluation (LREC,* 211–218. Athenes, Greece.

———. 2004. "The MATE/GNOME Proposals for Anaphoric Annotation, Revisited." In *Proceedings of the 5th SIGDIAL Workshop,* 154–162. Boston, MA, USA, April.

Poesio, Massimo, and Ron Artstein. 2008. "Anaphoric Annotation in the ARRAU Corpus." In *Proceedings of the Sixth International Conference on Language Resources and Evaluation (LREC-08).* Marrakech, Morroco: European Language Resources Association (ELRA), May.

Poesio, Massimo, Florence Bruneseaux, and Laurent Romary. 1999. "The MATE meta-scheme for coreference in dialogues in multiple languages." In *ACL'99 Workshop Towards Standards and Tools for Discourse Tagging,* 65–74. College Parc, MD, USA, June.

Pradhan, Sameer S., Eduard Hovy, Mitch Marcus, Martha Palmer, Lance Ramshaw, and Ralph Weischedel. 2007. "OntoNotes: A Unified Relational Semantic Representation." In *Proceedings of the International Conference on Semantic Computing,* 517–526. ICSC '07. Washington, DC, USA: IEEE Computer Society.

Pradhan, Sameer, Alessandro Moschitti, Nianwen Xue, Olga Uryupina, and Yuchen Zhang. 2012. "CoNLL-2012 Shared Task: Modeling Multilingual Unrestricted Coreference in OntoNotes." In *Proceedings of the joint Conference on Empirical Methods in Natural Language Processing (EMNLP) and Computational Natural Language Learning (CoNLL)*, 1–40. CoNLL '12. Jeju, Korea: Association for Computational Linguistics.

Rodríguez, Kepa Joseba, Francesca Delogu, Yannick Versley, Egon W. Stemle, and Massimo Poesio. 2010. "Anaphoric Annotation of Wikipedia and Blogs in the Live Memories Corpus." In *Proceedings of the Seventh International Conference on Language Resources and Evaluation (LREC'10)*. Valletta, Malta, May.

Romary, Laurent. 2017. "stdfSpec : A proposal for a stand-off element for the TEI Guidelines." July 7. `https://github.com/laurentromary/stdfSpec`.

Soraluze, Ander, Olatz Arregi, Xabier Arregi, Klara Ceberio, and Arantza Díaz de Ilarraza. 2012. "Mention detection: First steps in the development of a Basque coreference resolution system." In *Proceedings of KONVENS 2012,* edited by Jeremy Jancsary, 128–136. Main track: oral presentations. Wien, Austria: ÖGAI, September.

Taulé, Mariona, M. Antònia Martí, and Marta Recasens. 2008. "AnCora: Multilevel Annotated Corpora for Catalan and Spanish." In *Proceedings of the Sixth International Conference on Language Resources and Evaluation (LREC-08)*. ACL Anthology Identifier: L08-1222. Marrakech, Morroco: European Language Resources Association (ELRA), May.

TEI consortium, ed. 2016. "16 Linking, Segmentation, and Alignment." TEI P5: Guidelines for Electronic Text Encoding and Interchange. December 15. Accessed July 7, 2017. `http://www.tei-c.org/release/doc/tei-p5-doc/en/html/SA.html`.

Tutin, Agnès, François Trouilleux, Catherine Clouzot, Éric Gaussier, Annie Zaenen, Stéphanie Rayot, and Georges Antoniadis. 2000. "Annotating a large corpus with anaphoric links." In *Third International Conference on Discourse Anaphora and Anaphor Resolution (DAARC2000),* 2. United Kingdom.

Widlöcher, Antoine, and Yann Mathet. 2012. "The Glozz Platform: A Corpus Annotation and Mining Tool." In *Proceedings of the 2012 ACM Symposium on Document Engineering,* 171–180. DocEng '12. Paris, France: ACM.

Four Types of Temporal Signals

Kiyong Lee
Korea University, Seoul
`ikiyong@gmail.com`

Abstract

Temporal prepositions in English signal various temporal relations over events and times. In this
paper, we propose to categorize such signals into four types: **locative**, **measure**, **boundary**, and
orientation signals. We show that each of these signal types is constrained by its own semantic
restrictions. First, each of them takes as its argument a temporal entity structure either of an *atomic
type* such as dates, periods of time, and time lengths or amounts, or of a *complex type* such as bounded
intervals ("*from* dawn *till* dusk") and oriented intervals with their lengths specified ("an hour *after* the
sunset"). Second, each signal type determines the semantic type, called *aspect*, of an eventuality that
it is associated with. Such an analysis of temporal signals, as we claim, lays a basis of developing an
integrated spatio-temporal annotation scheme for language, especially involving motions.

Keywords: atomic type, complex type, entity structure, eventuality, interval, locative, oreinted span,
time amount, time length

1 Introduction

There is only a small set[1] of prepositions in English that function as spatial and temporal signals. Prepositions such as *at, in, during, by, since, from, to, through, till, before*, and *after* in English trigger various
temporal relations over events, times or locations.

ISO-TimeML (2012) puts these prepositions used as temporal signals under one single type **signal**,
tagged <SIGNAL>. In this paper, we propose to categorize this one signal type into four types of temporal
signals, each of which is tagged with the same element name <signal>, but is typed differently: **locative signal** <signal type="locative">,[2] **measure signal** <signal type="measure">,
boundary signal <signal type="boundary">, and **orientation signal** <signal type=
"orientation">.

Each of these temporal signal types is represented as an *element* in XML, following ISOspace (2014)
that represents the two types of spatial signals as *elements* <spatialSignal> and <motionSignal>.
Such a representation makes temporal signals structurally more comparable to spatial signals.

These signals are illustrated by example 1:

(1) Kim stayed in Europe during$_{loSignal}$ the fall of 2010$_{timePeriod}$, visiting
various cities in Europe for$_{meSignal}$ three months$_{timeLength}$ from$_{boSignal}$
September$_{calMonth}$ through$_{boSignal}$ November$_{calMonth}$. She had left Seoul
a week$_{timeLength}$ after$_{orSignal}$ her graduation.

Each of the four types of signals is illustrated in (1) as being associated with a temporal entity structure of
some type. The preposition *during* as a locative signal in (1, line 1) anchors the event of Kim's staying in
Europe to the fall of 2010, a period of time. As is illustrated by (1), locative signals such as *during* trigger
the anchoring of an event to an extended interval of time, while locative signals such as *at* and *on* anchor
an event to a minimal interval of time, often called *instants*. This difference comes from differences in
the aspectual semantic features of eventualities.

---

[1]Bennett (1975) lists 38 prepositions one of which he claims is a dialectal variation.

[2]The term *locative* here is used in a temporal sense.

The signal *for* as a measure signal that occurs in (1, line 3) associates that eventuality with the temporal expression *three months* that denotes a length of time. The signals *from* and *through* as a pair in (1, lines 4 and 5) mark a bounded interval (duration) with its boundaries, start and end, of Kim's stay in Europe or traveling around there. The signal *after* in (1, line 7) places Kim's departure from Seoul some time later than her graduation with a forward orientation, but with the length of an intervening interval specified between her graduation and departure as being a week. That time of Kim's departure is thus identified with the endpoint of that interval.

The ultimate purpose of this paper is to provide a basis for designing an integrated spatio-temporal annotation scheme on an enriched system of temporal signals which are interoperable with spatial signals. This paper, however, focuses solely on the classification of temporal signals which depends on how each of the signals is related to a different type of temporal entity structures.

The rest of the paper is organized into four sections. In section 2, we restructure temporal entity structures into two types: *atomic* and *complex*. In section 3, we relate four types of temporal signals to these two types of temporal structures. We finally show in section 4 how these signals interact with various semantic types of eventualities that they modify.[3] Section 5 concludes the paper with a summary.

2 Re-structuring Temporal Entity Structures

2.1 Overview

Both TimeML and ISO-TimeML (2012)[4] put every type of temporal expressions referring to times, dates, durations, measures, frequencies, and quantified times under one category, tagged <TIMEX3>. However, following Hobbs and Pan (2004), Bunt (2011) classifies them into three types: *instants* that refer to temporal points, time *intervals*, and then *time amounts*. Frequencies and quantified temporal entities also form different classes, but are treated in a different domain.

We propose to classify all of the temporal entity structures, except for frequencies and quantifications,[5] by generalizing entity structures into two types, *atomic* and *complex*. We then treat temporal entity structures as particular cases of those sub-typed entity structures.

2.2 Atomic vs Complex Entity Structures

Bunt (2007) and his subsequent works (Bunt, 2010, 2011) introduce the notion of *entity structures* as a pair $<m, A>$, where m is a markable in text and A a list of annotations on m. Lee (2012) then proposes to categorize entity structures into two types: *atomic* and *complex*, for there are some entity structures, as to be treated of the complex type, which refer to two or more entity structures like link structures.

Some entity structures such as spatial or temporal locations (e.g., *Seoul, the city, December 2016, the morning*)[6] are annotated by themselves without making any reference to other entity structures. In contrast, entity structures like paths or durations (e.g., *California Highway 1 from San Francisco to Carmel* or *half a day from noon to midnight*) are annotated with reference to other spatial or temporal entities.

This distinction can be stated, as follows:

(2) **Complex Entity Structure**
   Given a markable m and a list A of annotations on m, an entity structure $<m, A>$ is called *complex* if and only if any of the components in A refers to another entity structure; otherwise, it is *atomic*.

---

[3]The term *eventuality* was coined by Bach (1986) as a cover term that comprises all of the aspectual types of states or events or other Vendler classes.

[4]TimeML is briefly introduced in Pustejovsky et al. (2005) and ISO-TimeML in Pusejovsky et al. (2010) and Pustejovsky (2017a).

[5]These two types have been discussed by Pratt-Hartmann (2005), Bunt and Pustejovsky (2010) and Lee and Bunt (2012) withtin the framework of TimeML or ISO-TimeML.

[6]In this paper, we often talk about entities without differentiating them from their annotated structures.

We apply the notion of *atomic* vs *complex* entity structure, as stated above, directly to a way of differentiating temporal entity structures into two types, *atomic* and *complex*, as to be discussed in 2.3 and 2.4, respectively.

Exceptions to the definition of complex entity structure as given in (2) are three kinds: (1) indexical expressions (e.g., *today, last year*), (2) pronominal or anaphoric expressions (e.g., *they, she, that time*), and (3) markables as targets in semantic annotations. Indexical expressions refer to discourse entities introduced in a discourse situation or model, anaphoric expressions to their antecedents, and markables to morpho-syntactic annotations. Entity structures referred to by these expressions are not treated as of the complex type, although they refer to other entity structures or entities.

2.3   Atomic Temporal Structures

There are two sorts of atomic temporal structures: *simple intervals* and *temporal measures*.[7]

2.3.1   Simple Intervals

Simple temporal intervals are either minimal (instances) or extended (periods). They include dates, times of day (e.g., morning, noon, afternoon, evening, night), clock times (hour, minute, second), and periods of time (season, year, decade, century, millennium). They all can be viewed as either minimal intervals (instances) or extended intervals (periods), depending on what type of eventualities they modify. These entities are directly referenced to by temporal expressions such as dates, clocktimes or periods of time, without referring to other temporal entities.

Here are examples in (3):

(3)   a.   Mia got up$_{e1}$ at seven$_{t1}$ in the morning$_{t2}$.

     b.   Mia stayed home during the summer$_{t3}$ of 2016$_{t4}$.

The clocktime *seven$_{t1}$* refers to the seventh hour of a day. The time expression *the morning$_{t2}$* refers to the first half period of a day. Both *summer$_{t3}$* and *2016$_{t4}$* refer to periods of time, a season and a year, respectively. All of them refer to definite times without referring to other times. They are thus treated as referring to temporal entity structures of the *atomic* type.

2.3.2   Temporal Measure: Length vs Amount

There are two closely related notions of time measure: *time length* and *time amount*. They refer to different dimensions of measure. In general, a length is a property of an interval, either spatial or temporal, which constitutes either a path or a duration. A length is quantitatively measured in terms of a real number and a unit, which is either spatial or temporal: e.g., *15 meters* vs *15 minutes*. We thus define the notion of *temporal length*, as in:

(4)   **Time Length**
    length is a function $l : I \rightarrow R \times U$,
    where I is a set of time intervals, R a set of reals and U a set of temporal units.

There is another term *time amount*. We use it in a technical sense to refer to a time measure, sometimes called *runtime*, which is the time consumed by an eventuality. The *time amount* is thus defined, as in:

(5)   **Time Amount**
    A *time amount* is a function $\tau : E \rightarrow R \times U$,
    where E is a set of eventualities, R a set of reals, and U a set of temporal units.

According to these definitions, as given in (4) and (5), both a length of time l and an amount of time τ may have the same measure of values, such as $<10, hour>$ (*ten hours*), but their domains are different. Formally speaking, the domain of length l is a set of time intervals I, whereas that of amount τ is a set of eventualities E.

---

[7]Frequencies and quantified times are also of the atomic type.

2.4 Complex Temporal Structures

Temporal entity structures of the *complex* type, in contrast, are characterized in their reference to other temporal entity structures. These entity structures may be either (1) bounded intervals (durations) or (2) oriented intervals (directed spans).

2.4.1 Bounded Intervals (Durations)

Bounded intervals, more often called *durations*, have their boundaries, start or end, or both, specified by boundary signals (`<signal type="boundary">`) such as *from* and *till* as a pair. These intervals are temporal entity structures of the complex type, for they refer to their boundary points (minimal intervals), being represented as a triplet below:

(6) A bounded interval t, delimited either partially or totally by its specifically mentioned boundaries, t_i and t_j: $<t, t_i, t_j>$, or $\lambda t[starts(t_i, t) \wedge ends(t_j, t)]$.

Here are examples:

(7) a. Mia slept$_{e1}$ $\emptyset_{t3}$ *from* ten$_{t1}$ *till* seven$_{t2}$.

b. Mia will get$_{e2}$ better $\emptyset_{t5}$ *from* now$_{t4}$ on.

Example (7a) above contains the two time expressions, ten_{t1} and $seven_{t2}$, each referring to a clock time, an atomic entity structure type. Because of the temporal signals, these times, however, refer to the two boundaries, *start* and *end*, of an interval which is marked up as a non-consuming empty tag, $\emptyset_{t3}$.[8] Hence, this interval $\emptyset_{t3}$ forms an entity structure of the *complex* type, delimited by its two boundaries, t_1 and t_2.

Likewise, example (7b) also marks up an interval $\emptyset_{t5}$ with its start boundary t_4 explicitly mentioned and referred to by *from now*, while its end boundary is not mentioned and left open. This semi-open interval is also a temporal entity structure of the complex type with a temporal signal *from* that is triggering a temporal entity *now* to be its start boundary.

2.4.2 Oriented Intervals

There are temporal intervals which are oriented either forward or backward,[9] as triggered by signals such as *after, before,* and *ago*[10].

Here is an example:

(8) Mia left$_{e1}$ for Busan two hours$_{t6}$ after$_{s1}$ her breakfast$_{e2}$.

Determining the orientation type and the anchoring ground depends on the type of signals as well as the semantic type of eventualities. The signal *after* triggers a forward oriented interval t at the end t_j of which the event e_1 of Mia's leaving is anchored, as shown by Figure 1. The semantic type of Mia's leaving is a transition (accomplishment) type.

---

[8] In parsing or semantic annotation, an element (in XML) which has no reference to a textual fragment is called a *non-consuming tag*. For example, in a gapping structure such as *Bill loves apples and Ben $\emptyset$ pears*, a verb is missing in the right conjunct. This missing verb, marked by $\emptyset$, is treated as a non-consuming tag. The tag is there, but it is not *consumed by* nor refers to any markable expression in text.

[9] Quirk et al. (1985) (section 8.5) use the *forward* or *backward span* to explain phenomena that are related to these orientation signals.

[10] Unlike other temporal triggers that are mostly prepositions, *ago* is an adverbial trigger.

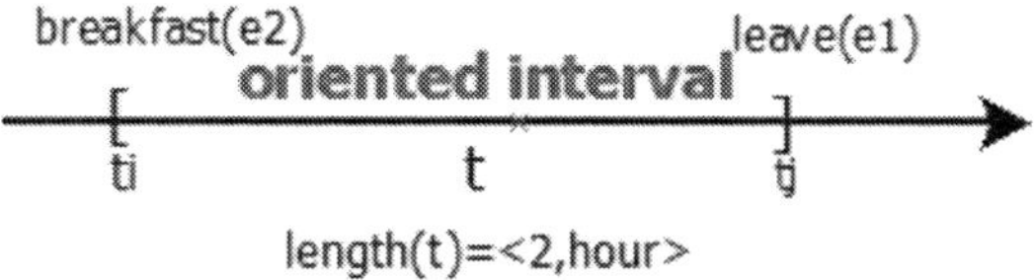

Figure 1: Forward Oriented Interval

3 Four Types of Temporal Signals Revisted

3.1 Overview

Temporal signals are classified into four types, depending on the type of a temporal entity structure which each of them is associated with, as shown in:

(9) a. Associated with Atomic Temporal Entity Structures:
 (1) Locative signals `<signal type="locative">` for times proper;
 (2) Measure signals `<signal type="measure">` for temporal measure.

 b. Associated with Complex Temporal Entity Structures:
 (3) Boundary signals `<signal type="boundary">` for bounded intervals;
 (4) Orientation signals `<signal type="orientation">` for oriented intervals with their lengths specified.

3.2 Locative Signals

Locative signals such as *at, in, on, during*, and *by* are used in both temporal and spatial senses. These signals all refer to temporal locations, also called *time-positions* by Quirk et al. (1985).[11] Unlike the prepositions such as *at, in*, and *on*, the preposition *during* is used in a temporal sense only. The preposition *by* is used in both spatial and temporal senses, but these two senses are not related.

The locative signals *at* and *in* in examples (10) each anchor an eventuality to an atomic-type time.

(10) a. Mia arrived$_{e1}$ at$_{loS1}$ nine-fifteen$_{t1:clocktime}$.
 $[arrive(e_1) \land past(e_1) \land occurs(e_1, t) \land t = t_1 \land hour(t_1) \land clocktime(\text{KST}, t_1) = 9 : 15]$[12]

 b. Mozart lived$_{e2}$ in$_{loS2}$ [the eighteenth century]$_{t2:period\,of\,time}$.
 $[live(c_2) \land past(e_2) \land holds(e_2, t) \land t \subset t_2 \land century(t_2) \land period(\text{CE}, t_2) = 18]$[13]

The time-related event predicates **occurs** and **holds**[14] are accompanied by their respective constraints. The predicate **occurs** is constrained by an equality relation $=$ between an event time t and a mentioned or referenced time t_1 as in (a), whereas the predicate **holds** is constrained by an inclusion relation, represented by a subset relation $\subset$, between the two times, t and t_2. The length of the time t in the interval t_2 is, however, determined by a pragmatic factor. It is a historical fact that Mozart did not live throughout the whole period of the eighteenth century, but for only a portion of it.

3.3 Measure Signals

Measure signals such as *for* and *in* take temporal measure entities, time lengths or time amounts, as their arguments. Here is an example:

---

[11] See Quirk et al. (1985), 8.51 Adjuncts of time.

[12] KST stands for the Korean Standard Time, which is GMT + 9 hours.

[13] CE stands for the Current or Christian Era, replacing AD, *Anno Domini*.

[14] We follow the interval temporal logic of Allen (1984) and Allen and Ferguson (1994) and their definition of these predicates.

(11) I taught at a university ($for_{meSignal}$) *almost 40 years*$_{tMeasure}$, but have to retire $in_{meSignal}$ *a year*$_{tMeasure}$.

As shown in the example, the signal *for* may be omitted, but the signal *in* may not.

The temporal entities referred by these measure expressions, however, are of two different types. The time measure associated with the signal *for* is an amount time that is consumed by an eventuality, involving an extended time interval, called *time span*. This amount can be a cumulative quantity. The signal *in*, in contrast, is simply associated with a length of a time interval at the end of which an associated event comes to a culmination point, thus being called *time frame*. Differences in their use have been discussed by Vendler (1967), Kenny (1963), Mourelatos (1978), Croft (2012), and many others in relation to the semantic aspectual types, especially *achievement* and *accomplishment* types, of eventualities that those measure signals are used with. In section 4.3, we resume this topic discussing the use of temporal measure signals related to such eventuality types.

3.4 Boundary Signals

Intervals are often bounded by their boundaries, represented by the predicates **starts** and **ends**. Here are examples:

(12) a. Mia visited Thailand *from* **January 5** *to* **20** this year.

     b. Some workmen have to work *from* **dusk** *till* **dawn**.

Bounded intervals may occur with specific measure expressions:

(13) a. Mia slept **the whole morning** *from early morning till noon*.

     b. Kim has been sick *for* **six straight days** *from Monday through Saturday*.

The measure expressions supplement the meaning of their respective bounding intervals.

3.5 Orientation Signals

As Quirk et al. (1985) suggest, the main function of orientation signals is to locate event times either forward (future oriented) or backward (past oriented) with respect to their reference times. Here is a short list:

(14) a. Forward: *after, since, from*
     b. Backward: *before, ago*

These signals may occur with or without any oriented intervals. Here are examples:

(15) a. Gio left for Paris *two weeks*$_{orInterval}$ after$_{orSignal}$ Easter$_{rTime}$. [forward]

     b. Gio will return home *a week*$_{orInterval}$ before$_{orSignal}$ Christmas$_{rTime}$. [backward].

The forward orientation signal places each oriented time interval at a later position with respect to the reference time,[15] whereas the backward orientation places that interval at a position earlier than the reference time. The event time is grounded to one of the boundary points, depending on the directionality of the signal: if a given interval is forward oriented as in (15a), then the anchoring ground point is the end of that interval, whereas the anchoring ground is its start point if the interval is backward oriented.

There is, however, an ambiguity in interpreting these so-called oriented intervals especially when such an interval modifies *state*-type or *process*-type eventualities. Consider:

(16) a. Mia has lived in Seoul *12 years*$_{orInterval}$ since$_{orSignal}$ 2005$_{rTime}$.

     b. Mia has lived in Seoul *for 12 years*$_{orInterval}$ since$_{orSignal}$ 2005$_{rTime}$. [state]

     c. Jon has been smoking *(for) six years* after$_{orSignal}$ his military service. [process]

Sentence (16a) is acceptable only if it is interpreted as (16b). In this case, the eventuality of Mia's having lived in Seoul is anchored to the whole interval. The same type of interpretation applies to (16c).

---

[15]See Reichenbach (1947) for the notion of reference time in contrast to that of event time.

4 Types of Eventualities Interacting with Temporal Structures

The interpretation of temporal structures, consisting of time signals and entities, which syntactically function as temporal adjuncts, is much restricted by the type of an eventuality which they occur with. In this section, we discuss how they interact with each other.

4.1 Basic Assumptions

We assume an ontology of eventualities that amalgamates Allen (1984) and Pustejovsky (1991), which is then modified by Pustejovsky et al. (2017) (page 32, (10)) that subcategorize the type of *transition* into *achievement* and *accomplish* types, as in Vendler (1967).[16]:

```
(17) eventuality types = state (property) | occurrence;
     state (property) = e;
        (*e stands for a single homogeneous eventuality.*)
     occurrence = process (activity) | transition;
     process (activity) = e_1...e_n; (* where n ≥ 2 *);
        (*A process is defined to be a sequence of more than one
          eventualities that may not be homogeneous.*)
     transition = transition_ach | transition_acc;
     transition_ach = e_1e_2; (*where e_1 and e_2 are states.*);
     transition_acc = e_1...e_ne_c;
        (* The sequence e_1...e_n is a process and e_c, a culminating state.*)
```

The notion of *achievement* here is understood as consisting of a state followed by another state, but we extend it to include a case in which a state is followed by a process as the inverse of an accomplishment. This is represented as below:

(18) Extended Notion of Achievement:
$$\text{transition}_{ach^e} = e_i\ e_1...e_n;$$
(*where e_i is an initial state and $n \geq 1$.*);

We also assume, as stated earlier in section 3.2, the interval temporal logic of Allen (1984) and Allen and Ferguson (1994) with their definitions of two predicates **holds** and **occurs**. A *state* or *property* is a static eventuality that *holds* over an interval of time and every subinterval of it. An *occurrence* is of a dynamic type that consists of a sequence of sub-events which may not be uniform nor contiguous as it develops. There are two subtypes of *transition*: *transition_ach* for achievements and *transition_acc* for accomplishments.[17] *John woke up at seven* is an example of achievements in which a state of John's being asleep changes to the state of his being awake. The activity of *John wrote a novel* involves a process of writing and then reaches the culminating state of finishing a novel. This is an example of accomplishments.

We then understand that an *instance* is a minimal interval, thus treating the two boundary points of a time interval as two minimal intervals, called *start* and *end*. The predicates corresponding to them are **starts** and **ends**, each representing a relation between an interval and its begin-point and endpoint, respectively.

4.2 Locative Constructions

Locative constructions represent simple intervals, each triggered by locative signals. Consider:

(19) a. John woke up at seven thirty-five$_{clocktime}$. [transition$_{ach}$]

     b. Mozart lived$_{t_e}$ in the eighteenth century$_{t_r}$. [state]

---

[16] We represent the structure of eventuality types in extended BNF (ISO/IEC 14977, 1996)

[17] See Pustejovsky et al. (2017) page 32, (10).

The interpretation of (19a) is represented by the predicate **occurs** because the verb *woke up* is of a transition type. That of (19b), in contrast, is represented by the predicate **holds** because the verb *lived* is of a state type. Note, however, that there is a subinterval constraint between an event time t_e and a reference time t_r which affects the interpretation **holds** relation.

4.3 Measure Constructions

The *for*-measure expression provides an answer to a *how long*-type question, whereas the *in*-measure expression provides an answer to a *when*-type question as well as *how long*-type question with *it takes*, as illustrated by (20).

(20) a. *How long* did you teach at a university?
     (For) almost forty years.

    b. *When* will you retire?
     In a year.

    c. *How long* did it take for Mia to write a book?
     It took almost six months. In fact, she wrote it in exactly five months and three weeks.

The semantic content of the *for*-measure expressions can be represented as shown by (21):

(21) a. We worked$_{e1}$ for$_{meS1}$ 10 hours$_{me1}$.
     $[work(e_1) \wedge past(e_1) \wedge occurs(e_1, t) \wedge \tau(e_1) = <10, hour>]$[process]

    b. John waited$_{e2}$ for$_{meS2}$ more than 2 days$_{me2}$ to get a visa.
     $[wait(e_2) \wedge past(e_2) \wedge occurs(e_2, t) \wedge t \subset t_2 \wedge l(t_2) \geq <2, day>]$ [process]

The *for*-measure expressions are associated with *process*-type eventualities. Their temporal properties are represented by the time amount τ that each process has taken. The time amount of the occurrence *worked*$_{e1}$ was $10\,hours_{me1}$, which might have been measured cumulatively. The length l of the time interval in which the event of *waited*$_{e2}$ lasted was a stretch of *more than 2 days*$_{me2}$.

    The semantic content of the *in*-measure expressions can be represented as illustrated by (22):

(22) a. Mia wrote$_{e1}$ a book *in*$_{meS1}$ six months$_{me1}$.
     $[write(e_1) \wedge past(e_1) \wedge occurs(e_1, t) \wedge t \subseteq t_1 \wedge ends(t, t_1) \wedge l(t_1) = <6, month>]$ [transition$_{acc}$].

    b. I will retire$_{e2}$ in$_{meS2}$ a month$_{me2}$.
     $[retire(e_2) \wedge future(e_2) \wedge occurs(e_2, t) \wedge ends(t, t_2) \wedge l(t_2) = <1, month>]$ [transition$_{ach}$]

Unlike the signal *for*, which is associated with *process*-type eventualities, the signal *in* is, in contrast, associated with *transition*-type eventualities. The time t is the culmination point of an interval t_1 or t_2, as represented with the predicate **ends**. These two, however, differ from each other: (22a) is an accomplishment involving a process, represented as $t \subset t_1$, through which the activity of writing a book holds, whereas (22b) is an achievement which just occurs at the end of the given time interval.

    The signal *for* can also be used with *state*-type eventualities, as illustrated by (23):[18]

(23) a. James Pustejovsky *was CTO* for five years.
     $[be\text{-}CTO(e_1) \wedge past(e_2) \wedge holds(e_1, t) \wedge t \subseteq t_1 \wedge l(t_1) = <5, year>]$ [state]

    b. They *lived* in U.N.-run refuge camps for two and a half years.
     $[live(e_2) \wedge past(e_2) \wedge holds(e_2, t) \wedge t \subseteq t_2 \wedge l(t_2) = <2.5, year>]$ [state]

These two states lasted throughout the entire time intervals (durations) as mentioned.

---

[18]These examples are taken from ISO-TimeML (2012), A.2.1.3.3 (35).

4.4 Bounded Intervals

Eventualities of the type *process* or *state* occur during a bounded interval. Accomplishment types are also allowed during a bounded interval, while achievements are not.

(24) a. My mother has been ill since last year. [state]

    b. My girl friend worked there till Christmas. [process]

    c. I have been writing a novel from the spring of last year till this autumn. [transition$_{acc}$]

    d. *My girl friend arrived there till Christmas.[19] [transition$_{ach}$]

These examples show that bounded intervals occur with *state, process* or *accomplishment*-type eventualities only. The *accomplishment* type occurs in a bounded interval because it involves a process, unlike the *achievement* type.

4.5 Orientation Intervals

Oriented intervals, triggered by orientation signals, can easily occur with *achievement*-type eventualities. Here are examples for the *achievement* type:

(25) a. Mia left for France a month before Easter. [transition$_{ach}$]

    b. We will meet a week from today. [transition$_{ach}$]

    c. Jon died an hour before midnight. [transition$_{ach}$]

    d. I submitted a paper an hour before the deadline. [transition$_{ach}$]

In the case of an *achievement*-type eventuality as in the above example, its anchoring ground is a boundary point of a given oriented interval.

States and processes are allowed if the oriented intervals are interpreted as so-called time spans like the *for*-measure expressions.[20]

(26) a. My family lived in Osaka *(for) almost 15 years* before the end of World War II. [state]

    b. My family was living in Osaka *up till almost a year* before the end of World War II. [state]

In these cases, each state is anchored to the whole oriented interval.

(27) a. Mia studied French in Paris *(for) a semester* after her arrival. [process]

    b. Mia studied French in Paris *a semester* after her arrival. How she managed to put it off for this long I can't understand.[21] [transition$_{ach^e}$]

Example (27a) is ambiguous: it can either mean that Mia started studying French a semester after her arrival in Paris or that she spent a semester studying it after her arrival. In the case of example (27b), it is clear that Mia started studying French a semester after her arrival, but her study lasted for an indeterminate period of time. The semantic type of the eventuality involved here is considered not a simple achievement ($transition_{ach}$), but an achievement ($transition_{ach^e}$) in an extended sense which defines an achievement as consisting of an initial state followed by either a state or a process, as defined in (18) Extended Notion of Achievement.

---

[19]Taken from Quirk et al. (1985), 9.37

[20]Gary Rector, a native speaker of English and a professional translator, has noted the ambiguous interpretation of oriented intervals. He also provided some of the examples.

[21]This example was provided by an anonymous native speaker of English, who reviewed a penultimate version of this paper.

5 Concluding Remarks

Table 1 summarizes the whole discussion. There are four types of temporal signals proposed: **locative, measure, boundary**, and **orientation** signals. Some prepositions in English are listed for illustration. Each signal type is associated with a certain type of temporal structure. The first two types mark temporal entity structures of the atomic type such as dates, periods of time, times of day, and an amount or length of time. The other two mark temporal entity structures of the complex type such as intervals with their boundaries specified or oriented spans with time distances, either quantitatively or non-quantitatively specified, or totally unspecified.

Table 1: Summary

signalType	preposition	timeStructure	semanticType
locative	*at, in, on, during*	dates, times, periods	any
measure	*for*	time amounts	state, process
	in	time lengths	transition
boundary	*from – till, since*	bounded intervals	state, process, transition$_{acc}$
orientation	*before, after*	oriented spans	state^c, process^c, transition$_{ach^e}$

Note: The two *c*-superscripted cases require additional context to allow a durational interpretation.

The last column of Tabel 1 shows what type of eventuality each of the four types of temporal signals is associated with. The locative signals allow an event of any of the semantic types except that *state* or *process*-type events require a more extended interval to anchor them, while *transition*-type events are anchored to minimal intervals, called *instants*. There are at least two types of measure signals, each triggered by *for* and *in*. The trigger *for* works with *state* or *process*-type eventualities, whereas the trigger *in* marks *transition*-type occurrences. The bounded interval signal works with *state*, *process* or *accomplishment*-type eventualities. The orientation signals create oriented spans, either forward or backward. States and processes are also interpreted as being anchored to the whole stretch of an oriented interval, but these interpretations are contextually determined. Achievements are each anchored at the boundary point of an oriented interval, but in an extended sense. Each achievement can consist of an initial state followed either by a single state or by a process.

As stated in section 1 Introduction, we have not discussed how our analysis of temporal signals applies to the design of an event-based temporal annotation scheme as a whole. Nor have we shown how these four types of temporal signals correspond to spatial signals. We can, however, point out easily that locative signals correspond to qualitative spatial signals, temporal measure signals to spatial measure signals, bounded temporal intervals to bounded paths, and oriented time distances to oriented spatial distances. Details of these issues are to be discussed on a separate occasion.

Acknowledgments

I owe many thanks to Suk-Jin Chang, Youngsoon Cho, Roland Hausser, Ghang Lee, Chongwon Park, Byong-Rae Ryu, and Gary Rector for their reading preliminary versions of this paper and also to the three anonymous reviewers with their most detailed and helpful comments.

References

Allen, James F. (1984). Towards a general theory of action and time. *Artificial Intelligence* 23: 123–154. Reprinted in Mani et al. (eds) (2015), pp. 251–276.

Allen, James F., and George Ferguson (1994). Actions and events in interval temporal logic. *Technical Report* 521 (July 1994), The University of Rochester Computer Science Department, Rochester, New

York and also in *Spatial and Temporal Reasoning*, ed. Oliveiro Stock, pp. 205–245. Dordrecht: Kluwer Academic Publishers, 1997.

Bach, Emmon (1986). The algebra of events. *Linguistics and Philosophy*, 9:5–16. Reprinted in Mani et al. (eds) (2005), pp. 61–69.

Bennett, David C. (1975). *Spatial and Temporal Uses of English Prepositions: An Essay in Stratificational Semantics*. London: Longman.

Bunt, Harry (2007). The Semantics of semantic annotations. *Proceedings of the 21st Pacific Asia Conference on Language, Information and Computation*, pp. 13–28. Seoul: The Korean Society for Language and Information.

Bunt, Harry (2010). A methodology for designing semantic annotation languages exploiting semantic-syntactic ISO-morphisms. In *Proceedings of the Second International Conference on Global Interoperability for Language Resources* (ICGL 2010), ed. Alex C. Fang, Nancy Ide, and Jonathan Webster, pp. 29–45. Hong Kong: City University of Hong Kong.

Bunt, Harry (2011). Abstract syntax and semantics in semantic annotation, applied to time and events. Revised version of "Introducing abstract syntax + semantics in semantic annotation, and its consequences for the annotation of time and events." In *Recent Trends in Language and Knowledge Processing*, ed. Eunryoung Lee and Aesun Yoon, pp. 157–204. Seoul: Hankukmunhwasa.

Bunt, Harry, and James Pustejovsky (2010). Annotating temporal and event quantification. *Proceedings of the Fifth Joint ISO-ACL SIGSEM Workshop on Interoperable Semantic Annotation (ISA-5)*, ed. Harry Bunt, pp. 15–22. Hong Kong: Department of Chinese, Translation and Linguistics, City University of Hong Kong.

Croft, William (2012). *Verbs: Aspects and Clausal Structure*. Oxford: Oxford University Press.

Gagnon, Michel, and Guy Lapalme (1996). From conceptual time to linguistic time. *Computational Lingistics*, 22.1: 91-127.

Hobbs, Jerry R., and Feng Pan (2004). An ontology of time for the semantic Web. *ACM Transactions on Asian Language Information Processing (TAKIP)*, 3.1:66–85.

Ide, Nancy, and James Pustejovsky (eds.) (2017). *Hanbook of Linguistic Annotation*. Dordrecht: Springer.

ISO/IEC (1996). *ISO/IEC 14977 Information technology – Syntactic metalanguage – Extended BNF*. Geneva: The International Organization for Standardization.

ISO (2012). *ISO 24617-1:2012(E) Language resource management - Semantic annotation framework - Part 1: Time and events (SemAF-Time, ISO-TimeML)*, drafted by TC 37/SC 4/WG 2. Geneva: The International Organization for Standardization.

ISO (2014). *ISO 24617-7:2014(E) Language resource management - Semantic annotation framework - Part 7: Spatial information (ISOspace)*, drafted by TC 37/SC 4/WG 2. Geneva: The International Organization for Standardization.

Katz, Graham (2007). Towards a denotational semantics for TimeML. In *Annotating, Extracting and Reasoning about Time and Events*, ed. Frank Schilder, Graham Katz, and James Pustejovsky, pp. 88–106. Berlin: Springer.

Kenny, Anthony (1963). *Action, Emotion, and Will*. New York: Routledge.

Lee, Kiyong (2012). Towards interoperable spatial and temporal annotation schemes. *Proceedings of The Joint ISA-7, SRSL-3 and I2MRT Workshop on Interoperable Semantic Annotation*, ed. Harry Bunt, pp. 61–68. Workshop of The Eighth Edition of Language Resources and Evaluation Conference (LREC 2012), Istanbul.

Lee, Kiyong (2013). Multi-layered annotation of non-textual data for spatial information. In *Proceedings of the 9th Joint ACL SIGSEM-ISO Workshop on Interoperable Semantic Annotation (ISA-9)*, ed. Harry Bunt, pp. 15–24. Workshop of the 10th International Conference of Computational Semantics (IWCS 2014), March 2013, Potsdam, Germany.

Lee, Kiyong (2015). The semantic annotation of measure expressions in ISO standards. In *Proceedings of the Eleventh Joint ACL-ISO Workshop on Interoperable Semantic Annotation (ISA-11)*, ed. Harry Bunt, pp. 55–66. Workshop of the 11th International Conference on Computational Semantics (IWCS 2015) London: Queen Mary University of London, U.K., April 14, 2015.

Lee, Kiyong, and Harry Bunt (2012). Counting time and events. In *Proceedings of the Eighth Joint ISO-ACL SIGSEM Workshop on Interoperable Semantic Annotation (ISA-8)*, ed. Harry Bunt, pp. 34–41. January 3–5, 2012, University of Pisa, Faculty of Foreign Languages and Literatures and Istituto di Linguistica Computazionale Antonio Zampolli.

Mani, Inderjeet, James Pustejovsky, and Robert Gaizauskas (eds) (2005). *The Language of Time: A Reader*. Oxford: Oxford University Press.

Mourelatos, Alexander P.D. (1978). Events, processes, and states. *Linguistics and Philosophy*, 2: 415–434.

Pratt-Hartmann, Ian (2005). From TimeML to TPL. http://drops.dagstuhl.de/opus/votexte/2005/318. [date of citation: 2006-12-01].

Pustejovsky, James (1991). The syntax of event structure. *Cognition* 41: 47–81. Reprinted in Mani et al. (eds.) (2005), pp. 33–60.

Pustejovsky, James, Robert Ingria, Roser Saurí, Jose castaõ, Jessica Littman, Rob Gaizauskas, Andreas Setzer, Graham Katz, and Inderjeet Mani (2005). The specification language TimeML. In Inderjeet Mani, James Pustejovsky, and Robert Gaizauskas (eds.), pp. 545–557.

Pustejovsky, James, Kiyong Lee, and Harry Bunt (2010). ISO-TimeML: An international standard for semantic annotation. In *Proceedings of LREC 2010, the Seventh Edition of the International Conference on Language Resources and Evaluation*, pp. 394–397. Malta.

Pustejovsky, James (2017a). ISO-TimeML and the annotation of temporal information. In Nancy Ide and James Pustejovsky (eds.), pp. 941–968.

Pustejovsky, James (2017b). ISO-Space: Annotating static and dynamic spatial information. In Nancy Ide and James Pustejovsky (eds.), pp. 941–968.

Pustejovsky, James, Harry Bunt, and Annie Zaenen (2017). Designing annotation schemes: from theory to model. In Nancy Ide and James Pustejovsky (eds.), pp. 21–72.

Quirk, Randolph, Sidney Greenbaum, Geoffrey Leech, and Jan Svartvik (1985). *A Comprehensive Grammar of the English Language*. London and New York: Longman.

Reichenbach, Hans (1947). *Elements of Symbolic Logic*. New York: The Free Press.

Vendler, Zeno (1967). Verbs and times. *Linguistics in Philosophy*, chapter 4. Ithaca, NY: Cornell University Press. Reprinted in Mani et al. (eds.) (2005), pp. 21-32.

Temporal@ODIL Project: Adapting ISO-TimeML to Syntactic Treebanks for the Temporal Annotation of Spoken Speech

Jean-Yves Antoine[1], Jakub Waszczuk[2], Anaïs Lefeuvre-Halftermeyer[3], Lotfi Abouda[4], Emmanuel Schang[5], and Agata Savary[6]

[1,2,6]LI, University François Rabelais of Tours
[2,3]LIFO, University of Orléans
[4,5]LLL, University of Orléans

Abstract

This paper presents Temporal@ODIL, a project that aims at building the largest corpus annotated with temporal information on spoken French. The annotation is based on an adaptation of the ISO-TimeML standard that consists in grounding the annotation on a treebank and not on raw text.

1   Introduction

The representation and the processing of temporal information is important for most understanding tasks on linguistic data. Temporal annotation has benefitted from the normalization efforts of the ISO TC37/SC4 committee which has led to the definition of the ISO-TimeML standard (ISO 24617-1:2012), following the seminal proposal of Pustejovsky et al. (2003). While originally developed for English, ISO-TimeML has been applied on a large variety of languages (Italian, Korean, Romanian, Chinese...) with only slight idiomatic adaptations. This is a clear indication of its relevance and genericity.

Only one French corpus (French Time Bank) has been annotated following the ISO-TimeML standard (Bittar et al., 2011). It was built on an extract of the French Tree Bank, FTB (Abeillé et al., 2003). Its size is reasonable (15,876 words) for pilot linguistics studies but is too restricted for computational purposes. In addition, the syntactic information that is present in the FTB was not considered during the annotation phase.

In this paper, we present Temporal@ODIL, a project which aims precisely at enlarging and deepening the seminal work conducted with the French Time Bank in two directions :

- The temporal annotation is not conducted on written text but on speech transcripts. Several language registers are considered, ranging from socio-linguistic interviews to highly interactive dialogues. The annotation is conducted on ANCOR (Muzerelle et al., 2014), the largest French coreference corpus and one of the largest ones of spoken language. Temporal@ODIL provides a complementary annotation layer, allowing studies combining coreference and temporal data. It will concern 20,000 words, which doubles the size of existing French TimeML-based resources.

- Temporal@ODIL proposes modifications to the ISO-TimeML standard and its main originality is to delimit temporal mentions not by their minimal chunk but by the range of the syntactic subtree that covers the temporal mention. In order to favor re-usability, we watch out carefully to maintain upward compatibility between the ISO standard and our annotation scheme.

The second section presents and substantiates the modifications we propose to the standard. The third section describes the semi-automatic treebank annotation procedure we are following. The discussion between dependency and constituency parsing is presented there. Finally, the fourth section introduces the annotation tool that has been developed for the project. This tool is not restricted to temporal annotation, it can also be used for treebank edition and correction.

2   Annotation scheme : modifications of the ISO-TimeML standard

The changes that are proposed in Temporal@ODIL involve some extensions that do not imply any modification of the structure of the XML TimeML documents. They are indeed limited to the definition of values that instantiate some attributes of the norm and preserve a structural compliance with the norm. These changes are largely detailed in (Lefeuvre-Halftermeyer et al., 2016). For the sake of clarity, we recall however briefly our main proposals[1].

- TIMEX: temporal functions. The attribute temporalFunction expresses whether the temporal reference of a time expression needs to be calculated considering its linguistic expression or an other reference. Instead of defining temporalFunction as binary value, three values based on the seminal work of Reichenbach (1947) are considered in the Temporal@ODIL project: Null (absolute references), S (enunciation-based relative references) and R (discourse-based relative ones). The details of the function (temporalFunctionID) themselves have never been described by the norm. Temporal@ODIL adopts a typology of function classes defined in Drat (2014).

- TLINK relation. TLINK types available in the norm are the ones identified by Allen (1983), in addition to a fourteenth one, IDENTITY. Like other authors of (MERLOT, 2016), we have decided to ignore this type which is a proper coreference relation, and to add a few more relations (Drat, 2014).

The last proposal of modification is deeper: it involves a move from a word-based to a tree-based annotation. ISO TimeML guidelines request <EVENT> tags to be delimited by their minimal event-denoting chunks. This restrictive delimitation was questioned by Pustejovsky et al. (2006). The Temporal@ODIL project follows a broader annotation that covers the whole event-denoting expression, in order to keep all the relevant information that is useful for temporal reasoning without asking the annotator to resolve the syntactic structure in addition to the semantic annotation.

A first interest of a broader annotation is obvious with temporal abstract anaphora, whose resolution often needs the consideration of a whole clause (Zinsmeister and Dipper, 2011). This large-span annotation questions the ability for the annotators to delimit the eventualities with a satisfactory reliability. To ease this delimitation, we adopt a solution that was investigated for multi-word expressions in the Prague Dependency Treebank (Bejček and Straňák, 2010): eventualities are defined on the syntactic structures of a treebank. Then, the delimitation task boils down to the selection of one specific node. Data reliability is favored by a reduction of the annotator's cognitive load. For this, we propose to only annotate the two syntactic nodes implied in a supposed SLINK (in a constituency paradigm) and to resolve the SLINK automatically by overloading the syntactic link. We conducted pilot experiments that showed that a phrase-structure treebank is required for temporal annotation: the annotators indeed encountered difficulties to characterize the span of time-denoting items on dependency trees. This tree-based annotation does not violate the XML structure of the ISO-TimeML annotation files: the span of the eventualities in the standoff annotation is simply based on tree nodes identifiers rather than on token identifiers.

3   From a syntactic annotation towards a semantic one

Temporal@ODIL adopts an incremental process of annotation: the annotation is divided in several successive stages that combine automatic and manual procedures. The annotation is composed of 5 phases:

- automatic pre-processing of the corpus: the first stage consists in a preprocessing of the speech transcripts to ease the parsing. We proceed in the sidelining of noises interjections, and phatic expressions not carrying patent temporal information: *"oui"* for *'yes'*, *"bonjour"* for *'good morning'*, etc., whereas verbal expressions like *"excusez-moi"* for *'excuse-me'*, *"s'il vous plaît"* for *'please'* are kept[2].

- automatic syntactic annotation: this phase consists of using a parser to build the constituency-based treebank on which the temporal annotation will be conducted. Two strategies have been considered: using a robust dependency parser and building afterwards the constituency treebank from the

---

[1]Our proposals have been updated recently on some points: these changes are integrated in this paper.

[2]We expect the studies lead during this project to help us confirm or disprove this choice.

parsing dependency trees; using directly a constituency-based parser, provided it presents a satisfactory behaviour. Temporal@ODIL focuses on spontaneous speech transcripts, which challenge the robustness of the syntactic analysis. We conducted pilot experiments that show dependency parsers do not outperform noticeably constituency ones on spoken French. We thereby decided to use the Stanford parser trained on the FTB. All the analyses are lead on speech turns separately, further boostrapping of the parser on speech data will be also considered.

Figure 1 illustrates this parsing output for the sentence :

(1) *oui bonjour madame j'aurais voulu parler à madame Nom mais je crois que sa ligne directe ne répond pas*
'yes good morning Madam I would like to talk to madam Name but her direct phone line does not answer'

One should note that the phatic expression *"oui bonjour madame"* (*'yes good morning Madam'*) has been automatically put aside in the pre-processing phase: it does not appear in the syntactic structure whereas the whole dialogue (before pre-processing) is available on the right side of the interface.

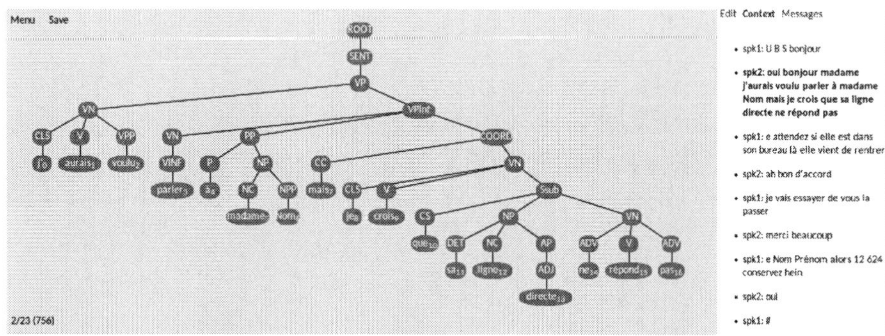

Figure 1: Output of the second phase: Standford parse tree on the pre-processed sentence (1).

- revision of the syntactic annotations: this phase is required to correct parsing errors but also to reach additional purposes. The parsing trees have to be adapted in order to allow the representation of speech disfluences and to obtain deeper constituency trees.

First, annotators are asked to put aside all the interjections and noises not dealt with in the first phase[3], and speech repairs are annotated following the Rhapsodie project guidelines (Lacheret et al., 2014). Annotators are asked to readdress the right POS if wrongly labeled, then a new analysis can be invoked respecting the new declared POS if needed.

FTB annotation scheme leads to rather flat syntactic trees that do not fulfill all the need of our temporal annotation. This phase aims at correcting this problem: it combines the contextual activation of automatic deepening rules and a fully manual revision. These deepening rules consist of:

- a VN followed by a VPInf under a node SENT, VPInf or SRel are grouped into a single VP in the same context, as one can see in figure 2 for *"j'aurais voulu parler à madame Nom"*.

- a VN followed by a NP under a node SENT, SSub, COORD or Sint are grouped into a VP.

- a VN followed by a PP under a node VPinf or SSub are grouped into a VP.

- a VN followed by an ADV under a node SENT are grouped into a VP.

- manual eventualities annotation: the detection of the linguistic items that denote eventualities or signals is achieved completely through a manual procedure. This annotation is conducted directly on the treebank built during the two previous phases.

- manual temporal relations annotation: the relations between eventualities are also defined manually. Every relation is characterized manually by several temporal features[4].

---

[3]The annotator visualizes the whole dialogue containing the disfluences as one can see in the right part of the figure 1. Noises and interjections are kept in the context even if put aside for syntactical purposes.

[4]We hope to detect automatically some semantic relations carried by syntactic links like SLINKs. In the figure 3, the two red subgraphs are good candidates for carrying a SLINK: VP-VPINF-VP and VP-SSUB-VP added to the annotation of the first

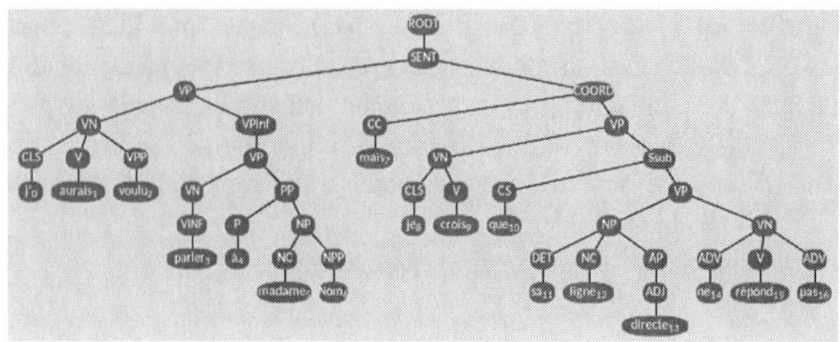

Figure 2: Output of the third phase: correction process and application of the automated rules.

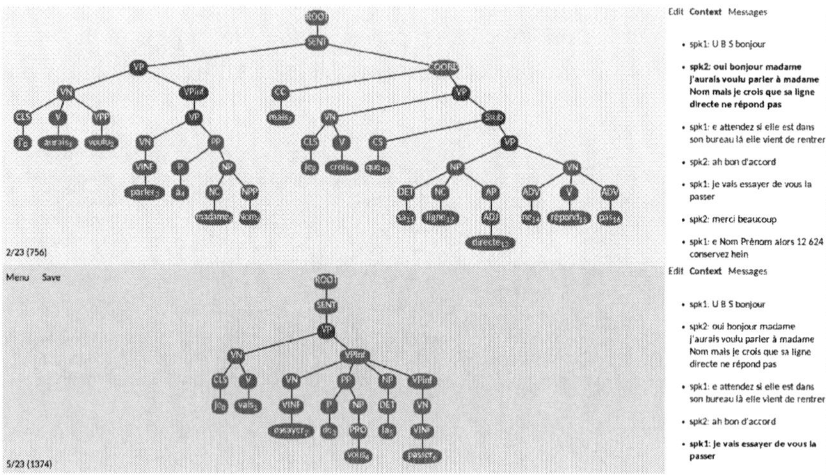

Figure 3: Full interface of the tool and first hint for locating interesting SLINK schemes.

4   Annotation tool

All of the manual annotation phases are conducted using a single annotation tool, which has been specifically implemented for the purpose of the project.

The tool's workspace consists of two vertically arranged annotation windows, showing two syntactic trees assigned to two (typically different) speech turns in a given file. As mentioned in the previous section, one of the primary functionalities provided by the tool is to allow correction of syntactic trees. To this end, the tool allows annotators to perform several structure-modifying operations: adding and deleting nodes, changing the parent of a node, changing the position of the node w.r.t. its parent, etc. Only the operations which preserve the well-formedeness of syntactic structures are allowed.

Duplication of the annotation workspace facilitates, among others, viewing and editing the temporal relations occurring between different trees. Such relations can be created by selecting the corresponding nodes and using an appropriate keyboard command. The newly created events and temporal relations are supplied with default ISO-TimeML-related attribute values, which can be subsequently changed manually in the side windows. We plan to later experiment with a semi-automatic annotation of the attribute values, where the corresponding machine-learning annotation model is being gradually bootstrapped from the already annotated part of the corpus.

The tool is implemented in a client/server architecture. The frontend annotation tool is written in Elm (http://elm-lang.org/), which compiles to JavaScript, thus the tool can be used in any modern internet browser. The client annotation tool communicates with a Haskell server via websockets, with

---

VNs under the first VPs as L_STATEs should raise SLINKs between *"j'aurais voulu"* (*'I would like'*) and *"parler à madame Nom"* (*'to talk to Madam Name'*) and between *"je crois"* (*'I think'*) and *"sa ligne directe ne répond plus"* (*'her direct phone line does not answer'*) .

the annotated files serialized to JSON before being sent. On both sides, annotation data is represented with appropriate data types, which guarantees, among others, that malformed data is never sent to the server to be stored in the database.

Such an architecture has a couple of advantages. The annotator does not have to install anything locally, and the server can provide the user with more advanced functionality. The server can be requested to syntactically re-analyze a given sentence in a way which takes the constraints specified directly by the annotator (e.g. a particular tokenization) into account. In the long run, the client/server architecture should also allow a more collaborative annotation style.

The Temporal@ODIL project will end in spring 2018. The resulting corpus, providing a 100,000 words syntactic annotation layer, and a 20,000 words temporal annotation layer, will be freely available from June 2018 under Creative Commons CC-BY-SA license[5].

References

Abeillé, A., L. Clément, and F. Toussenel (2003). Building a treebank for french. *Treebanks*, 165–187.

Allen, J. F. (1983). Maintaining knowledge about temporal intervals. *Communications of the ACM 26*.

Bejček, E. and P. Straňák (2010, Apr). Annotation of multiword expressions in the prague dependency treebank. *Language Resources and Evaluation 44*(1), 7–21.

Bittar, A., P. Amsili, and P. Denis (2011). French TimeBank : un corpus de référence sur la temporalité en français. In *TALN 2011*, Montpellier, France, pp. 259–270.

Drat, L. (2014). Projet TourInFlux. Annotation des expressions temporelles. Master's thesis.

ISO (2012). Language resource management - Semantic annotation framework (SemAF) Part 1: Time and events. ISO 24617-1:2012, International Organization for Standardization, Geneva, Switzerland.

Lacheret, A., S. Kahane, J. Beliao, A. Dister, K. Gerdes, J.-P. Goldman, N. Obin, P. Pietrandrea, and A. Tchobanov (2014, July). Rhapsodie: un Treebank annoté pour l'étude de l'interface syntaxe-prosodie en français parlé. In *4e Congrès Mondial de Linguistique Française*, Volume 8, Berlin, Germany, pp. 2675–2689.

Lefeuvre-Halftermeyer, A., J.-Y. Antoine, A. Couillault, E. Schang, L. Abouda, A. Savary, D. Maurel, I. Eshkol-Taravella, and D. Battistelli (2016). Covering various Needs in Temporal Annotation: a Proposal of Extension of ISO TimeML that Preserves Upward Compatibility. In *LREC 2016*, Portorož, Slovenia.

MERLOT (2016). Annotation scheme for the merlot french clinical corpus. Technical report.

Muzerelle, J., A. Lefeuvre, E. Schang, J.-Y. Antoine, A. Pelletier, D. Maurel, I. Eshkol, and J. Villaneau (2014). ANCOR_Centre, a Large Free Spoken French Coreference Corpus: description of the Resource and Reliability Measures. In *LREC 2014*, Reyjavik, Iceland.

Pustejovsky, J., J. M. Castao, R. Ingria, R. Sauri, R. J. Gaizauskas, A. Setzer, G. Katz, and D. R. Radev (2003). Timeml: Robust specification of event and temporal expressions in text. In M. T. Maybury (Ed.), *New Directions in Question Answering*, pp. 28–34. AAAI Press.

Pustejovsky, J., J. Littman, and R. Saurí (2006). Argument structure in timeml. In *Dagstuhl Seminar Proceedings*. Schloss Dagstuhl-Leibniz-Zentrum für Informatik.

Reichenbach, H. (1947). *Elements of Symbolic Logic*. New York, Macmillan.

Zinsmeister, H. and S. Dipper (2011). *Towards a Standard for Annotating Abstract Anaphora*.

---

[5]This licence is inherited from the original oral corpus.

Towards Efficient String Processing of Annotated Events

David Woods
ADAPT Centre
Trinity College Dublin, Ireland
dwoods@tcd.ie

Tim Fernando, Carl Vogel
Computational Linguistics Group
Trinity Centre for Computing and Language Studies
School of Computer Science and Statistics
Trinity College Dublin, Ireland
tim.fernando@tcd.ie, vogel@tcd.ie

Abstract

This paper explores the use of strings as models to effectively represent event data such as might be found in a document annotated with ISO-TimeML. We describe the translation of such data to strings, as well as a number of operations, such as superposition, which may be used to manipulate these strings in order to infer new information. Some advantages and limitations of the operations are discussed, including issues of over-generation, which can be mitigated though the use of suitable constraints. In particular, we look at how Allen Relations, which might be extracted from a document annotated with ISO-TimeML, can be understood as useful constraints, and translated to strings.

1 Introduction

This paper explores the use of strings as models to effectively represent event data such as might be found in a document annotated with ISO-TimeML. It is described how such data may be simply translated to strings, and how to infer information through operations on these strings. Strings are basic computational entities that can be more readily manipulated by machines than the infinite models of predicate logic. Finite sets of strings serve as finite models.

We fix a finite set A of fluents (temporal propositions), and encode sets of these fluents as symbols to allow any number of them to hold at a time (as in Fernando, 2016). A string $s = \alpha_1 \cdots \alpha_n$ of subsets α_i of A can be construed as a finite model consisting of n moments of time $i \in \{1, \ldots, n\}$ with α_i specifying all fluents (in A) that (as unary predicates) hold simultaneously at i.

Throughout this paper, a fluent $a \in A$ will be understood as naming an event, and the powerset 2^A of A will serve as an alphabet $\Sigma = 2^A$ of an *event-string* $s \in \Sigma^+$. Such strings are finite models of Monadic Second Order logic, and are amenable to finite state methods. We will further restrict them in Section 6, with a focus on using Allen Relations adopted in ISO-TimeML, in order to analyse inference over a finite search space.

An event-string $\alpha_1 \cdots \alpha_n$ is read from left to right chronologically, so that any predicates which hold at the moment at index i are understood to have held before another moment indexed by j if and only if $i < j$. The precise duration of each moment is taken as unimportant in the current discussion, and thus the strings model an inertial world, whereby *change* is the only mark of progression from one moment to the next – "But neither does time exist without change" (Aristotle, *Physics IV*). Thus, if $\alpha_i = \alpha_{i+1}$ for any $1 \leq i < n$, then either α_i or α_{i+1} may be safely deleted from s without affecting the interpretation of the string, as the remaining symbol is simply taken as representing a longer moment. This operation of removing repetition from the event-string is known as *block compression* (Fernando, 2016). The inverse of this process introduces repeated elements in an event-string for greater flexibility in manipulating strings. These operations are detailed in Section 3.

We see that strings may provide useful finite models for event data, once sufficiently constrained. This is in order to avoid a large combinatorial blow-up when reconciling information from different strings.

In the following section, we see an example from ISO-TimeML which we might convert to an event-string, and why it would be useful to do so. Sections 3 and 4 provide the formal string operations used to manipulate and combine information from event-strings. How these operations are useful in regards to Allen Relations is described in Section 5, and Section 6 explores constraints to prevent malformed event-strings. Finally, Section 7 shows how the framework can be applied to data from an ISO-TimeML document.

2 Motivation in ISO-TimeML

ISO-TimeML (Pustejovsky et al., 2010) is a standard markup language used for the annotation of events (and their interrelations) in texts. Of particular interest to us here are the TLINK elements, which indicate the relations between pairs of fluents found in the document. Though not every fluent will necessarily be linked with another in this manner, a majority will be. The TIMEBANK Corpus (Pustejovsky et al., 2003) provides a large number of documents annotated using the 1.1 TimeML standard (a predecessor to ISO-TimeML), which we may extract TLINKs from.

According to the markup specification (TimeML Working Group, 2005), a TLINK is required to have the following attributes: either a `timeID` or `eventInstanceID` attribute, referring to some fluent in the text, as well as either a `relatedToTime` or `relatedToEventInstance` attribute, which will refer to another fluent, and also a `relType` attribute, declaring the relation between the two fluents. Other attributes are optional and not relevant to the current discussion.

In order to give a more concrete understanding, let us take a small fragment from an ISO-TimeML document, which will give us three TLINK nodes:

```
(1a)    <TLINK lid="l2" relType="IS_INCLUDED" eventInstanceId="ei1"
                              relatedToTime="t1" origin="USER"/>
(1b)          <TLINK lid="l9" relType="IS_INCLUDED" timeID="t1"
                  relatedToEventInstance="ei9" origin="USER"/>
(1c)      <TLINK lid="l10" relType="BEFORE" eventInstanceID="ei9"
                  relatedToEventInstance="ei10" origin="USER"/>
```

The value of `relType` will correspond to exactly one of the relations described in Allen (1983), though it should be noted that some of these Allen Relations can correspond to multiple `relTypes` (for example, `IDENTITY` and `SIMULTANEOUS` are both covered by the Allen Relation *equal*). The other attributes (`lid`, `origin`) in each TLINK may be ignored for now.

We can represent the information in (1a)–(1c) in predicate logic as follows:

$$(2a) \qquad\qquad\qquad Includes(t1, ei1)$$

$$(2b) \qquad\qquad\qquad Includes(ei9, t1)$$

$$(2c) \qquad\qquad\qquad Before(ei9, ei10)$$

where *Includes* (the inverse of `IS_INCLUDED`) and *Before* are binary relations, corresponding to the Allen Relations *during (inverse)* and *before*, respectively (see Section 5).

An issue with this representation is that the full picture of the chronological sequence of events is not intuitively obvious from the three predicates. It is possible to create a set of inference rules (see Setzer et al., 2005) which allow for drawing new conclusions from the given information – for example, that the predicate *Before*$(t1, ei10)$ also holds. However, the amount of information that can be obtained from any single binary relation is relatively small, and reasoning about more than two fluents at once can require the conjunction of multiple relations.

Using an event-string, we may include all of the above information in a single, readable string, which allows us to reason about the relations between any number of fluents. Additionally, we provide facilities to infer new relations from this event-string (see Section 6).

3 Superposition and Block Compression

In order to usefully collect information from multiple strings into a single string, we define here the operation of *superposition*. With two strings s and s' of the same length n built from an alphabet Σ, the powerset of some fixed set A, the superposition $s\ \&\ s'$ of s and s' is their componentwise union:

$$(3) \qquad \alpha_1 \cdots \alpha_n\ \&\ \alpha_1' \cdots \alpha_n' \ := \ (\alpha_1 \cup \alpha_1') \cdots (\alpha_n \cup \alpha_n')$$

For convenience of notation, we will use boxes rather than curly braces { } to represent sets in Σ, such that each symbol α in a string s corresponds to exactly one box. For example, with $a, b, c, d \in A$:

$$(4) \qquad \boxed{a\,|\,c}\ \&\ \boxed{b\,|\,d} \ = \ \boxed{a,b\,|\,c,d} \ \in \Sigma^2$$

Extending superposition to languages L and L' over the same alphabet is a simple matter of collecting the superpositions of strings of equal length from each language:

$$(5) \qquad L\ \&\ L' \ := \ \bigcup_{n \geq 0} \{s\ \&\ s' \mid s \in L \cap \Sigma^n \text{ and } s' \in L' \cap \Sigma^n\}$$

For example, $L\ \&\ \boxed{\ }^{*} = L$. If L and L' are regular languages computed by finite automata with transitions $\rightarrow$ and $\rightarrow'$, then the superposition $L\ \&\ L'$ is a regular language computed by a finite automaton with transitions $\Rightarrow$ formed by running $\rightarrow$ and $\rightarrow'$ in lockstep according to the rule

$$(6) \qquad \frac{q \xrightarrow{\alpha} r \qquad q' \xrightarrow{\alpha'}{}' r'}{(q, q') \xRightarrow{\alpha \cup \alpha'} (r, r')}$$

A disadvantage of this operation is that it requires the string operands to be of equal length, which is an overly specific case. In order to generalise this procedure to strings of arbitrary lengths, we may manipulate the strings to move away from the synchrony of the lockstep procedure. One such manipulation is that we can cause a string $s = \alpha_1 \cdots \alpha_n$ to *stutter* such that $\alpha_i = \alpha_{i+1}$ for some integer $0 < i < n$. For example, $\boxed{a\,|\,a\,|\,a\,|\,c\,|\,c}$ is a stuttering version of $\boxed{a\,|\,c}$. If a string does not stutter, it is *stutterless*, and we can transform a stuttering string to this state by using "block compression":

$$(7) \qquad \mathrm{bc}(s) \ := \ \begin{cases} s & \text{if } length(s) \leq 1 \\ \mathrm{bc}(\alpha s') & \text{if } s = \alpha\alpha s' \\ \alpha\,\mathrm{bc}(\alpha' s') & \text{if } s = \alpha\alpha' s' \text{ with } \alpha \neq \alpha' \end{cases}$$

This function can be applied multiple times to a string, but the output will not change after the first application: $\mathrm{bc}(\mathrm{bc}(s)) = \mathrm{bc}(s)$. We can also use the inverse of this function to generate infinitely many stuttering strings:

$$(8) \qquad \mathrm{bc}^{-1}\!\big(\boxed{a\,|\,c}\big) = \{\boxed{a\,|\,c}, \boxed{a\,|\,a\,|\,c}, \boxed{a\,|\,c\,|\,c}, \boxed{a\,|\,a\,|\,c\,|\,c}, \ldots\}$$

We can say that any of the strings generated by this inverse block compression are bc-*equivalent*. Precisely, a string s' is bc-equivalent to a string s iff $s' \in \mathrm{bc}^{-1}\mathrm{bc}(s)$.

We can now define the *asynchronous superposition* $s\ \&_* s'$ of strings s and s' as the (provably) *finite* set obtained by block compressing the *infinite* language generated by superposing the strings which are bc-equivalent to s and s':

$$(9) \qquad s\ \&_* s' \ := \ \{\mathrm{bc}(s'') \mid s'' \in \mathrm{bc}^{-1}\mathrm{bc}(s)\ \&\ \mathrm{bc}^{-1}\mathrm{bc}(s')\}$$

For example, $\boxed{a\,|\,c}\ \&_* \boxed{b\,|\,d}$ will comprise three strings:

$$(10) \qquad \{\boxed{a,b\,|\,c,d}, \boxed{a,b\,|\,a,d\,|\,c,d}, \boxed{a,b\,|\,b,c\,|\,c,d}\}$$

In order to avoid generating all possible strings when using the inverse block compression, we introduce an upper bound to the length of the strings which will be superposed. It can be shown that with two strings of length n and n', the longest bc-unique string (one which has no shorter bc-equivalent strings) produced through asynchronous superposition will be of length $n + n' - 1$.

4 Upper Bound on Asynchronous Superposition

The aforementioned bound on the length of superposed strings can be established as follows. For all $s, s' \in \Sigma^*$, we define a finite set $s \mathbin{\hat{\&}} s'$ of strings over Σ with enough of the strings in $\mathrm{bc}^{-1}\mathrm{bc}(s) \mathbin{\&} \mathrm{bc}^{-1}\mathrm{bc}(s')$ to form $s \mathbin{\&_*} s'$. The definition proceeds by induction on s and s', with

$$\tag{11a} \epsilon \mathbin{\hat{\&}} \epsilon := \{\epsilon\}$$

$$\tag{11b} \epsilon \mathbin{\hat{\&}} s := \emptyset \quad \text{for } s \neq \epsilon$$

$$\tag{11c} s \mathbin{\hat{\&}} \epsilon := \emptyset \quad \text{for } s \neq \epsilon$$

and for all $\alpha, \alpha' \in \Sigma$,

$$\tag{12} \alpha s \mathbin{\hat{\&}} \alpha' s' := \{(\alpha \cup \alpha')s'' \mid s'' \in (\alpha s \mathbin{\hat{\&}} s') \cup (s \mathbin{\hat{\&}} \alpha's') \cup (s \mathbin{\hat{\&}} s')\}$$

Note that a string in $s \mathbin{\hat{\&}} s'$ might stutter, even if neither of the operands s or s' do (e.g. $\boxed{a,c}\,\boxed{a,c} \in \boxed{a}\,\boxed{c} \mathbin{\hat{\&}} \boxed{c}\,\boxed{a}$). However, it can be made stutterless through block compression.

Proposition 1. *For all $s, s' \in \Sigma^+$ and all $s'' \in s \mathbin{\hat{\&}} s'$,*

$$\tag{13} length(s'') \leq length(s) + length(s') - 1$$

Proposition 2. *For all $s, s' \in \Sigma^+$,*

$$\tag{14} s \mathbin{\hat{\&}} s' \subset \mathrm{bc}^{-1}\mathrm{bc}(s) \mathbin{\&} \mathrm{bc}^{-1}\mathrm{bc}(s')$$

and

$$\tag{15} \{\mathrm{bc}(s'') \mid s'' \in s \mathbin{\hat{\&}} s'\} = s \mathbin{\&_*} s'$$

Now, for any integer $k > 0$ and string $s = \alpha_1 \cdots \alpha_n$ over Σ, we introduce a new function pad_k which will generate the set of strings with length k which are bc-equivalent to s:

$$\tag{16a} pad_k(\alpha_1 \cdots \alpha_n) := \alpha_1^+ \cdots \alpha_n^+ \cap \Sigma^k$$

$$\tag{16b} = \{\alpha_1^{k_1} \cdots \alpha_n^{k_n} \mid k_1, \ldots, k_n \geq 1 \text{ and } \sum_{i=1}^{n} k_i = k\}$$

$$\tag{16c} \subset \mathrm{bc}^{-1}\mathrm{bc}(\alpha_1 \cdots \alpha_n)$$

For example, $pad_4(\boxed{a}\,\boxed{c})$ will generate $\{\boxed{a}\,\boxed{a}\,\boxed{a}\,\boxed{c}, \boxed{a}\,\boxed{a}\,\boxed{c}\,\boxed{c}, \boxed{a}\,\boxed{c}\,\boxed{c}\,\boxed{c}\}$. We can use this new function in our calculation of asynchronous superposition, to limit the generation of strings from the inverse block compression step. Since we know from Proposition 1 that the maximum possible length we might need is $n + n' - 1$, we can use this value in the *pad* function to just generate the strings of that length, giving us a new definition of asynchronous superposition:

Corollary 3. *For any $s, s' \in \Sigma^+$ with nonzero lengths n and n' respectively,*

$$\tag{17} s \mathbin{\&_*} s' = \{\mathrm{bc}(s'') \mid s'' \in pad_{n+n'-1}(s) \mathbin{\&} pad_{n+n'-1}(s')\}$$

Neither $s \mathbin{\hat{\&}} s'$ nor $pad_{n+n'-1}(s) \mathbin{\&} pad_{n+n'-1}(s')$ need be a subset of the other, even though, under the assumptions of Corollary 3, both sets block compress to $s \mathbin{\&_*} s'$.

5 Event Representation

Now we may use asynchronous superposition to generate the 13 strings in $\boxed{\ }\,e\,\boxed{\ }\ \&_*\ \boxed{\ }\,e'\,\boxed{\ }$, each of which corresponds to one of the unique interval relations in Allen (1983). No more than one of these relations may hold between any two fluents, and thus each of the 13 generated event-strings exists in a distinct possible "world". We use the empty box $\boxed{\ }$ as a string of length 1 (not to be confused with the empty string ϵ, which is length 0) to bound events, allowing us to represent the fact that they are finite – they have a beginning and ending point. It is prudent to assume that we will deal only with finite event data, such that there are no fluents which do not have both an associated start-point and end-point. If such a non-finite fluent without a begining and ending were to occur, it could trivially appear in every position in the event-string.

The bounding boxes represent the time before and after the event occurs, during which no other fluents $a \in A$ are mentioned. The event-strings associated with the Allen Relations are laid out below:

$e = e'$	$\|\;e, e'\;\|$	equal
e **s** e'	$\|\;e, e'\;\|\;e'\;\|$	starts
e **si** e'	$\|\;e, e'\;\|\;e\;\|$	starts (inverse)
e **f** e'	$\|\;e'\;\|\;e, e'\;\|$	finishes
e **fi** e'	$\|\;e\;\|\;e, e'\;\|$	finishes (inverse)
e **d** e'	$\|\;e'\;\|\;e, e'\;\|\;e'\;\|$	during
e **di** e'	$\|\;e\;\|\;e, e'\;\|\;e\;\|$	during (inverse)
e **o** e'	$\|\;e\;\|\;e, e'\;\|\;e'\;\|$	overlaps
e **oi** e'	$\|\;e'\;\|\;e, e'\;\|\;e\;\|$	overlaps (inverse)
e **m** e'	$\|\;e\;\|\;e'\;\|$	meets
e **mi** e'	$\|\;e'\;\|\;e\;\|$	meets (inverse)
$e < e'$	$\|\;e\;\|\;\|\;e'\;\|$	before
$e > e'$	$\|\;e'\;\|\;\|\;e\;\|$	after

These Allen Relations are included in the attributes of ISO-TimeML, as types of relation annotated by TLINKs (though some relations are named slightly differently). By extracting the TLINKs from an annotated document, and translating them to our event-string representation (see Section 7), we may begin to reason about the relationships between annotated events which do not have an associated TLINK in the markup. For example, the document may give us a relation between events e and e', and another relation between e' and e'', and from this we may infer the possible relations between e and e''.

As asynchronous superposition is commutative and associative, we may superpose arbitrary numbers of event-strings: $s_1 \,\&_*\, \cdots \,\&_*\, s_n$. We can show that superposing n unconstrained bounded event-strings will generate strings of maximum length $2n+1$.[1] Note, however, that superposing even a relatively small number of unconstrained bounded events leads to a massive combinatorial blow-up in the number of

---

[1] The proof is by induction:

Let each string to be superposed $s_i \in \{s_1, \ldots, s_n\}$ be $\boxed{\ }\,e_i\,\boxed{\ }$, with each $e_i \in A$.

For $n = 2$: $s_1 \,\&_*\, s_2$.

From Proposition 1, the maximum length of the result is $3 + 3 - 1 = 5 = 2(2) + 1$.

We assume true for $n = p$, thus the maximum length of $s_1 \,\&_*\, \cdots \,\&_*\, s_p$ is $2(p) + 1$.

Next, we prove for $n = p + 1$: $s_1 \,\&_*\, \cdots \,\&_*\, s_{p+1} = s_1 \,\&_*\, \cdots \,\&_*\, s_p \,\&_*\, s_{p+1} = s_{1\ldots p} \,\&_*\, s_{p+1}$.

From Proposition 1, the maximum length of the result is $(2(p) + 1) + 3 - 1 = 2(p + 1) + 1$.

Thus true for $p + 1$, and by induction, true for any $n \geq 2$.

outcomes, or possible worlds, as each event-string generated from one superposition (*e.g.* $s_1 \mathbin{\&_*} s_2$) will in turn be superposed with each generated from another (*e.g.* $s_3 \mathbin{\&_*} s_4$). Additionally, with each event, the maximum possible length of the strings grows, meaning a larger set of strings will be generated at the *pad* stage. Table 1 shows the maximum lengths of the stutterless strings generated from n unconstrained bounded events, up to $n = 5$. For $n \geq 2$, one can show that $2^n < b(n) < (2n^2 - n)^n$, where $b(n)$ represents the number of distinct outcomes generated by asynchronously superposing n unconstrained bounded events.[2] Table 1 also sets out these numbers.

Clearly, simply superposing bounded events in this manner is not feasible, given the huge growth in the

Number of events: n	Maximum length: $2n + 1$	Lower bound: 2^n	Number $b(n)$ of outcomes from $s_1 \mathbin{\&_*} \cdots \mathbin{\&_*} s_n$	Upper bound: $(2n^2 - 1)^n$
2	5	4	13	36
3	7	8	409	3,375
4	9	16	23,917	61,456
5	11	32	2,244,361	184,528,125

Table 1: Outcomes of asynchronous superposition of n bounded events

number of possible outcomes, and it is unreasonable to expect that any given document should contain five or fewer events. In order to avoid generating such a large number of computed event-strings, it is necessary to add constraints to limit the strings that may be considered allowable for a particular context.

Interestingly, because each unconstrained bounded event-string $\boxed{\;\boxed{e}\;}$ contains exactly one fluent, we may determine the maximum possible length of a string generated by superposition, $2n + 1$, from the size of the set A of fluents, where $n = |A|$. By keeping track of $|A|$, we ensure that the length of the string will always be finite, opening up the possibility of using methods from constraint satisfaction, exploiting the finite search space.

6   Constraints on Event-Strings

Two approaches to constraints may be implemented, which are not mutually exclusive. The first is to prevent unwanted strings from being generated, based on the nature of the operand strings, and the second is to remove disallowed strings from the set of outputs. The former approach is preferred from a computational standpoint, as there is less data to store and process. For either, we define some properties of what we may consider to be a *well-formed event-string*.

We assume that every fluent we encounter has exactly one beginning and one ending – that is, that events do not *resume* once they have ended. Events of the same type may stop and start frequently, but by assuming that every instance of an event will have a uniquely identifying fluent, we can discard any strings which feature such a resumption.[3] In this way, fluents are *interval-like*. We define the function ρ_X on strings of sets to component-wise intersect with X for any $X \subseteq A$ (Fernando, 2016):

$$(18) \qquad \rho_X(\alpha_1 \cdots \alpha_n) := (\alpha_1 \cap X) \cdots (\alpha_n \cap X)$$

Applying block compression to an event-string which has been reduced with $\rho_{\{a\}}$ should produce a single string: $\boxed{\;\boxed{a}\;}$. For example, with $a, b \in A$:

$$(19) \qquad \mathrm{bc}\!\left(\rho_{\{a\}}\!\left(\boxed{\;\boxed{a}\,\boxed{a,b}\,\boxed{b}\;}\right)\right) = \boxed{\;\boxed{a}\;}$$

---

[2] A single bounded event may be represented in a (possibly stuttering) string of length $2n + 1$ in $\sum_{i=1}^{2n-1} i = 2n^2 - n$ ways. Together, n of these leads to $(2n^2 - n)^n$.

[3] We adopt simplifying assumptions made in Allen Relations, though it should be noted that the distinction between event instances and event types (see Fernando, 2015) is not imposed by the event-string framework itself, allowing for discontinuous events (such as *judder*) in future work.

Additionally, fluents may be referred to multiple times by different TLINKs in an annotated document, and we assume that they will be *consistent* within the context of that document *i.e.* if a relation holds between e and e', and a relation holds between e' and e'', then both instances of e' refer to the same fluent. In this case, if a relation also holds between e and e'', then this relation should not contradict the other two relations. For example, if $e > e'$ and $e' > e''$, then it should be impossible for a well-formed event-string to also have the relation $e < e''$, as this would break the interval-like fluent constraint mentioned above.

These last two points are interesting in particular, as they lead to a specific kind of superposition between strings $s, s' \in \Sigma^+$ when some symbol $\alpha \in s$ is equal to some other symbol $\alpha' \in s'$. In this scenario, the symbols must unify when superposing the strings, in order to create a well-formed event-string in accordance with the above two constraints. To achieve this, when a symbol α in s is also present in s', and the asynchronous superposition of these strings is desired, padding is carried out as normal, but superposition is only permitted of those results of padding in which the indices of the matching symbols are equal. To do otherwise would permit event-strings which are not well-formed.

Allen (1983) gives a transitivity table showing the inferred possible relations between two events a and c, given the relation between each and an intermediary event, b. Each cell of the table shows simply the symbol which represent the binary relation – we may improve on the readability of this by showing explicitly the well-formed event-string(s) formed by the asynchronous superposition in each case. A fragment of the entire table is shown in Table 2 below:

	"before" [b | c]	**"during"** [c | b,c | c]	**"meets"** [b | c]	**"starts"** [b,c | c]
"before" [a | b]	[a | b | c]	[a | | c | b,c | c], [a | a,c | c | b,c | c], [a | c | b,c | c], [c | a,c | c | b,c | c], [a,c | c | b,c | c]	[a | | b | c]	[a | | b,c | c]
"during" [b | a,b | b]	[b | a,b | b | c]	[c | b,c | a,b,c | b,c | c]	[b | a,b | b | c]	[b,c | a,b,c | b,c | c]
"meets" [a | b]	[a | b | c]	[a | a,c | b,c | c], [c | a,c | b,c | c], [a,c | b,c | c]	[a | b | c]	[a | b,c | c]
"starts" [a,b | b]	[a,b | b | c]	[c | a,b,c | b,c | c]	[a,b | b | c]	[a,b,c | b,c | c]

Table 2: Fragment of Allen Transitivity Table using event-strings

Here and in the original table, only three events are mentioned: a, b, and c. We can see that the asynchronous superposition of an event-string $s_{a,b}$ mentioning a and b with an event-string $s_{b,c}$ mentioning b and c gives a language L of event-strings mentioning all three events. Applying the reduct $\rho_{\{a,b\}}$ to any string in L (and block compressing the result) should give back exactly $s_{a,b}$, and likewise applying $\rho_{\{b,c\}}$ to any string in L should give back exactly $s_{b,c}$. It should, in theory, be possible to generalise this to any number of events, ensuring the same level of readability by using event-strings. Then for an event-string of arbitrary length featuring any number of fluents, we can apply the reduct $\rho_{\{e,e'\}}$ and block compress the result to obtain the Allen Relation between fluents e and e' by comparing with the event-strings corresponding to each Allen Relation, laid out in Section 5.

Finally, we may also introduce further constraints if external information is available, and these might be simply intersected with the result of a superposition: $(s \mathbin{\&_*} s') \cap C$, where C represents the constraints to be applied, for example, "e is among the first events to occur in the string s" (true iff $s \mathbin{\&} \boxed{\;\boxed{e}\;}^{*} = s$). This allows for extension beyond Allen Relations in the future.

7 Application to TLINKs

As mentioned in Section 5, attempting to generate all of the possible worlds becomes difficult when using just the unconstrained bounded event-strings alone, as there are just too many (rarely, if ever, featuring five fluents or fewer). Instead, we begin by looking at just those fluents which are linked to another by Allen Relation, which we may extract from the TLINKs in a document annotated with ISO-TimeML, as noted in Section 2.

As each relation corresponds exactly to one possible model, we translate the TLINKs immediately to the appropriate event-strings, and superpose these according to the constraints mentioned in Section 6. This allows us to avoid simply superposing based on the fluents, and bypasses having to generate the initial 13 possibilities. In this way, we may generate a much smaller set of possible outcomes from a larger number of bounded events.

We can now rewrite the information given in the TLINKs (1a)–(1c) as the following event-strings:[4]

$$(20\mathrm{a}) \qquad \boxed{\;\boxed{t1}\;\boxed{ei1,t1}\;\boxed{t1}\;}$$

$$(20\mathrm{b}) \qquad \boxed{\;\boxed{ei9}\;\boxed{t1,ei9}\;\boxed{ei9}\;}$$

$$(20\mathrm{c}) \qquad \boxed{\;\boxed{ei9}\;\boxed{ei10}\;}$$

We may asynchronously superpose these event-strings while respecting the established constraints in order to generate a new event-string which contains all of the information from each of the inputs:

$$(21) \qquad \boxed{\;\boxed{ei9}\;\boxed{t1,ei9}\;\boxed{ei1,t1,ei9}\;\boxed{t1,ei9}\;\boxed{ei9}\;\boxed{ei10}\;}$$

A clear advantage here is the compact, readable representation. Furthermore, we can infer the Allen Relation between any two fluents in this event-string s by applying a reduct and block compressing the result. For example, to infer the relationship between $ei1$ and $ei10$, we obtain $s' = \mathrm{bc}(\rho_{\{ei1,ei10\}}(s)) = \boxed{\;\boxed{ei1}\;\boxed{ei10}\;}$, from which we can conclude that the Allen Relation $ei1$ *before* $ei10$ holds.

A drawback here is that for this to be effective, it relies on the events being heavily constrained by their interrelations. If there are too few TLINKs relative to the number of events, we still run into the problem of combinatorial explosion. What's more, as seen in Table 2, some asynchronous superpositions will still generate multiple disjoint possibilities (such as a *before* b with b *during* c), which will also impact the combinatorial problem.

An additional issue in computation of the superposition of events arises as multiple superposition operations are be carried out in sequence, meaning unordered data may lead to a much less efficient calculation of final results. For example, $\boxed{\;\boxed{a}\;\boxed{b}\;} \mathbin{\&_*} \boxed{\;\boxed{b}\;\boxed{c}\;} \mathbin{\&_*} \boxed{\;\boxed{c}\;\boxed{d}\;}$ and $\boxed{\;\boxed{a}\;\boxed{b}\;} \mathbin{\&_*} \boxed{\;\boxed{c}\;\boxed{d}\;} \mathbin{\&_*} \boxed{\;\boxed{b}\;\boxed{c}\;}$ should produce the same, single output: $\boxed{\;\boxed{a}\;\boxed{b}\;\boxed{c}\;\boxed{d}\;}$, which they do. However, due to the respective orderings, the first sequence will arrive at that conclusion much faster as $\boxed{\;\boxed{a}\;\boxed{b}\;} \mathbin{\&_*} \boxed{\;\boxed{b}\;\boxed{c}\;}$ has one possible outcome ($\boxed{\;\boxed{a}\;\boxed{b}\;\boxed{c}\;}$), which can immediately be asynchronously superposed with $\boxed{\;\boxed{c}\;\boxed{d}\;}$ to produce the final output. However, $\boxed{\;\boxed{a}\;\boxed{b}\;} \mathbin{\&_*} \boxed{\;\boxed{c}\;\boxed{d}\;}$ has 321 possible outcomes, each of which must be individually asynchronously superposed with $\boxed{\;\boxed{b}\;\boxed{c}\;}$, only to come to the same conclusion, as only one of these results is well-formed.

---

[4]Using https://www.scss.tcd.ie/~dwoods/timeml/ to quickly extract TLINKs from an ISO-TimeML document and translate them to event-strings. A non-trivial extension of this program which computes results of superposition is in the works.

One potential way to work around this pitfall is a grouping and ordering stage, where initially only events linked by some relation may be superposed, and only after the operand strings have been sorted to some optimal order, whereby the event-strings with the most shared fluents are grouped. It may be prudent to only perform superposition at all on event-strings which may be linked through one or more relations or shared fluents. In this way, new, underspecified events may be formed from the output strings. Consider the scenario with $e_1, \ldots, e_8 \in A$, and the following Allen Relations:

(22a) $$e_1 < e_4$$

(22b) $$e_1 \textbf{ m } e_2$$

(22c) $$e_2 \textbf{ di } e_3$$

(22d) $$e_5 \textbf{ s } e_7$$

(22e) $$e_8 > e_5$$

Let us cluster the fluents as follows: for each fluent $a \in A$, fix a set $P = \{a\}$, and a set S whose members are these sets P.

(23) $$S = \{\{e_1\}, \{e_2\}, \{e_3\}, \{e_4\}, \{e_5\}, \{e_6\}, \{e_7\}, \{e_8\}\}$$

Next, check for an Allen Relation between each pair of fluents a and a'. If a relation exists, add the fluent a' to the set P.

(24) $$S' = \{\{e_1, e_4, e_2\}, \{e_2, e_3\}, \{e_3\}, \{e_4\}, \{e_5, e_7\}, \{e_6\}, \{e_7\}, \{e_8, e_5\}\}$$

Finally, for each pair of sets P, Q, if $|P \cap Q| > 0$, form $R = P \cup Q$, adding R to the set S'' and discarding P, Q. Add the remaining sets from S' to S''.

(25) $$S'' = \{\{e_1, e_4, e_2, e_3\}, \{e_5, e_7, e_8\}, \{e_6\}\}$$

We might form the underspecified event groups E_1 and E_2 to refer to these first two clusters, at which point we may freely treat these groups as normal bounded events, and perform asynchronous superposition on their event-strings, as well as with that of e_6 – reducing the number of inputs from 8 to 3.

Additionally, various weightings might be considered as a method of priority-ordering in the case of a large A, such as the number of component events in an underspecified event group, or the number of relations linking to a particular event.

8 Conclusion

We have explored in this work the possibility of using strings as models for event data, motivated by their nature as computational entities. The operation of asynchronous superposition was described for composing strings which represent finite, bounded events, as well as its limits in terms of massive growth in the number of outputs when the operation is repeated in sequence. The problem is addressed by constraining the strings which may be superposed, with the 13 Allen Relations forming the main part of these, as these can be found in annotated corpora such as TIMEBANK, using the ISO-TimeML standard.

Future work on this topic will further develop the constraints on asynchronous superposition and expand on the features of the current framework, while also examining the use of alternative models to approach the same issue, such as using finite state automata, or a hybrid string/FSA approach. We will additionally explore the potential of employing methods from distributed computing in order to tackle the combinatorial explosion that occurs in asynchronously superposing unconstrained bounded events.

Acknowledgements

This research is supported by Science Foundation Ireland (SFI) through the CNGL Programme (Grant 12/CE/I2267) in the ADAPT Centre (https://www.adaptcentre.ie) at Trinity College Dublin. The ADAPT Centre for Digital Content Technology is funded under the SFI Research Centres Programme (Grant 13/RC/2106) and is co-funded under the European Regional Development Fund.

References

Allen, J. F. (1983). Maintaining Knowledge About Temporal Intervals. *Communications of the ACM 26*(11), 832–843.

Fernando, T. (2015). The Semantics of Tense and Aspect: A Finite-State Perspective. In S. Lappin and C. Fox (Eds.), *The Handbook of Contemporary Semantic Theory*, pp. 203–236. John Wiley & Sons.

Fernando, T. (2016). On Regular Languages Over Power Sets. *Journal of Language Modelling 4*(1), 29–56.

Pustejovsky, J., P. Hanks, R. Sauri, A. See, R. Gaizauskas, A. Setzer, D. Radev, B. Sundheim, D. Day, L. Ferro, et al. (2003). The TIMEBANK Corpus. In *Corpus Linguistics*, Volume 2003, pp. 647–656. Lancaster, UK.

Pustejovsky, J., K. Lee, H. Bunt, and L. Romary (2010). ISO-TimeML: An International Standard for Semantic Annotation. In *LREC*, Volume 10, pp. 394–397.

Setzer, A., R. Gaizauskas, and M. Hepple (2005). The Role of Inference in the Temporal Annotation and Analysis of Text. *Language Resources and Evaluation 39*(2), 243–265.

TimeML Working Group (2005). TimeML 1.2.1. A Formal Specification Language for Events and Temporal Expressions. `http://www.timeml.org/publications/timeMLdocs/timeml_1.2.1.html#tlink`. Accessed: 2017-07-12.

Enriching the Notion of Path in ISOspace

James Pustejovsky[1] and Kiyong Lee[2]

[1]Dept. of Comp. Science Brandeis University, Waltham, MA, USA
[2]Korea University, Seoul 137-767, Korea
jamesp@cs.brandeis.edu, ikiyong@gmail.com

Abstract

This paper proposes a modification to the notion of PATH as used in ISOspace, in order to both simplify the semantics of the MOVELINK tag as well as improve its coherence as a link structure, as defined in Bunt et al. (2016). This follows a suggestion by Lee (2016), where a reformulation of MOVELINK is proposed, in effect restoring an earlier proposal by Pustejovsky et al. (2010), where a motion is a relation between a MOVER and an EVENT_PATH. This simplifies the specification in ISOspace, maintains a coherent abstract syntax, and avoids redundancy with the annotation of semantic role labels.

1   Elements of ISOspace

As part of an ISO international standard on semantic annotation, ISOspace (ISO-24617-7, 2014) provides an abstract syntax, represented in UML diagrams, two concrete syntaxes, and a set of guidelines for the annotation of spatial entities and motions in language. It specifies: (a) how to annotate spatial entities such as places, paths, and spatially involving non-locational objects and motions and other non-motion events in language; and (b) how to annotate and represent their relations in a concrete format, either XML or predicate-logic-like form. The specification for ISOspace distinguishes between four major types of spatially relevant elements for markup in natural language (Pustejovsky, 2017).

(1) a. PLACES AND SPATIAL ENTITIES: natural or artificial locations in the world, as well as objects participating in spatial relations.

   b. EVENTS AND MOTION EVENTS: Eventualities involving movement and static situations.

   c. SPATIAL SIGNALS AND SPATIAL MEASURES: linguistic markers that establish relations between places and spatial entities.

   d. SPATIAL RELATIONSHIPS: The specific qualitative configurational, orientational, and metric relations between objects.

In the discussion below, we focus on those elements of ISOspace that are most relevant for modeling motion events. We begin with the six basic entity types, given below.

(2) a. PLACE   d. MOTION events

   b. PATH   e. EVENT (non-motion)

   c. SPATIAL_ENTITY (non-locational)   f. SIGNAL (three types)

The PLACE tag is used for annotating geographic entities like lakes and mountains, as well as administrative entities like towns and counties. (3) shows extents that should be captured with PLACE.

(3) a. [**Boston**$_{pl1}$] is north of [**New York**$_{pl2}$].

   b. John entered the [**store**$_{pl3}$].

   c. Kiyong flew to [**Montpellier**$_{pl6}$].

"

With the exception of implicit, non-consuming tags, a PLACE tag in ISOspace must be directly linked to an explicit span of text.

The PATH tag is used to capture locations where the focus is on the potential for traversal or functions as a boundary. This includes common nouns as in (4a) and (4b) as well as proper names as in (4c). The attributes of the PATH tag are a subset of the attributes of the PLACE tag, but with the additional `beginID`, `endID`, and `midIDs` attributes.

> (4) a. … I arrived at the end of the [**road**$_{p1}$].
>
> b. … a massive mountain [**range**$_{p2}$] that hugs the west [**coast**$_{p3}$] of Mexico.
>
> c. I followed the [**Pacific Coast Highway**$_{p4}$] along the coastal mountains …

Finally, a SPATIAL_ENTITY is a named entity that is both located in space and participates in an ISOspace link tag. It is generally anything that is spatially relevant but does not fit into either the PLACE or PATH categories. In practice, moving objects and objects that have the potential to move are most commonly tagged as a SPATIAL_ENTITY. In both (5a) and (5b), *car* should be marked as a SPATIAL_ENTITY. In the first case, it is the mover and, in the second case, it behaves like a PLACE. Note, though, that it should still be annotated as a SPATIAL_ENTITY and not be annotated as a PLACE since cars still have the potential for movement.

> (5) a. The [car$_{sne1}$] drove down the street.
>
> b. [**John**$_{sne1}$] arrived at the [car$_{sne2}$].
>
> c. My [**father**$_{sne1}$] and [**I**$_{sne2}$] biked for two days.

ISOspace has four types of relation tags, called *links*, holding between entity structures, illustrated below.

> (6) a. QSLINK – qualitative spatial links; c. MOVELINK – movement links;
>
> b. OLINK – orientation information; d. MLINK – measuring dimensions of locations

A QSLINK captures the topological relationship between two spatial objects, and are usually triggered by topological SPATIAL_SIGNALs. Topological information primarily refers to containment and connection relations between a pair of locations. ISOspace uses the Region Connection Calculus (RCC) as the basis for its qualitative spatial relationships (Randell et al., 1992). RCC8 is concerned with how regions (spatial objects) are *connected* to each other. The combination of RCC8's jointly exhaustive and pairwise disjoint relations, along with IN (the disjunction of TTP and NTTP) is referred to in ISOspace as RCC8+. Figure 1 visualizes the basic RCC8 relations.

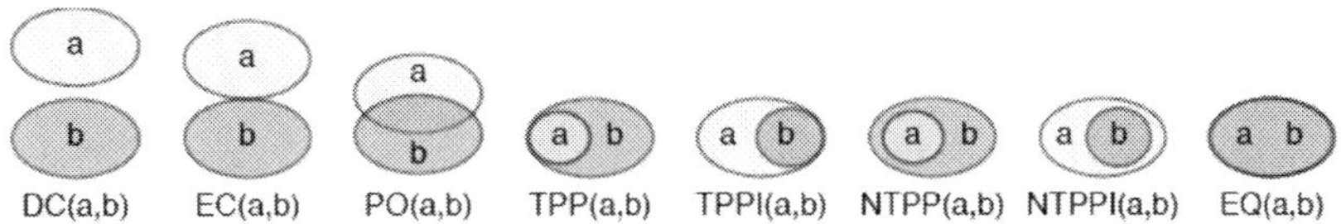

Figure 1: Visual Correspondence of RCC8 Relations

Briefly, the OLINK tag covers those relationships that occur between two locations that are non-topological in nature. Orientation links essentially fill in information that QSLINKs fail to capture, including direction, orientation, and frame of reference. Finally, the MLINK tag serves two purposes in ISOspace: to capture the distance between two spatial objects; or to describe the dimensions of a single object. See Pustejovsky (2017) for details on both of these relation types.

Finally, we come to the MOVELINK. The MOVELINK tag is used to connect all of the elements that are involved in a motion event, including the MOTION event itself, the `mover`, the `source`, `goal`, `midPoints`, and `ground` of the MOTION, an explicit path, if there is one, (i.e., `pathID`) and any adjuncts that are present (i.e., `adjunctID`). The `trigger` of a MOVELINK is always a MOTION ID and the `mover` is normally a SPATIAL_NE. Table 1 shows the attributes for the MOVELINK tag.

`id`	mvl1, mvl2, mvl3, …
`trigger`	identifier of the motion event that triggered the link
`source`	identifier of the place, path, spatial named entity, or event at the beginning of the path
`goal`	identifier of the place, path, spatial named entity, or event at the end of the path
`midPoint`	identifier of the place, path, spatial named entity, or event in the middle of the path
`mover`	identifier of the entity that moves along the path
`ground`	identifier of a place, path, spatial named entity or event that the `mover`'s motion is relative to
`goal_reached`	TRUE, FALSE, UNCERTAIN
`pathID`	identifier of a path that is equivalent to the one described by the MOVELINK
`adjunctID`	identifier of the spatial_signal that participates in the link

Table 1: Attributes for MOVELINK

2 Problems with MOVELINK

It is perhaps important to understand that the motivation for the MOVELINK tag in ISOspace comes originally from an interest in tracking objects in motion, as described in texts, and then linking them to maps or other visual geographic displays (Pustejovsky and Moszkowicz, 2008). As such, this results in a conflation of two kinds of information structures: (i) a relation between a motion and the mover in the motion; and (ii) all of the semantic roles that are involved in a motion event. This has the unintended consequence of creating a link structure that overlaps with efforts to annotate semantic roles generally, i.e., SemAF-SR (24617-4, 2014), and specifically within spatial language (Kordjamshidi et al., 2012). Moreover, it is unlike the other relational structures in ISOspace, in that it identifies no actual relation type, independent of the motion event itself. In this sense, it fails to conform to the definition of a link structure, as proposed in Bunt et al. (2016). For these reasons, following Lee (2016), we propose to simplify the structure of the MOVELINK tag as a relation between a MOVER and the path created by the movement, namely the EVENT_PATH.

3 The Return of EVENT_PATH

In ISOspace version 1.3e, Pustejovsky et al. (2010) introduced an additional tag to the elements listed in Section 1 above, namely an EVENT_PATH. The original intuition behind this type was to have a record of the movement as carried out by the mover: that is, to encode the path created by the traversal of an entity in motion. In order to make this more transparent, following Mani and Pustejovsky (2012), Pustejovsky and Yocum (2013) introduce two axioms of motion into the abstract syntax of ISOspace, given below.

(7) a. Axiom 1: Mover Participants
Every motion-event involves a mover.
$\forall e \exists x [motion\text{-}event(e) \rightarrow mover(x, e)]$

b. Axiom 2: Event Paths
Every motion-event involves an event-path.
$\forall e \exists p [motion\text{-}event(e) \rightarrow [event\text{-}path(p) \land loc(e, p)]]$

These axioms presuppose the following definitions[1]:

(8) MOVER: participant in a motion-event that undergoes a change in its location.[2]
PATH: non-null sequence of locations (places).

---

[1] See Pustejovsky and Yocum (2013).

[2] Langacker (2008) (p.356) introduces **mover** as one of the six archetypal roles associated with actions and events, while defining it as "anything that moves (i.e. changes position in relation to its external surroundings)". He also treats the mover as a *trajector* in contrast to a *landmark* that provides a ground for the activity or motion of a *trajector*. These two terms, *trajector* and *landmark*, correspond to the terms *figure* and *ground* in our use related to motion-events.

EVENT-PATH:

Formal: path which is directed, finite, and bounded with a begin-point, an endpoint, and a sequence of midpoints between them;

Functional: path triggered by a motion-event, that traces or represents the locational (physically necessary spatio-temporal) transition or trajectory of the *mover*, of a motion-event.

To illustrate the role of EVENT_PATH in the context of motion, let us consider some examples.

(9) a. John$_{mover}$ walked from Boston to Cambridge.
  b. An arrow$_{mover}$ hit the target.
  c. John pushed a big rock$_{mover}$ over the hill.

As shown above, the mover is not necessarily an agent or the cause of a motion. Whatever their semantic roles, however, all these movers above have the characteristics of moving from one location to another. Hence, to understand what is meant by **mover**, some locational change of an object must be implied from a motion.

By the two definitions given above, the **mover** in Axiom 1 is understood to be locationally related to the **event-path** in Axiom 2. By Axiom 1, an object x is related to a motion-event e and then by Axiom 2 the motion-event e to an event-path p with the relation loc. Hence, the mover x is *locationally* related to the path p, provided that transitivity is assumed to hold. Following Pustejovsky and Moszkowicz (2011); Lee (2016), to make the relation between the mover and the path more explicit, we introduce the following additional axiom:

(10) Every motion-event has a path to which it is anchored, and the mover traverses that path.
  $\forall e \exists \{p, x\}[motion\text{-}event(e) \rightarrow [event\text{-}path(p, e) \land \land mover(x, e) \land traverse(x, p)]]$[3]

We assume that traversal can be defined as follows:

(11) TRAVERSE:
  a. A binary relation between an object x and a path p such that $traverse(x, p)$ holds if and only if, for any path p, represented as $<l_0, .., l_k>$ with two endpoints l_0 and l_k, and any object x, each of the locations of x, represented as $l(x)_i$, in its transition from one location to another, corresponds to each location l_i in p.
  b. For an object x and a path p such that p is a sequence $< l_o, ..., l_k >$, $\sigma(traverse(x, p))$ implies:
  $\forall t_{i \in N}[t_0 \preceq t_k \quad \rangle [loc(x, t_0), ..., \lor loc(x, t_k)]]$.

4 Reformulation of MOVELINK

Given these observations, we propose that MOVELINK can be recast as a proper link structure, as a relation between a FIGURE and GROUND, to be defined below. A link structure, $<\eta, E, \rho>$, within the abstract syntax $\mathcal{ASyn}_{isoSpace}$ of ISOspace, has the following properties (Bunt et al., 2016).

(12) a. η is an entity structure of the **spatial entity** type functioning as the *mover* of a motion-event and as its *figure*,

  b. E is a singleton containing an entity structure of the **event-path** type functioning as a *ground*;

  c. ρ is a relation over η and E triggered by a motion-event.

---

[3] *event-path* is here treated as a relation between a path and an event because, unlike a (static) path, an event-path is created by a motion-event. $loc(e, p)$ holds if and only if $traverse(x, p)$ holds for each l in p.

We assume the mover of a motion to be a *figure*, as suggested by Talmy (1975, 1985). For its interpretation then, each event-path or traversal of the mover of a motion-event requires a reference location, either a place or a path, called *ground*.

The movement link is triggered by a motion-event. In the modified version of ISOspace, this link is viewed as relating the mover of that motion-event to an event-path traversed by the mover. The MOVER and EVENT-PATH are then treated as the *figure* and *ground* of the movement link, respectively.[4] The revised structure for MOVELINK is shown below.

id	mvl1, mvl2, mvl3, ...
trigger	identifier of the motion event that triggered the link
relType	relation value of motion, defaults to traverse
figure	identifier of the entity that moves along the path
ground	identifier of the event-path of the motion

Table 2: Revised MOVELINK

To illustrate how this plays out, consider the different ways in which a mover can relate to the event-path, as it unfolds in a motion event. We demonstrate this with the distinction that Talmy and others have observed between *internal motion* and *external motion*: below, *se* is SPATIAL_ENTITY, m is MOVE_EVENT, and *ep* is EVENT_PATH.

(13) a. John swam around the lake.

   $\text{John}_{se1:figure}$ $\text{swam}_{m1:trigger}$ around $[\text{the lake}]_{ep1:ground}$

   b. John walked around the lake.

   $\text{John}_{se1:figure}$ $\text{walked}_{m1:trigger}$ $[\text{around the lake}]_{ep1:ground}$

In (13a), the motion that John is involved in is internal to the region identified as the *figure*, hence the notion of "internal motion". In (13b), on the other hand, John is engaged in motion external to the PLACE identified by the park, and the *figure* is some path defined functionally as: $\lambda p[around(p, \text{the\_park})]$.

The abstract syntax $\mathcal{ASyn}_{isoSpace}$ of ISOspace specifies the value of the relation type ρ to be CDATA, allowing any possible values. In a concrete syntax proposed here, we specify this value to be TRAVERSE, as defined above, a single value for each of the <moveLink> instances. If a mover x traverses a path p, then x goes through p by being located at its begin-point, midpoints, or endpoint, sequentially as time progresses.

5   Conclusion

In this paper, we propose a reformulation of the MOVELINK tag in ISOspace, motivated by two major concerns: it currently fails to satisfy the conditions on link structures in abstract syntax, as defined in Bunt et al. (2016); and it contributes no additional information to the annotation beyond the identification of the semantic roles involved in motion. Since this is information that is already annotated or accounted for by other specifications, it was seen as largely uninformative. The new formulation of MOVELINK structures it as a relation between a MOVER and the EVENT_PATH created by the traversal in the movement event. This accords with both Talmy's typological observations regarding how motion is encoded in language, as well as the qualitative spatial interpretation of motion provided in Pustejovsky and Moszkowicz (2011) and Mani and Pustejovsky (2012).

---

[4]In Mani and Pustejovsky (2012), the *mover* is treated as the figure of a movement link.

6 Acknowledgements

We would like to thank Harry Bunt for discussion and input concerning the proposed changes in the specification for ISOspace.

References

24617-4, I. (2014). Language resource management - semantic annotation framework - part 4: Semantic roles (semaf-sr).

Bunt, H., V. Petukhova, A. Malchanau, and K. Wijnhoven (2016). The tilburg dialogbank corpus. *Proceedings of 10th Edition of the Language Resources and Evaluation Conference (*LREC2016*).*

ISO-24617-7 (2014). Iso 24617-7:2014(e) language resource management - semantic annotation framework - part 7: Spatial information (isospace).

Kordjamshidi, P., S. Bethard, and M.-F. Moens (2012). Semeval-2012 task 3: Spatial role labeling. In *Proceedings of the First Joint Conference on Lexical and Computational Semantics-Volume 1: Proceedings of the main conference and the shared task, and Volume 2: Proceedings of the Sixth International Workshop on Semantic Evaluation*, pp. 365–373. Association for Computational Linguistics.

Langacker, R. W. (2008). *Cognitive Grammar: A Basic Introduction.* Oxford: Oxford University Press.

Lee, K. (2016). An abstract syntax for isospace with its ¡movelink¿ reformulated. *Proceedings of The isa-12 Workshop on Interoperable Semantic Annotation 2016.*

Mani, I. and J. Pustejovsky (2012). *Interpreting Motion: Grounded Representations for Spatial Language.* Oxford: Oxford University Press.

Pustejovsky, J. (2017). Iso-space: Annotating static and dynamic spatial information. In *Handbook of Linguistic Annotation*, pp. 989–1024. Springer.

Pustejovsky, J. and J. Moszkowicz (2011). The qualitative spatial dynamics of motion. *The Journal of Spatial Cognition and Computation.*

Pustejovsky, J. and J. L. Moszkowicz (2008). Integrating motion predicate classes with spatial and temporal annotations. *Proceedings of* COLING *2008*, 95–98.

Pustejovsky, J., J. L. Moszkowicz, and M. Verhagen (2010). ISO-space specification: Version 1.3 (october 5, 2010). includes discussion notes from the workshop on spatial language annotation, the airlie retreat center, VA, september 26-29. *2010.*

Pustejovsky, J. and Z. Yocum (2013). Capturing motion in ISO-spacebank. In H. Bunt (Ed.), *Proceedings of isa-9*, pp. 25–34. Germany: Potsdam.

Randell, D., Z. Cui, and A. Cohn (1992). A spatial logic based on regions and connections. In M. Kaufmann (Ed.), *Proceedings of the 3rd Internation Conference on Knowledge Representation and REasoning*, San Mateo, pp. 165–176.

Talmy, L. (1975). Figure and ground in complex sentences. In *Annual Meeting of the Berkeley Linguistics Society*, Volume 1, pp. 419–430.

Talmy, L. (1985). Lexicalization patterns: Semantic structure in lexical forms. *Language typology and syntactic description 3(99)*, 36–149.

Association for Computational Linguistics
209 N. Eighth Street
Stroudsburg, Pennsylvania 18360

ISBN 978-1-5108-8133-4